DATE DUE			
GAYLORD 234			PRINTED IN U.S.A.

BENCE SZABOLCSI

A HISTORY OF MELODY

New York
ST MARTIN'S PRESS

Title of the Hungarian original:
A MELÓDIA TÖRTÉNETE

Translated by
CYNTHIA JOLLY
and
SÁRA KARIG

Published in cooperation with

CORVINA PRESS BUDAPEST

by
ST MARTIN'S PRESS
173 Fifth Avenue
New York 10,
N.Y.
Library of Congress Catalog Card Number 64-12334

Binding and jacket by Vera Csillag

© Corvina, 1965
Printed and bound in Hungary 1965
Franklin Printing House, Budapest

DEDICATED TO ZOLTÁN KODÁLY,
THE MASTER WHOSE TEACHINGS HAVE INSPIRED
THIS BOOK

Thou wast not born for death, immortal Bird!
No hungry generations tread thee down;
The voice I hear this passing night was heard
In ancient days by emperor and clown:
Perhaps the self-same song that found a path
Through the sad heart of Ruth, when, sick for home,
She stood in tears amid the alien corn;
The same that oft-times hath
Charm'd magic casements, opening on the foam
Of perilous seas, in faery lands forlorn.

. . .

Fled is that music: Do I wake or sleep?

Keats: Ode to a Nightingale

CONTENTS

7

PREFACE TO THE ENGLISH EDITION

This book—planned in 1930, written for the most part around 1940, and actually concluded in 1948—consists of a series of unconnected, single experiments in the history of musical styles. It was published in Hungarian first in 1950, followed by a second edition in 1957, and by a German edition entitled *Bausteine zu einer Geschichte der Melodie* in 1959. The great interval between its conception and completion may explain the lack of unity and the possible contradictions, while the period in which it was written—World War II—may account for the more or less narrow limits of the material used. At the time it was almost impossible to treat the problems of contemporary music, and the chapters of the Appendix often answer the questions in different ways. In spite of all these deficiencies and gaps it did not seem inappropriate to maintain the original rhapsodical draft of the text, as it may, to some extent, give a picture of the rise of 'melo-poetic' problems in contemporary musicology. Nevertheless, it is intended—no less than at the time of its preparation—to be a mere fragment, a first sketch of a great work that has not yet been written and can hardly ever be completed.

Budapest, 1965.

Bence Szabolcsi

THE WORLD OF PRIMITIVE MELODY:
FROM INFLECTION TO PENTATONICISM*

"Of the old songs, thousands have been scattered by the winds, thousands covered in snow; thousands have gone to their graves, and thousands have been wiped out in servitude." (Old Estonian song, in Pál Hunfalvy's *Journey through the Baltic.* 1871, vol. I, p. 326.)

Nature's capacity to create, nourish and stimulate is the starting-point for all music; rhythm informs the beat of the heart, the thrumming downpour of rain and the thud of horses' hooves; melody is evoked in the mind by a bird-call or the howl of a jackal; form can be produced quite casually through repetition or memory. The first music was born independently of man, yet it was man who created genuine music from natural sounds. Man was most strongly influenced by the natural sounds he experienced directly, through his own physical senses, or which he could produce himself: above all, he had his own voice, which, though it was incapable of refined articulation, served to communicate his emotions—a sound which was partly howling and whining, and partly already singing and speech. In fact, the two elements of music, pitch and rhythm, were both carried in the human body as natural, cosmic phenomena. "In the beginning was melody" . . . but obviously only natural melody, no more and no less.

Hence the earliest human manifestation to which the origin of music can be traced is to be found in inflection, or the accentuation of the spoken word—the 'music' which underlies articulated present-day speech, and separates human-

---

* The abstract term 'pentatonicism' or 'five-note-ism' has replaced the 'pentatonality' adopted in Kodály's *The Folk Music of Hungary* in order to bring it into line with diatonicism, chromaticism, etc. But it is none the less a form of tonality!   (Translators' note.)

The English translator would like to express her gratitude to Mr. Paul Hamburger for advice and assistance on various points throughout the book.

ity not only into nations and races, but into further subdivided groups as well.* Few scholars have as yet investigated the origin and development of inflection from the combined viewpoint of music and linguistics—in spite of a rich enough literature on phonetics. Since the work of Merkel, Sievers and Jespersen, there has been little scientific interest shown in this direction, although it is undoubtedly the point of departure for any musician who wants to explore the origin of his means of expression.

Inflection and melody are closely connected, and must in the distant past have had one and the same origin.[1] The best proof of this lies in the life of still surviving primitive peoples. At the earliest stage of development, speaking was the same as singing: raising the voice in emphasis turned willy-nilly into chanting and singing. A Santali Indian woman lamenting her dead would unconsciously start singing instead of sobbing.[2] Observers have recorded that Australian aboriginals in a state of excitement break into an avalanche of words, the set rhythms and regular cadences of which create an illusion of chanting.[3] (In other places, as amongst the Minang-Kabau, a Sumatran-Malayan tribe, an instrumental accompaniment is used to give musical shape to solemn speeches.[4]) The sing-song intonation of the Wapares, a Bantu tribe, carries the sound of their voices over great distances.[5] But there is no need to look so far afield for evidence: in its countless variants, the ancient Hungarian dirge, related to the Ostyak and Vogul melodies of Siberia, consists of a kind of melodious sobbing or sung declamation. In fact its chief characteristic is its dependence on the modulations of speech. True, the dirge was a ritualistic melody for a special occasion, and as such belonged to a later stage of development. Yet for all its improvised character it still showed the power of settled, collective tradition. The conventions of fixed form and set meaning naturally underlay every melodic shape and intonation, and without them even personal emotion could hardly find expression. An individual who expresses himself in an unknown and unintelligible way sooner or later cuts himself off from human society.

'Singing speech' clearly developed in line with social convention, obligation and ceremonial. In other words, the primitive world sometimes needs to be correlated with the life of early civilisations. For from the Hoang-Ho to the Nile and the range of the Andes, it was they which first defined and regulated life, assessing and evaluating its every aspect. Convention obviously had a strong hold on primitive peoples, and was soon applied to ceremonial and ritualistic

---

* Both *intonation* and *inflection* are used in this chapter as translations of the German word *Tonfall*, implying changes of tone or pitch in speaking or singing. We are indebted to Mr. Peter Crossley-Holland for the following distinction which has regulated their use:

Inflection: a slide of the voice in a certain direction (e.g., level, rising, or falling) *which alters the fundamental position*. *Intonation*: a slide or leap of the voice according to *a fixed system of definable relationships*. (Translators' note.)

practices; but only in the first civilisations was a really conscious effort made to cover every aspect of life, and regulate social behaviour according to universally-accepted notions. Even a way of life dominated by witchcraft presupposed a certain social pattern, which means that it cannot really be regarded as primitive: but complex social ceremonial, intricate religious beliefs and a coherent set of customs belonged more naturally to the early civilisations than to primitive communities. Rhythm was closely connected with these factors because it was the most 'communal' element of melody. Primitive rhythm could fluctuate a great deal; work-rhythms, like the organisation of labour itself, came at a later stage. It was the earlier phase which caused so many subtle refinements of rhythm to exist in the first civilisations. As in other fields, the influence of these civilisations was primarily selective; it eliminated and stabilised. Some of the magical elements of primitive rhythm were repressed as tribal superstitions, and others elevated to full consciousness as religious ceremonies. But to a later observer their primitive origin is unmistakable. Countless features of the early civilisations help to shed light on primitive life, so it is not surprising that their melodies also 'reflect' the explanation as to how primitive melody originated.

The first important question is how *regulated intonation is related to fixed pitch*. In numerous Asian and African languages there is a well-known system of intonation *(toneme)*. Zulus and Congolese, Yoruba, Bantu, Efik and Ibo tribes possess real 'melody languages'; Hottentots use six different levels of intonation, and Liberian Jabos four; an Ewe negro can recognize single words of his language even if their 'melody' is only whistled.[6] As for the eastern rim of Asia, region of the great civilisations, Chinese has four to nine tone-levels (or tone-distinctions, etc.) divided up into matching groups, so as to form a closed system. They differ from each other as much as the dialects of a language; the various pronunciations produce quite a different meaning in the spoken language, even though the same written symbol is used. The author has witnessed how two Chinese from different parts of the country could not understand each other in speech, and were forced to use written symbols in order to avoid using a third language which would have been alien to them both. In modern Swedish, Norwegian and Japanese, different intonations can alter the meaning of words, not unlike the way that the combined use of definite pitch and syllabic accent in ancient languages (i.e. 'tonic accent') introduced a musical element which overrode the normal function of verbal stress. But in Chinese, word- and phrase-melody is more extensive, so that the spoken language is built up into self-contained musical entities which are really melody-systems. What was the origin of 'Cheng', that complicated and far-reaching system of intonations? So far there has been no convincing explanation. The philologist Henry Sweet considered intonation to be the most tenacious element in a language,[7] and observed that "the complexity of the tone distinctions increases as we advance south-eastwards: Tibetan has no word-tones, Burmese has only two, Siamese has five, North Chinese four, while in South Chinese (Cantonese) and Annamite the number of tones reaches its maximum."[8] "These facts seem to show that the borrowing, if any, is on the side of Burmese and Chinese, but against this we must set the unexpected fact that Mon and Cambodian, which are apparently the real aboriginal languages of Further India, and which are similar in structure to, though unconnected with Annamite, have no word-tones at all." Hence Sweet imagines that "the distinction of word-tones must have developed and spread out from some small centre in South-Eastern Asia, without any regard to linguistic relationship."[9] In lands where the ear is so sensitive to the various shades of speech-melody, it is not surprising that the melodic prototypes of the language assumed decisive importance in social life. The Chinese distinguished whole families and even clans by musical signs and epithets, a melodic coat-of-arms as it were, conferred either by tradition or heredity.[10] Ancient China is not alone in this: amongst the Papuans of New Guinea, every member of a clan has his or her individual rhythmical formula, which forms his 'surname' in the language of drum-signals.[11] The high or low register of the voice plays an important part in the tribal ceremonies of the North American Navahos, and every secret group or military alliance of the Omaha Indians has its own particular rhythm.[12] At an early stage of development, patterns of sound and rhythm must have served as symbols in communities large and small, and even have been adopted by individuals—but invariably as a fixed sound and a definite rhythm. That is why it is necessary to study the cultural region where the pitching of sounds, or 'tuning', is thought to have originated: that is, China, Central and South-East Asia. This was the area where the English philologist Sweet looked for the origin of intonation, and where in his turn the Dutch musicologist Jaap Kunst considered pitch to have been invented and first practised. In the course of his comparative researches as a distinguished scholar of Indonesian instruments and tonal systems, Jaap Kunst discovered that the tuning of the *marimba* and *balafo*—played by negroes—is exactly the same as the Javanese gender.[13] All three instruments are based on the early Chinese circle of blown fifths—a tuning-system which had evidently reached Indonesia as well as Central Africa; Hornbostel too has shown that the same principle found its way to South America, particularly to Peru.[14] It may well be that analogous tuning-systems occurred independently of each other at different points on the earth's surface. "Since tonal systems derive from the physical phenomenon of overtones," says Kunst, "it is conceivable, though improbable, that one and the same system might arise in different regions and at different times, exactly identical in form and yet quite unrelated to one another; but there is not the slightest reason—psychological or physiological—why the same fundamental note should be adopted as a starting-point. Yet, curiously enough, in every case where tonal systems deriving from blown fifths are used, their basic-note, their starting-point is not only approximately, but exactly the same: a sound of the frequency of 366 vibrations per second." (This is slightly sharper than our F^1 sharp; recent investigations verified it as 358 vibrations.) If Kunst's and Hornbostel's calculations are right, the early method of tuning, which originated somewhere in Central or South-Eastern Asia, and which Chinese tradition dates back some 3000 years B.C., established itself in America as well as in Africa. (E.g., when the Javanese *pelog* or ancestral five-note scale, adopted from China, came into contact with a more recent seven-note scale, called *slendro*, adopted from India or Sumatra, the *pelog* merely conquered and displaced it.) Pan-pipes, genders and xylophones were all tuned to this old system. The *Huang-Chung* (diapason, 'Imperial note', or 'Yellow Bell'), selected by Ancient China as the basis of its tonal system, was retained as an unchanging basic note. It seems that with its help the Chinese anticipated all other peoples in the consistent use of tuning.[15] Thus the first fixing of sound by tuning began in the same culture-region that first fixed the intonation of the voice. These two achievements represented mastery over a notoriously variable phenomenon of acoustics—probably for the first time for thousands of years, with a likely validity of further thousands.

The second problem concerns the kind of melodies which came into being as the result of inflection, or which could clearly be traced back to speech. Dirges have already been mentioned: in Asia as in Europe, their basic structure departed little from the declamatory lament of ancient ritual. These laments, however, are already surprisingly developed from a melodic point of view: like their Ostyak and Vogul variants, ancient Hungarian laments are pentachordal or pentatonic, which is too rich a supply of tonal resources to be called primitive. As speech-melody developed, it reached a stage when a larger group of speech-sounds broke off from the normal speech-levels to form tunes. But it must have been a phase of this process, when only very few of the available notes were used, thus giving rise to *tunes of one, two, or three notes*. The singing voice was unable to manage any more at this stage—at least not in the form of song. It took a long time for the complete range of notes to be at the singer's disposal in singable fashion. At first the compass of singable notes was perhaps only a second, and probably increased later to a fourth or fifth, within which three, or at most four, notes were sung. They were not necessarily adjacent, and formed several two-note and three-note patterns. This meant that in primitive music fourths and fifths were as familiar as seconds and thirds. They were all adopted, and played a similar role in the formation of pentatonic scale-types in each culture-region. Only much later was this followed by accurately measured intervals and regularly adopted patterns, in other words, the transition to fixed patterns and the final selection of four or five notes. Any series of notes (i.e. scale) is after all the result of a retrospective abstraction; the melodic shape came first, together with the instinctive urge to create well-balanced structures. For a long time afterwards, this urge was bound up with the capacity of speech-melody to express and communicate. Melody probably began to make headway, independently of speech, at the point where the purely *musical* urge to form decorative and symmetrical structures began to predominate.

It is worth taking a look at tunes made up of a few notes, as sung to this day by primitive peoples. There is no dearth of available material: the most remarkable examples seem to be South American and Wedda melodies. In ancient times, it seems to have been the prevalent style of Tierra del Fuego, Central Brazil and Ceylon.[16] The mourning songs of the Bororo of Central Brazil, for instance (published by Von den Steinen), are important because they represent that stage in evolution when melodies consisted of a fixed pivotal note and almost nothing else. Anything else was incidental and fluctuating, and only assumed importance when the basic shape slowly became a structure of several notes under the influence of many variants:

I

Dirge (Central Brazil)

The second example (also from Von den Steinen) shows the same sort of ambivalence. Men and women alternate in singing a tune which is clearly meant to be the same, but the sliding to vague, adjacent notes in the men's version becomes a clear three-note shape when sung by the women:

2

Hunting song (Central Brazil)
Men:

Ba - ko - ro - ró   a - ró - e   a - ró - e
(=water)

si - bá - yu   a - ró - e   a - ró - e   dyure - tó - tó
(=sea-gull)   (=water-snake)

16

Ba-ko-ro-ró   a-ró-.e   a-ró-e

si-bá-yu   a-ró-e   a-ró-e   dyure-tó-tó

It is interesting that a single note unobtrusively formed others, depending on whether the dynamic stress was light or heavy. A more shrill and emphatic note rose, a muffled note fell. "It would hardly be wrong to consider even two-tone melodies as fluctuations of a single note due to accent"—Hornbostel writes of tunes sung by the Indians of Tierra del Fuego.[17]

Even at this early stage, it is important to realise that melody already showed a double nature where rhythm was concerned. The closed dance-form already existed alongside the free *parlando* style. This was a general characteristic: the two- and three-note Wedda tunes of Ceylon were normally *rubato* in type, but there were some in *tempo giusto*. Bushman tunes are normally in rhythmic dance-style, whilst Patagonian tunes and those of the Kubu of Sumatra are rhythmically free. Andaman solo-songs are also free, although their choral refrains are regulated by dancing.[18] If the noting down of Wedda melodies by English and German investigators is correct, a further characteristic is the appearance of a more or less definite semitone alongside the whole tone interval:

3

Wedda melodies
a)

b)

It is not known how far this chromatic tendency extended, nor what melodic shapes it was capable of creating at this stage. So it is all the more surprising that Andamanese music, in many ways stylistically related to Singalese music, shows a tendency to an almost over-developed chromaticism. At the time that M. V. Portman noted down the tunes, he resorted to thirds and quarters of a tone to fix the fluctuation.[19] This strange minuteness seems to be no chromaticism or over-refinement, but rather a genuine indecision; it is not beyond diatonicism but this side of it. So long as the tonal system was unfixed, intonation was uncertain and wavering. From a historical point of view, true chromaticism was at the opposite pole: when melody had developed to such an extent that diatonicism could contain it no longer, a process of fragmentation and greater refinement set in. This was what happened in Indian-Mohammedan chromaticism in the East, and in 16th-century Italian and 19th-century German chromaticism in the West. Yet it is worth noticing that nearly all archetypal European melodies which are half-way between speech and song are diatonic. These include the words and phrases for calling animals—of which more below—and the traditional street-cries of London, Paris, Florence and Vienna (*Kaufrufe, grida dei venditori*, etc.). They have constantly been noted down and used by composers during the course of the last five hundred years.[20]

An important stage was reached when primitive speech-melodies *began to be played on instruments*. The first instrumental melodies probably belong here. The primitive instrument imitated the primitive singing-voice, and the speech-melodies of the human larynx were transferred to 'dead matter'. Drums, animal horns, conches and pan-pipes were naturally the first instruments used to accompany or reproduce human melody (in fact the natives of Liberia call them 'speaking tools'). This 'instrumental speech' always occurred in centres of refuges of primitive culture, such as Melanesia, West Africa, certain parts of South Africa, and some almost completely isolated primitive folk-communities of the present day.

The most important instrumental speech was that of *drum-language*—a system of signals perfected by some Papuan and Negro tribes, to help them establish contact over vast distances.[21] The pitch of the drum could be altered in numerous ways, its rhythmic possibilities were almost endless, its carrying power depended chiefly on the player, and could be extended by relays. In this way communication was able to be almost unlimited. Systems of signal-signs have existed from very primitive times, and, as described above, a signal could be used to identify tribes, families, or single individuals. The rest was a question of drum-technique. The Duala Negroes use the drum at funerals to relate the life-history of the deceased, and a second drum repeats every rhythm and every signal at a higher or lower pitch. Amongst the Monumbo of New Guinea, a husband calls his wife home from her work in the fields by the generic female signal, followed by the signal of the waiting husband (the women have generic signals only, whilst the men have their own, many of them hereditary). If these two signs are followed by the death-signal, it means that the husband had died. Luba, the language of the Congolese Bantu, has only two tone-levels—one high, one low—yet their drum-language, *tchianda*, can convey the most complicated paraphrases: for instance, a man calls his wife home by the following phrase: "a woman's finest ornament is not her tattoo, but the fire she has lit in her husband's hut!" The courses of festive banquets, any dangers threatening the tribe, the formation of hostile groups, duels, battles and peace-treaties are all announced by drum. The rhythm and pitch of such signals are closely related to the corresponding inflections and stresses of speech. Sometimes the phonetic subtlety of speech survives in the signals, although it has been lost in the language, because there was no longer any need to preserve the musical nuances. (This is probably what happened in Arabic, where complex and ancient Bedouin rhythms have survived only in the *waznes*, the accompanying rhythms of drums.) A similar *parlando* style has survived in some South African drum melodies, built up on the rhythmical repetition of two-note motifs.[22]

At a certain stage, speech-melody seems to have been transferred to wind instruments too. Many of Melanesian pan-pipe tunes, published by Hornbostel, keep surprisingly close to speech accentuation and articulation.[23] The horn-signals of Liberian Jabos originated in the inflections of watchwords. Jewish *shofar* (ram's horn) signals reflect in their entirety the cantillation of sung bible-reading, and though their notation was not attempted until the 14th century, it is probable that they derived from ancient traditions, like the vocalised cantillation of prayers (ecphonetic recitation) and bible-cantillation itself.[24]

Short phrases for calling animals, and the horn melodies of swineherds and shepherds also need mentioning, as they are still played on their original primitive instruments, from Brittany to the villages of Hungary and Rumania, and the plains beyond. They originated in the inflections of calls for animals, to be heard on any farm, and obviously developed without reference to historical, geographical or ethnographical frontiers. How closely speech-stress and instrument were connected in these calls is clear even from medieval manuscripts.[25] Any text, apart from the onomatopoeic syllables, etc., imitates the instrument, which in its turn imitates human speech. This type of melody is just as genuine a primitive survival at the heart of European civilisation as the prehistoric rocks which lie at the base of skyscrapers.

*

Is there a connection between this primitive world of melody, involving the slightest quiver of melody in speech, and the more advanced forms? In other words, was this the course of melodic evolution, and can its traces still be seen?

Solution of the problem has been vastly stimulated in recent years by study of the five-note or pentatonic system, which, in the author's opinion, is the universal legacy of the first civilisation.[26] So far as cultural history is concerned, pentatonicism—or rather the melodic styles to which it gave birth—shows two different historical stages. As a tonal system, it preserved traces of primeval *community*, or a universally accepted central impulse. As a reservoir of melodic formulae, it points to an equally ancient *separation* of cultures, of continents and regions. The collective element reflected in pentatonicism may well belong to the primitive world, but the process of separation as shown by its various melodic patterns connects it indisputably with the emergence of ancient high-civilisations. Hence it possesses the Janus-like quality necessary to form a connecting link: its roots lie in the primitive world, but it flowers in highly developed musical cultures. It forms a bridge between primitive forms and highly developed styles. It may represent the first musical classicism; a synthesis and the result of long preparatory phases.

Some of the primary forms of pentatonia are in fact known: three-note tunes either confine themselves to trichords*, or else take the decisive step that leads to expansion into five-note forms. Three-note tunes are of many types: some are made up of three adjacent notes, whilst in others the interval of a third separates two of the three notes. Taking the series D—F—G—A—C as an example, the following formations may occur: F—G—A (e.g., Hebrew-Gregorian psalm-tones), D—F—G (Buriat songs), or A—C—D (most Hungarian children's singing-games) and, less often, C—D—F (Ostyak tunes).[27] In some regions, the three-note patterns, under the pressure of expansive and repetitive tendencies, spread out into five notes, and acquire the range and potential of D—F—G—A—C. The most interesting examples of this process come from the shores of the Mediterranean and certain parts of Eastern and Central Asia.

An ancient Indian type is important in this connection. The most valuable strata of ancient Indian music consists of a few melodies which have been preserved in connection with the texts of Vedic hymns.[28] They are characterized by few notes, which exactly correspond to the text and especially to the metre of the line-endings. They have a fixed and uniform number of syllables, but the definite rhythmical pattern appears only in the second half of the line. In the so-called *anustubh* metre, quoted below, the eight syllables of each line are so distributed that the first four are vague and variable, whilst the last are uncompromisingly iambic. Sometimes there are short, floating syllables of a passing nature, which the melody eases into the regular line-structure:

4

Vedic hymn

a - gnir naḥ pā .. tu kṛt - ti - kā - ḥ

---

* 'Trichord' — used here by analogy with tetrachord to indicate 3-note schemes. (Translators' note.)

20

nak - ṣa - traṃ de va-min-dri-yam idam āsāṃ

vicak - ṣaṇam ha-vir ā - sañ jo-ha ta - na

This tune clearly belongs to a three-note type that in certain parts of Asia (especially Central Asia, amongst the Buriat, for instance) would expand into a five-note form.[29] India of course is far from this Central Asian 'workshop', yet the original meaning of *anustubh* as "the metre of the north" probably points to some Central Asian connection. If this hymn-tune is stripped of its rhythm:

5

Vedic hymn (simplified, without rhythm)

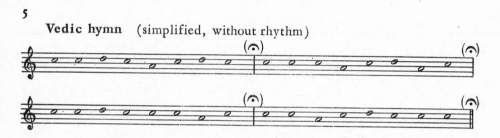

it lies revealed as a type of 'proto-pentatonicism', only one step removed from a fully pentatonic melody of the ancient Eurasian eight-syllable type, found from Mongolia to Transdanubia (Western Hungary).

In Central Asia, the most common way of extending the scale is by transposition, i.e. by repeating some of the melodic lines in a lower register. There are many examples of melodies based on a three-note pattern of A—C—D which has expanded into a five-note shape by having D—F—G added on below as its own counterpart, in other words, the basic idea has been doubled in a lower register. (Several African tribes, such as the Chewas, form tunes by linking two such three-note patterns.[30]) The melody grew down from above: it applies as well to primitive speech-melody as to the melodic feeling of ancient peoples, which manifested itself in the same way from China to classical Greece.

This may well have been the bridge between the primitive world and the early civilisations. Assuming a connection between the metres of Vedic hymns and those of ancient Greece,[31] India stood on an ancient crossroad between the Mediterranean world and Central Asia. The formative principles first embodied in the Vedic hymns were pursued in China and Central Asia in pentatonicism, in Greece in metrical systems, that is in different directions.

The opposite may also have happened: perhaps it was India which was the receptive party for both initiatives. The three-note elements leading to pentatonicism may well have come from Central Asia, and the principle of metre from some common Indo-European source. There is no certainty. What matters is that some part of a splendid ancient tradition has survived in Indian music. The historical evidence is ambiguous and vague, a faint light in the darkness: but it may still help the historian of melody to grope his way towards new discoveries.

NOTES

1. This point of view—which sometimes gives historical precedence to speech, and sometimes to singing—was first put forward by Rousseau and d'Alembert in the 18th century, and later by Spencer and Wagner in the 19th. (In more recent times it has been emphatically stated by F. Torrefranca: "Le origini della musica." *Riv. Mus. Ital.*, 1907; *cp.* also Della Corte: *Le teorie delle origini della musica e le musiche dei popoli antichi e primitivi.* 1932.) On European speech-melody see particularly Steele: *Essay Towards Establishing the Melody and Measure of Speaking.* 1776; Walker: *The Melody of Speaking.* 1787; L. Köhler: *Die Melodie der Sprache in ihrer Anwendung besonders auf das Lied und die Oper.* Leipzig, 1853; C. L. Merkel: *Physiologie der menschlichen Sprache.* Leipzig, 1866, pp. 348—397 and Musical Appendix; a wealth of data and comments in J. Storm: *Englische Philologie.* I, *Die lebende Sprache*, Section I, *Phonetik und Aussprache* (Leipzig, 1892, passim, especially pp. 205—208, e.g. p. 207: "*ein geübtes Ohr beobachtet in der Satzmelodie jeden Augenblick Anläufe zu einer musikalischen Melodie. Der Gesang liegt in der Redestimme als Keim . . .*" etc.). This opinion, shared also by Wagner, was taught in the 18th century by Lacombe (1758) and Grétry (1789):"*La parole est un bruit où le chant est renfermé . . .*" Further, see H. Siebeck: "Sprechmelodie und Tonmelodie in ihrem ästhetischen Verhältnis." *Riemann-Festschrift*, 1909; C. Stumpf: "Singen und Sprechen." *Zeitschr. f. Psychologie*, 1924; E. Waiblinger: "Beobachtungen über das Verhältnis von Gesang und Sprache." *Vox*, 1925; H. Chr. Wolff: "Die Sprachmelodie im alten Opernrezitativ" (*Archiv f. Sprach- und Stimmphysiologie*, 1940, on the basic differences between Italian, German and French operatic recitative in the 18th century); H. H. Unger: *Die Beziehungen zwischen Musik und Rhetorik im 16.—17. Jahrhundert.* Würzburg, 1941. For an independent enquiry into present-day phonetics, amongst others see Sievers: *Rhythmisch-melodische Studien.* Heidelberg, 1912; D. Jones: *Intonation Curves.* Leipzig—Berlin, 1909; by the same author: *An Outline of English Phonetics.* 4th edition, Leipzig, 1934, particularly pp. 241, 255—302; O. Rutz: *Musik, Wort und Körper.* Leipzig, 1911; by the same author: *Sprache, Gesang und Körperhaltung.* München, 1922; Eggert: "Untersuchungen über Sprachmelodie." *Zeitschr. f. Psychologie*, 1908; Jannuzzi: "Sulla melodia del linguaggio." *Soc. It. di Otorinolaringologia*, 1924; Griffith: "Time Pattern in Prose." *Psychol. Monogr.* XXXIX, 1929; Ipsen-Karg: *Schallanalytische Versuche.* Heidelberg, 1928; O. Jespersen: *Lehrbuch der Phonetik* (5th edition, Leipzig—Berlin, 1932, among others pp. 241—242 interesting comments on the major and minor modes in speech); G. Panconcelli-Calzia: *Die experimentelle Phonetik in ihrer Anwendung auf die Sprachwissen-*

schaft. Berlin, 1924, especially pp. 105—114; A. Rousselot: *Principes de la phonétique expérimentale*. 2nd ed. Paris, 1925; W. E. Peters: *Sprechmelodische Motive nachgewiesen in experimental-phonetischen Aufnahmen estnischer Versrezitation*. Tartu—Dorpat, 1927; by the same author: *Bericht über eine experimental-phonetische vergleichende Untersuchung der estnischen Sprechmelodie*. Hamburg, 1927; N. S. Trubetzkoy: *Grundzüge der Phonologie*. Prague, 1939; Gemelli—Pastori: *L'analisi elettroacustica del linguaggio*. Milan, 1934, especially I, pp. 237—243; H. Palmer: *English Intonation*. Cambridge, 1922; Armstrong—Ward: *Handbook of English Intonation*. 2nd ed. Cambridge—Leipzig, 1931; H. Krause: *Intonation und Lautgebung in der englischen Aussprache*. Berlin, 1938; J. Smits van Waesberghe: *Phonetics in its Relation to Musicology. Manual of Phonetics*. Amsterdam, 1957. A selected list of relevant Hungarian books (the titles are given in English): G. Mátray: *Basic Course of Recitation*. 1861; Gábor Egressy: *A School for Actors*. 1879; Studies by V. Tolnay, B. Csüry, Gy. Laziczius, L. Hegedüs, E. Jacobi-Lányi, and, most important, Z. Gombocz: "Musical Stress in Sentences." *Urania* VIII, p. 129; Z. Kodály: *On the Decline of Hungarian Pronunciation*. 1937; also S. Eckhardt: *Documents of Correct Hungarian Pronunciation*. 1941; B. Szabolcsi: *Speech and Melody* (Appendix of this book); János Horváth: *Hungarian Verse*. 1948; Imre Molnár: *System of Hungarian Intonation*. 1954. See also R. Lach's relevant comments in *Studien zur Entwicklungsgeschichte der ornamentalen Melopöie*. Leipzig, 1913.

2. Rev. P. O. Bodding: *Materials for a Santali Grammar*. I, Dumka, 1930, p. 155. For its Hungarian analogy, see Béla Gunda's description of a custom in Újbars (County Bars): "When a husband dies, his wife leaves the corpse, runs out into the courtyard, waves her arms about at shoulder-height, and cries out in a long drawn-out wail, which is close to singing. This is to announce the news to the neighbours." In villages in County Szabolcs (e.g. Balsa), the lament for a dead child imperceptibly turns into singing. (Contributed by György Kisfaludy.)

3. G. Grey: *Journals of Two Expeditions of Discovery in North-western and Western Australia*. 1841, II, p. 313. The 'sounding-calls' of the Mississippi Negroes are examples of work-songs based on primitive speech-melody. Some were recorded on discs by H. Halpert (Amer. Folklore Soc.) in 1939.

4. J. C. van Eerde: "Minangkabausche Poezie." *Tijdschr. voor Ind. Taal. Land- en Volkenkunde*. Deel 39, 1897, p. 572.

5. O. Baumann: *Usambara*, 1891, p. 219.

6. *Cf.* D. M. Beach: "The Science of Tonetics and its Application to Bantu Languages." *Bantu Studies*, 1924; by the same author: *The Phonetics of the Hottentot Language*. Cambr. 1938, p. 124 et *seq.*, p. 235 et *seq.*; K. E. Laman: *The Musical Accent or Intonation in the Kongo Language*. Stockholm, 1922; I. C. Ward: *The Phonetic and Tonal Structure of Efik*. Cambridge, 1933; by the same author: *An Introduction to the Ibo Language. Ibid.*, 1936; N. W. Thomas: "Some Notes on the Tones of the Ibo Language of Nigeria." *Assoc. Phonétique Internat., Miscellanea Phonetica*. I, 1914, pp. 38—43; W. Heinitz: "Ein Beitrag zur Reproduktion des musikalischen Elements in der Ewe-Sprache." *Vox*, 1916, p. 83; George Herzog: "Speech-Melody and Primitive Music." *Mus. Quart.* 1934; G. Révész: *Einführung in die Musikpsychologie*. Bern, 1946, pp. 274—289; Kenneth L. Pike: *Tone Languages*. Ann Arbor, 1948; C. Sachs: *The Wellsprings of Music*. The Hague, 1962, pp. 35—38.

7. *The History of Language*. London, 1909, p. 73.

8. For more details, see B. Karlgren: *Études sur la phonologie chinoise*. Leyden—Stockholm, 1915, pp. 254—259 and 581—597. Karlgren maintains that four 'chengs' are known in old Chinese, in present-day Pekinese and the language of Hankow, whilst Nankinese has five, Hakka six, Fu-chow seven, Swatow, Shanghi and Chinese-Annamite eight, and Cantonese

23

nine. M. Courant attempted to transcribe these tonemes into modern notation (*La langue chinoise parlée.* Paris, 1914); see also Chiu Bien-ming: "A Phonogram in Chinese." *Vox*, 1930, p. 33; M. Schneider: *La relation entre la mélodie et le langage dans la musique chinoise.* Barcelona, 1950, Sep. del Anuario Mus. V. For the Japanese material, see E. Meyer: "Der musikalische Wortakzent im Japanischen." *Le Monde oriental* I, 1906.

9. *Op. cit.*, pp. 78—79.
10. M. Granet: *La pensée chinoise.* Paris, 1934, pp. 49—50.
11. R. Neuhaus: *Deutsch-Neu-Guinea.* 1911, I, p. 316.
12. Herzog: *op. cit.*; A. C. Fletcher—F. La Flesche: "The Omaha Tribe." *Bureau of American Ethnology*, 27. Report, Washington, 1911, p. 503.
13. "Ein musikologischer Beweis für Kulturzusammenhänge zwischen Indonesien—vermutlich Java—und Zentral-Afrika." *Anthropos*, 1936, p. 131.
14. "Die Massnorm als kulturgeschichtliches Forschungsmittel." *W. Schmidt Festschrift*, 1928. See *Musik in Geschichte und Gegenwart* for M. F. Bukofzer's Critical comments in his article *Blasquinte*.
15. *Cf.* Chao Mei-pa: *La cloche jaune.* Bruxelles, 1932; J. H. Lewis: *Foundations of Chinese Musical Art.* Peiping, 1936 and Wang Kung-Ki: "Chinesische Musik." *Sinica*, 1927, Nos. 6—10.
16. Sources of the data quoted include K. von den Steinen: *Unter den Naturvölkern Zentral-Brasiliens. Reiseschilderung und Ergebnisse der zweiten Schingu-Expedition 1887—1888.* 2nd ed., Berlin, 1897, p. 381; M. Wertheimer: "Musik der Wedda." *Sammelb. d. Internat. Mus. Gesellsch.* XI, 1910; Seligmann—Brenda: *The Veddas.* 1911; H. Werner: *Ursprünge der Lyrik.* 1924, pp. 133—158. Cp. also a Turcoman tune, transcribed by Uspenski, known from a work of G. Lobatchev: *Turkmenskiye pyesni.* Moscow, 1937, No. 14. It consists of frequent repetitions of the following motifs:

viz. a two-note tune with a ditty-like rhythmic structure. *Cf.* the 'Villő' tune used in winter folk-ritual from County Nyitra, published by Z. Kodály and János Manga (*Ethnographia*, 1909, p. 121, and *Report of the Budapest Ethnographical Museum*, 1941, p. 283):

Australian 'spell-songs' of one or two basic notes, similar to those published by v. d. Steinen, are contributed by A. W. Howitt: *The Native Tribes of S.E. Australia.* London, 1904, pp. 420—421; Bedouin dirges with up to four notes appear in the collection of G. H. Dalman: *Palästinischer Diwan.* Leipzig, 1901, pp. 358—359.

17. *Ethnos.* Stockholm, 1948, p. 68. (The Music of the Fuegians) includes the following:

Like their Lapp equivalents, these tunes accompany dances in imitation of animals, and are used at initiation ceremonies. (The melody quoted is the 'Dance of the white seagull'.)

18. Werner: *op. cit.*: pp. 151—152; E. v. Hornbostel: *Über die Musik der Kubu.* (In Hagen's *Die Orang-Kubu auf Sumatra.* 1908.)
19. "Andamanese music." *Journal of the R. Asiatic Soc.* XX, 1888. For a European musician, melody at this stage of evolution is pre-melodic, because it slides about uncertainly by means of portamento. Articulated tonal structure (i.e., with regular intervals) clearly only

developed later. It is worth noticing how composers nearer our own day often seem to recapitulate the slow processes of historical development, as though they too have to 'emerge from the mists.' Ferdinand Ries relates how Beethoven in 1806 conceived the last movement of the *Appassionata* during a walk, "mumbling and howling all kinds of sounds, up and down the scale, without any definite pitch."

20. E.g., the Florentine Messer Zacharias, about 1420 (words of such cries had already been noted by Guillaume de Villeneuve in the 13th century), Jannequin in the 16th century, Weelkes, Gibbons and Deering at the beginning of the 17th century, Handel (*Serse*, 1738), Werner (*Der Wienerische Tandelmarkt, c.* 1740), more recently Clapisson (1856), Charpentier (1900), Vaughan Williams (*London Symphony*, 1917), and Gershwin (*Porgy and Bess*, 1935). In 1748, Lady Luxborough quotes Handel's remark that the memory of street cries had inspired his most beautiful arias. *Cf. Journal of the Folk-Song Soc.* XXII (1919) and P. A. Scholes: *The Oxford Companion to Music.* 2nd ed., London—New York, 1939, article on 'Street Music', pp. 900—903. Russian material: K. A. Yantchuk: "Vykriki raznostchikov" (Russian street-cries, etc., with transcripts of Gretchaninov, Listopadov, Nevstruyev, Yantchuk and Araktcheiev), "Materiali i isslyedovania po isutsheniu narodnoi pessni i musiki." *Isvj. Imper. Obshtch. Lub. Yest. Antrop. i Etnogr. Trudi Etnogr. Otdyela XV, Trudy Muzikalno-Etnogr. Komissii*, Tom. I, Moscow, 1906, pp. 497—516. For recent French material, see J. Sempé: *France qui chante.* Paris, 1945, p. 20, for Italian, F. Ghisi: *I canti carnascialeschi nelle fonti musicali del XV e XVI sec.* Firenze—Roma, 1937, pp. 171—172. For Rumanian: G. Suliţeanu: "Din strigătele muncitorilor, mestesugarilor, vînzătorilor, distribuitorilor ambulanti." *Revista de Folclor* V, Nos. 1—2. Bucureşti, 1960, pp. 75—113.—The street-cries, or *exclamationes* of Roman merchants were referred to by Seneca, *Epist.* 56, 2. (See Walter Wiora: *Europäische Volksmusik und abendländische Tonkunst.* Kassel, 1957, p. 41).—About modern street-cries in European towns see Wiora *l. c.* p. 102.—In recent literature see M. Proust: La prisonnière (*A la recherche* ... VI, 1) 61. éd., pp. 159—163, 172—175, 186—188. (About the street-cries of Paris.)

21. For the most important literature on drum signals see: R. Betz: "Die Trommelsprache der Duala," *Mitteilungen a. d. deutschen Schutzgebieten* XI, 1898; Thilenius — Meinhof — Heinitz: "Die Trommelsprache in Afrika und in der Südsee." *Vox*, 1916, and *Phonetische Vorträge.* Hamburg, 1917; C. Meinhof: *Die afrikanische Trommelsprache.* 1918; W. Heinitz: "Ein Beitrag zum Problem der Trommelsprache." *Vox*, 1927; Amaat Burssens: "Le Luba, langue à intonation et le tambour-signal." *Proc. of the III. Internat. Congress of Phonetic Sciences*, Ghent, 1939, pp. 503—507; M. Schneider: "Zur Trommelsprache der Duala." *Anthropos* XLVII, 1952. Old Chinese military drums were probably used for intonation in the same way (*cf.* De Groot: *Die Hunnen der vorchristlichen Zeit.* 1921, p. 166).

22. Percival R. Kirby: *The Musical Instruments of the Native Races of South Africa.* London, 1934, p. 31.

23. "Notiz über die Musik der Bewohner von Süd-Neumecklenburg," in Stephan and Graebner: *Neumecklenburg*, 1907, also in *Sammelb. f. vergl. Musikwiss.* I, 1922, pp. 356—357.

24. See *Memorial Vol. for B. Heller*, Budapest, 1941, p. 279. So far as the author is aware, the fixing of *Shofar* signals was first attempted in the metrical neums of the 10th-century Saadya prayer-book. (*Cf.* Davidson-Assaf-Joel; *Siddur R. Saadja Gaon, Kitab Gāmi at salawāt wat-tarābih.* Jerusalem, 1941, p. 397.) The ancient connection between intonation and instrument is also evident elsewhere. According to Cicero and Gellius (*De Oratore*, III, 60, resp. *Noctes Atticae*, I, 11) some classical authors memorised and performed their speeches with the help of a flute-player, so as to ensure the right level of intonation. The instrument provided the melodic line of the oration; this was the characteristic use of the *tibia* or *fistula concionatoria*. According to Isocrates, the perfect oration was really a musical composition!

There are some interesting comments on the relationship between intonation, compass and instrument in Max Weber: *Die rationalen und soziologischen Grundlagen der Musik*. München, 1921, pp. 26—29. Flute music, which represented the 'voice of the ancestors' in primitive rituals, is mentioned by Huizinga: *Homo ludens*. Amsterdam, 1939, p. 37.

25. P. Verrier: *Le vers français* I, Paris, 1931, pp. 96—98. Most Hungarian swineherd horn-tunes come into this group. *Cf.* Bartók's entry in the *Hungarian Dict. of Music* II, 1931, p. 62. (Bartók draws attention to their *parlando* character.) These may be supplemented with material from the Hungarian Plains; a herdsman of Péterréve (County Bács-Bodrog, now Yugoslavia) was heard blowing the following in the summer of 1941 (the horn's ground-note was *F* sharp):

In the course of repetition, the first or second bar was omitted, as well as an occasional crotchet: this emphasised even more clearly the speech character of the tune. *Cf.* also Chr. Vakarelski: *Izrazi za primamvanye i otpushdanye na nekoi domashni shivotni*. Sofia, 1937.

26. Zoltán Kodály: *Folk Music of Hungary*. 1960, pp. 23—55; *Hungarian National Character in Music*. 1940, pp. 15—16 (in Hungarian); W. Danckert: "Musikwissenschaft und Kulturkreislehre." *Anthropos*, 1937; by the same author: "Musikwissenschaftl. Erschliessung der Kulturkreise." *Mitt. d. Wiener Anthropolog. Ges.* LXVII, 1937; *Das europäische Volkslied*. Berlin, 1939, pp. 29, 208, 298, 354; *Grundriss der Volksliedkunde*. Berlin, 1939, p. 80; "Melodiestile der finnisch-ugrischen Hirtenvölker." *Studia Memoriae Belae Bartók Sacra*. Budapest, 1956; W. Wiora: *Älter als die Pentatonik. Ibidem;* L. Bárdos: *Natürliche Tonsysteme. Ibidem;* in Hungarian: Barna Kishonti: *The Physical Foundations of Musical Pentatonicism*. 1939; B. Szabolcsi: "Five-note Scales and Civilisation." *Acta Musicol.*, 1944 (also in Appendix in the present vol.). Further J. Yasser: *A Theory of Evolving Tonality*. New York, 1932, pp. 25—61, chaps. 6 and 7 (Historic Survey of Chinese Scales, resp. The Infra-Diatonic System).

27. A few examples:

Hebrew - Gregorian melody

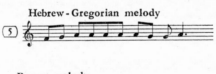

Buryat melody

(Bashkuyev: *Sbornik buriat mongolskikh pyesen*. Moscow, 1935, No. 13);

Ostyak melody

(W. Steinitz: *Ostjakische Volksdichtung und Erzählungen*. II, Stockholm, 1941, No. 36);

Hungarian nursery rhyme

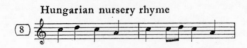

(international type, *cf.* also W. Tappert: *Wandernde Melodien*. Leipzig, 1890, pp. 39—41);
Z. Kodály: *Folk Music of Hungary*. 1960, pp. 69—70. The intervals of the 3-note pattern
g—a—c are the same as those of *c—d—f*, so that the same pattern occurs twice in the scale,
but is capable of being differently combined. *Cf.* the following plainchant litany:

Ky-ri - e   e - le - i - son,   Chri-ste   e - le - i - son

(later develops into a Lydian scale, i.e. f^1—e^2).

28. E. Felber: "Die indische Musik der vedischen und der klassichen Zeit." *Sitzungsberichte
der Akad. d. Wiss.* Wien, 1912; *cf.* also J. M. van der Hoogt: *The Vedic Chant Studied in its
Textual and Melodic Form*. 1929.

29. There are other examples amongst Chinese Confucius melodies (*cf.* Laloy: *La musique
chinoise*. 1910, Appendix; also in an article by A. Cimbro, *La Rassegna Musicale*. 1929,
p. 596):

30. See the communication of George Herzog: *Mus. Quart.* XX, 1934, p. 457.

31. A. Meillet: *Les origines indo-européennes des mètres grecs*. Paris, 1923, p. 32, *et seq.* Note also
the interesting review of this theory by G. Pasquali: *Preistoria della poesia romana*. Firenze,
1936, pp. 16—19.

MELODY IN THE FIRST CIVILISATION:
FROM PENTATONICISM TO DIATONICISM

"Subjects are lasting, and are handed down from one generation to the next. Most of them stem from antiquity, but their meaning was different at that time from what it was in the Middle Ages." (Huizinga: *Culturhistorische Verkenningen.* 1930.)

"Fundamentally ... all folk-music will be reduced to a few primary forms, primary types, primary styles." (Bartók: *Folk Music and Nationalism.* 1937.)

The first high-civilisations of mankind did not occur in isolation, but with almost chain-like continuity, practically simultaneously in Western Asia and along the shore-regions of Eurasia. The two thousand years from 4000 to 2000 B.C. were decisive for their growth to maturity: at the end of this period, the powerful civilisations of Mesopotamia, Egypt, China, India and Crete were either at their peak, or already in decline. Some scholars consider their growth to be a triumph of 'water-civilisation', but their almost simultaneous appearance may also imply a common ancestor in some vanished Atlantis, of which they were colonies or settlements. One thing, however, is certain: in the light of present-day knowledge, these cultures represented human self-awareness and skill in their first highly developed, organised form—and they had a similar importance in musical history.

Musical material, after all, is like any other raw material, and every community or cultural group selects and rejects, combines and constructs in relation to its own nature and purpose. This selective process is highly 'individual', and betrays the nature of its origin. In this way, tonal systems came into being without an abstract series of notes having necessarily taken shape in the musician's mind. Particular three-note combinations came to distinguish this or that culture, and pentatonicism was adopted as a common language, however varied in form and type. For to the extent that the ancient style can be reconstructed, pentatonicism was clearly universal: scattered remains from peripheral regions still bear eloquent witness to this fact. They also make it very clear that a few thousand years of melodic history is a very brief period; pentatonicism is alive as a musical language even today.

How did this world-language develop, and gain its supremacy? All explanations perforce involve guesswork and inconsistency. The question is complicated by the fact that development was not simultaneous and uniform, even though it is difficult to dismiss the idea of a common region of origin. Some three-note schemes probably developed into five-note schemes, either through transposition or addition. This would explain why so many different pentatonic styles exist within the same tonal system. Yet whenever a higher culture resorted to pentatonicism, a more or less conscious process of *selection* took place from some general note-supply, for basically every classical style involved sorting, sifting and selecting. The instruments of any pentatonic region show this very clearly—e.g., flutes and pipes in India, Mongolia, Melanesia and Transdanubia are used for pentatonic music although they are all capable of producing more notes. The legendary traditions of all great civilisations referring to the origins of music allude in fact to a multi-note stage, which occurred before the transition to pentatonicism. Chinese legend relates how in prehistoric times, i.e. before pentatonicism existed, Ling-Lun constructed a twelve-note system. In Greek tradition, Terpander and Olympos omitted the third, or the third and sixth from a seven-note scale, and so arrived at the classic five- or six-note scale. (The *tropos spondeiazon* or *spondeiakos* of Olympos—the libation mode—was possibly the same as the later form of 'ditone' pentatonic, to be found in Japan,* although a minor pentatonic form without semitones has recently been discovered to have been the common mode of ancient Hebrew, Greek, Syrian, Byzantine and Latin psalmody.[1]) Advanced cultures realized that five was a sacred number, but they also knew that it represented a reduction from larger numbers. This appears to contradict the idea of three-note schemes, for in the classical systems, five tended to be *less* than what had gone before, not *more*. But the paradox is an illusion: five may have displaced three as a sacred and practical number, although both theory and practice had long been concerned with seven and twelve. There is also another paradox. The spread of pentatonicism as a world-system of sound presumably came first, followed much later by the development of melodic schemes with their regional characteristics. Yet how was this possible, given that a tonal system never existed as an abstract

---

* I.e. involving the interval of two tones (or the major third in just intonation, which is wider and sharper than the western major third). (Translators' note.)

principle, but always took its shape from actual melodies? Even this objection may prove groundless if the growth of pentatonicism is seen in relation to the following phases:

(*1*) In some centres, three-note schemes hardened into basic, traditional formulae, instead of adopting the greater tonal possibilities available through singing and instruments, resulting e.g. in a three-note scheme with a third, in Western Asia, and a three-note scheme with a fourth, in Central Asia.

(*2*) Pentatonicism of fixed pitch spread as the result of the organic and continuous growth of three-note schemes, simultaneously with rigorous selection from a wider compass.

(*3*) The various pentatonic styles sprang from the stylistic tendencies of the various regions.

The possibilities of invention inherent in these styles are discussed elsewhere (see Appendix). Here it is only important to stress that all these various 'dialects' were divided into clear stylistic regions: Central Asia and Western Asia; the Mediterranean; Africa; Central and South America; Western Europe. Even so sketchy a summary shows how even relatively recent cultural centres need to be included in the classification, since *many hundreds, if not thousands, of years elapsed between the various phases of pentatonic development.*

At the height of pentatonicism, what were the representative melody-types in the various regions? What melodic patterns did it encourage? To make a brief survey of its various forms: the chain-like continuity of the Central Asian pentatonic style is shown by a Mongolian—Cheremissian—Hungarian parallel, which points to the familiar link between Central Asia and Hungary, the still traceable path trodden by Turkish tribes during the great migrations. Of the three tunes, the Cheremissian is obviously the oldest and most complete: the Hungarian has discarded the transposed answering phrase, and the Mongolian is shrunk and atrophied.[2]

6

a) **Mongolian tune**

b) **Cheremissian (Mari) tune**

c) **Hungarian tune**

This is the transposing bipartite type. The transposing of motives is mostly connected with the fourth or fifth. This was the simplest form of transposition known in pentatonicism, and sprang out of the system itself, clearly playing an important part in its development. In this style-region it is applied not only to fourths and fifths, but sometimes to intervals of seconds, as in this Tibetan prayer-tune, which has recently been recorded:[3]

7

Tibetan tune

An Indian melody from Peru, on the other hand, is an interesting example of transition to the next style-region. In this four-line tune it is clear that transposition was an inherent principle of its structure, but so was the ground-motive of the single line. This is heard first at the original pitch, and then a fourth (and sometimes a fifth) lower, so that the form $AA_1A_vA_{v1}$ practically turns into AA_1BB_1:[4]

8

Indian tune from Peru

31

A further step in the same direction is shown by a Negro flute melody recorded in Haiti, but probably of Congolese origin (Haiti is populated by Congolese). It is an almost pure, three-line type of ABA$_v$, viz. ternary song-form. The fourth line has shrunk to an abortive appendix at the end of the third line.[5]

9

Negro tune from Haiti

By contrast, an English folk-ballad from the Appalachians can be quoted to represent the 'modern' pentatonic style of the West. Of its five lines, the second and fifth—in correspondence—apply the Eastern transposing principle, yet the fourth and fifth lines together form the reprise of the first line. In other words, in spite of irregular articulation, it is a symmetrical, three-line form.[6]

10

English tune from the Appalachians

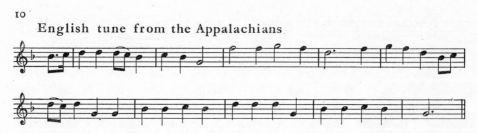

Mediterranean types have been left to the end because they are the most problematical. It seems as though geography was the deciding factor in the varying fortunes of pentatonicism. In Eastern and Central Asia it remained unchanged, in South-East Asia it blended into 'distance' scales through various changes in tuning, in South and South-West Asia it was submerged under various chromatic systems, but on the shores of the Mediterranean it was decisively transformed into seven-note scales. Gregorian plainchant is the richest and most complete summary of ancient Mediterranean music: it probably incorporates practically everything that has been salvaged of ancient Greek and Hebrew melody-style. In its pentatonic elements it seems to preserve an earlier stage of pentatonicism than appears in most known Jewish melodies, or

Chinese Pan-Pipe. One of the earliest and most authentic representations of the Chinese pan-pipe, the *pai'siao* (from the time of the T'ang dynasty, between the 7th and 10th centuries). It appears that the pan-pipe came into general use in much of the ancient world together with pentatonic scales; the instrument shown in the clay statuette has twelve pipes.

in the entire *corpus* of extant Greek music. Study of the oldest forms of Hebrew psalmody shows that Gregorian chant took and fixed these reciting patterns from authentic sources. The patterns then served as models for the rhythmically free articulation of Mediterranean music.

11

Hebrew melodies

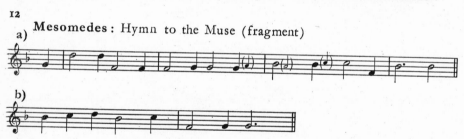

(The Oriental authenticity of Hebrew-Gregorian psalm-style is confirmed by the fact that simple three-note psalmody also exists in Indian Veda melodies.[7])

In ancient Greek music, pentatonic idioms are much more fragmentary. There are passages in the first Delphic Hymn to Apollo, which are reminiscent of Japanese 'ditone' pentatonicism; apart from these, the best example occurs at the beginning and end of the so-called *Hymn to the Muse* of Mesomedes.

12

a) Mesomedes: Hymn to the Muse (fragment)

b)

Here the archaic is evidently the result of a conscious later effort (1st—2nd century A.D.); the broad melodic lines and intervals of fifths and sixths suggest a rich and ripe diatonic culture and only allow a glimpse of early Greek pentatonicism. By contrast, Gregorian chant summed up the most diverse and distant stages of evolution, and included much earlier, and probably more authentic, Greek forms. Nor was this surprising: about 400 A.D., Latin chant drew heavily on the written and unwritten sources of Byzantium and Antioch (as did the ancient Slav liturgy five hundred years later), and at that time these were permeated with the ancient Orient. Traces of ancient Hebrew music survive for the most part in ancient choral music, in the melodies of lessons, orations and psalm-tones, the psalm and antiphonal settings of Introits, the liturgical recitatives of Graduals and Verses[8]—(the Gradual is the oldest sung part of the Mass)—whilst Greek traces occur particularly in the Hymns, and older settings of the Credo and Offertory. Here the most striking examples are not the fully pentatonic melodies (e.g., the psalm verse of the Advent Introit and the small added Doxology), but various pentatonic incipits and jubilations, which occur even in chants that are quite clearly of later origin. Here and there the disparity is obvious: particularly at cadences, the diatonic feeling of a later age found it hard to adapt a purely pentatonic turn of phrase, and solved the problem by making a small circular detour as a kind of modulation:

13   Gregorian melodies

34

Something new was happening: five-note schemes, no longer adequate, were expanding into seven-note schemes and seven-note scales, as had clearly happened in ancient Greek music. *Diatonicism* was developed in the Mediterranean area in the centuries before Christ, and settled itself into definite fixed patterns.

★

How did a pentatonic scale expand? Melodic material from East Europe and West Asia shows various ways. Pentatonic melody, in some areas at least, has a characteristic tendency to expansion: it likes to repeat itself at a lower range, forming what Robert Lach calls a 'cascade' (Central Asian, Hungarian and Indian types). Kodály has shown how it then had two possibilities. If the feeling for tonal system was stronger than the feeling for the melodic line, both the melody and its transposition remained in the same pentatonic system, and used adjacent notes to supply any *pien* notes needed. But if the sense for the melodic shape was stronger than the feeling for tonal system, the transposition became strict, the melody expanded into a two-system type, which adopted *pien* notes, and hence supplementary passing-notes, to complete the diatonic formation.[9] This need of 'completion' shows itself even at modest levels, and there is no need to study extensive two-line tunes. Typical examples are two recently published Ostyak tunes: in the first, the four-note range of the three-note tune is unexpectedly completed at the end, whereas in the second, the 'reply' (the transposed half of the tune) seems to stimulate the first half (second beat) to a similar 'bulge', so that the five-note scheme grows into a six-note one.[10]

14

Ostyak (Hanti) tunes

As yet they are still passing-notes, but once a melodic contour has been transitionally outlined, with time it easily becomes fixed. When diatonic feeling took root, it tried to weaken the traditions of pentatonic discipline by pushing its way into any gaps in the tradition. At first it acted through passing-notes, until with ever greater persistence it introduced elements which were foreign and forbidden in pentatonic schemes. Naturally the first to break through was pure diatonicism (Dorian or Aeolian). In some Transylvanian tunes, diatonic variants occur alongside pentatonic versions:

At a later stage, diatonic consciousness was replaced by a new awareness of the major-mode, the result of a shift of stress towards harmony, which caused an instinctive reassessment of melodies. It suddenly emerged after lying dormant for some long period: the pentatonic 'trichord' was taken to be a major triad, and gaps in the pentatonic melody (previously not considered as such) were filled by *pien* notes with major implications. The various stages of the process can be observed in certain Hungarian melodies, as they once adopted the pentatonic scale of *f-g-b flat-c-d* in common with most Chuvash and Cheremissian tunes from the Volga area:

Gradually, as may be seen, the unaccented 'supplementary' notes appeared as essential notes on accented beats, giving the pentatonic system its distinctive Dorian, Aeolian or Mixolydian quality, later transformed into major or minor melodies. The Hymn of Mesomedes (already quoted) shows this process in an embryonic form:

17 From **Mesomedes'** Hymn to the Muse

etc.

New modal awareness is another important characteristic at this stage. The Greek tetrachord and the octaves deriving from it, i.e. modes built up of fourths and fifths, made musicians aware of the vicinity of notes, even without fixed tonal sense.[11] Even today, by reason of its structural differences, true West European diatonicism is utterly distinct from the disguised pentatonicism prevailing in East Europe (e.g., in most Hungarian melodies of Dorian type, and the *Bogurodsitza* melody of Poland). Later on a similar discrepancy appeared between the major octave of popular music and the hexachordal major scale of later medieval art-music. This is inevitable when streams of evolution meet: there were several forms of diatonicism and of the major scale, because they converged from different directions, and were only merged with their 'doubles' at a later stage.

Even more important was the new conception of tonality, which built the component parts of the melody, and single degrees of the scale, around a ground-note and pivotal-note in a balanced and functional arrangement. Melody and scale now had perceptible and imperceptible pivots, round which they could unfold, rise and fall. The ground-note and final were the same *(Basis* and *Finalis):* the chief pivotal-note *(Dominant* or *Tenor)* controlled the curve of the melody as it rose and fell. One type of ground-note has already been discussed— the Chinese tuning-note, the 'Yellow Bell' *(huang chung),* and the Greek *mese,* or central note. But there is an important difference between the ancient conception and the new one. Pentatonicism was sufficiently self-contained to be complete in itself, and its notes had more or less equal importance. (Bartók considered that dominant function did not exist in pentatonicism, and that since

37

pentatonic intervals were all consonances, its harmony was entirely static in function, without direction, tension, or counter-balance.) Its final, too, was only a *primus inter pares*, and often varied.[12] The fact that in Hungary only one predominant pentatonic form survived is probably due to its being regarded as diatonic (minor mode); forms that still flourish amongst related peoples are now to be found here only in a 'disguised' plagal form (see Ex. 16). Finals that determined tonality were quite unknown in ancient Greek theory, as were the authentic and plagal systems found in Byzantine *echoi* and medieval modes; later on the ground-note acquired a significance that it did not possess even in early Christian chant, and Eastern chant probably only recognised two modes, later described as the second and eighth of the 'plagal' series. The varying endings (or *differentiae*) of antiphonal psalms show that even later chants maintained a traditional indifference to the final. Yet it assumed exceptional importance in the later development of the diatonic church modes. Where did the new conception of the final note originate, and where did it appear for the first time? Ottó Gombosi confirms Peter Wagner's hypothesis, which maintained it to be of Syrian or Byzantine origin.[13] Anyway it was reflected in medieval melody-styles, from England to Italy. *Musica Enchiriadis*, a 9th-century treatise attributed to Hucbald, declared that melodies could only begin within an upper or lower fifth of the final. In the 10th and 11th centuries, Odo of Cluny and Guido d'Arezzo unequivocally declared that the final should be the same as the starting-note. Later, Engelbert of Admont added that the starting-note had at least to be in strict consonance with the final. *Finalis vox est, quam melius intuemur* (the final is the note that we respect most), taught Guido in his *Micrologus*, and in the 11th century John Cottoniensis added *Tota vis cantus ad finales respicit* (all the force of a chant is directed towards the final). *A finali reguntur omnia, disponuntur et dijudicantur* (everything is governed, arranged, and judged by the finals), wrote Wilhelm von Hirsau, and Engelbert of Admont and John de Muris were only summarizing in the 14th century in their assertion that the close was the most important part of the melody, because it served to clarify the mode. (*Omnis tonus musicus speciem sumit a fine*—every type of musical mode takes its character from the final.) The functions of the dominant or tenor (i.e. the pivotal reciting-note), the tonal compass (rule of the Cistercians on the 10th interval), and the building of melodies in relation to central pivots, were all elaborated about the same time and in the same way: everything, that is, that musicians of that time and later regarded as being essential to the ordering of tonality and tonal compass, or which at the least conferred balance and proportion through the new system. Melody with its notes and intervals came to be managed in such a way that the final and dominant were not 'exploited' in the wrong places: stepwise movement succeeded wide intervals (fourths and particularly fifths), and slowing down occurred at the end of larger groups of notes:

in general now it was realized that smaller intervals usually quickened the pace, and wider intervals slowed it up (see the semitone rules of Aribo, Odo and Muris, Guido's theory of cadence, and Odo's rules about *distinctio, intervallum*, etc.) The first theory of tonal composition came into existence as a theory of melodic style which was purposely concerned with musical texture. It transformed whatever was left of the old five-note way of thinking just as much as it changed diatonicism.

*

Diatonic style differed from all earlier styles not only in character and structure but also because it was written down and preserved in writing. Yet certain special circumstances occurred in the process of this fixation. In any culture, the adoption of written records is known to cause a deep crisis, and the clash of opposing forces. The early medieval chroniclers took great pains to dissociate themselves and their profession from the vague, shifting world of oral tradition. The problems were the same as those that had previously been encountered in European melodic history. What was unusual was that the codifiers of melody were outsiders both in time and space, and clarified the issues objectively at a much later period: they were peripheral commentators. Aristoxenos, of Southern Italian origin, was the first great codifier of Greek music, and lived in the 4th century B.C., long after the flowering of classical Greek music; the scale names connected with the classical system turned up only in the 3rd century A.D., in the writings of Aristides Quintilianus and Gaudentius. The Byzantine-Greek scales, called *echoi*, were first codified in the 3rd century A.D. by Zosimus of Panopolis, an Alexandrian alchemist: the first codifier of Western church modes was Flaccus Alcuin, a Carolingian scholar of Anglo-Saxon extraction, who lived in the 8th century. All of them worked retrospectively, outside the arena, as it were. The splendour of classical Greek music was already waning when Plato first mentioned in his *Republic* (III[10]) the various effects of Mixolydian, Syntonolydian, Ionian, Lydian, Dorian and Phrygian modes *(harmoniai)*, and found them to be, as the text makes clear, 'imitated inflections', or melodies that most likely had a local origin of different character. Pindar was the only writer before Plato who referred to Aeolian and Lydian melodies, Dorian lyres, and other local specialities, which leads one to imagine that diatonicism was also formed from local variants as the result of the regional nature of Greek development. Aristotle and Plutarch mostly echoed Plato, and even Apuleius, in the 2nd century A.D., limited himself to describing Phrygian melody as 'soft', Ionian as 'varied', Dorian as 'bellicose', and Lydian as 'sweet'. (According to him, Phrygian was adopted in the orgiastic cult of the Goddess Syria, whilst the other modes occurred in the pantomime music of a Greek play, all of them normally in conjunction with the *aulos* or *tibia*.) Clement of Alexandria, *c.* 200 A.D., was much more concerned with classification; for him the Dorian mode stood for fire, the Lydian for air. He showed that the Dorian *harmonia* (or mode) was associated with the 'consonant' enharmonic genus, sometimes derived from the Psalms of David and sometimes from Thamyris of Thrace. The Phrygian *harmonia*, on the other hand, had been invented by the Phrygian Marsyas, and was associated with the 'fierce' or 'shrill' diatonic genus (Paidagogos). The *Republic* both of Plato and Aristotle inferred that the *ethos* (or character) of the instrument was at least related to that of the mode, and it seems even more natural to assume that both melody and instrument sprang in their *ethos* from a common root, a normal connection in archaic high-cultures. The scale lives only in the expert's mind, whether as a series of sounds on an instrument, or a theoretical abstraction; the untutored layman can only hear a melody, and is not conscious of the scale. The type of scale depends on the melodic shape, for the formula, pattern, or figure is always more important than the single note. In ancient civilisations, this was what caused the formation of definite melodic patterns. For instance, psalmodic melody-patterns connected with definite texts—such as the Syrian-Hebraic *Riš-qolo*, the Arabian *Lahan*, the Hebrew *Ne'ima*, the Byzantine *Heirmos*, the Latin *psalmitonus*, or the ancient Hungarian dirge—acquired significance by settling on a few typical diatonic formulae which were easily memorized and more or less freely organised in terms of intervals, numbers of syllables, and melodic line. In Arabic, Indian, Indonesian and Greek culture respectively the *maqam*, *raga*, *patet* and *nomos* represented a higher stage of development of the same principle.[14]

Another striking point is concerned with the authenticity of preservation in writing. Even if melodies could be written down (which Isidore of Seville doubted), was the written version the final one? Melodies had in no way reached the end of their development when they came to be written down: the written record was not a complete and finished product. The melodies in existence at the beginning of Europe's continuous history were destined to survive for thousands of years. The metrical and chromatic features of Gregorian chant, inherited from Greece and the Orient, had only disappeared because 11th-century notation was unable to preserve them. 20th-century musicology, for example, still finds that the *melismas* of Ambrosian chant are formed in a 'somewhat obscure' way.[15] Chromaticism, or the semitonal style, appears early on, in primitive melodies and in the music of antiquity. A form of chromatic melody appeared *between* the pentatonic and the diatonic, between the five-note and seven-note scale-system; this is proved by Greek and Indian melodies, by the Arab-Persian *maqam* system, and by some still surviving idioms of Oriental (Syrio-Armenian) liturgies. True, it existed as a deviation, a rejected line of development, yet it was only rejected for a certain time, and only by European sensibility. There was also the added effect of regional and national differences. The ancient principle affecting peripheral areas became active here in the sense that the peripheral Roman liturgies, i.e. Gallican and Mozarabic, preserved the older forms, whereas centrally placed Rome changed its style.[16] In German areas, a new type of Gregorian chant was in process of formation, in which wider intervals were preferred to semitone intervals and the unfamiliar tritone.[17] Finally, the Greeks preferred asymmetrical rhythms both in their language and their melodies, whereas Latin metrical system was rather simple and symmetrical. Nobody knows how these principles asserted themselves in writing, but Gregorian chant plainly absorbed them both, and assisted Latin rhythmical principles to become more acceptable than Greek in the European mind—in other words, European conceptions of rhythm are based on Latin rather than on Greek.

In this sense, since melodic material was still in a state of flux, the organisation of melody came too late and too early as well. Although it was already enjoying the first taste of classicism, the diatonic music of the early Middle Ages had in no way attained a settled or self-contained existence. Its real period of high classicism only came some five centuries later. Diatonic melody of the early Middle Ages was a summing up of ancient Mediterranean culture, whereas for the North and West of Europe it was a new language: it was still developing, still in a state of fluctuation, always changing its shape and surmounting new crises. Although as plainchant it had already attained its first consolidation, and begun its world-wide conquest, it still appeared crude and hesitant. In Europe, Gregorian chant was a popularly accepted form of classicism, and represented the impersonality of the Church inasmuch as it was an intruder from a strange and semi-Oriental world. Only towards the end of the Middle Ages did European diatonic melody reach its own *individual* greatness. From then on, European musical history seemed to be made up of a series of alternating phases. Early diatonicism was followed by the early affirmation of the major mode (in troubadour melodies). This was succeeded by a period of classical and transformed diatonicism (respectively Renaissance and Baroque), and then by major-minor classicism and its transformation (respectively Classicism and Romanticism).

Yet it cannot be said that the flowering of diatonicism in the late Middle Ages came unheralded. Its harbingers were the diatonic melodies of ecclesiastical character which already showed distinct Western influence within a closed and song-like form. They appeared with Latin texts in collections of early sequences, and—as a later product of the Latin-inspired Carolingian Renaissance —in neumatic manuscripts in Florence and Montecassino (11th and 12th centuries) and the Vatican (13th century):[18]

18 Spring Song

Au - re - a per - so - net ly - ra cla - ra mo - du - la - mi - na!
Sim - plex chor - da sit ex - ten - sa vo - ce quin - de - na - ri - a.

Pri - mum so - num me - se red - dat le - ge hy - po - do - ri - ca.

Cum tel - lu - ris ve - re no - vo pro - du - cun - tur__ ger - mi - na etc.

19 Pilgrim's Hymn

O Ro - ma no - bi - lis___ or - bis et do - mi - na,___
cun - cta - rum ur - bi - um___ ex - cel - len - tis - si - ma___

Sa - lu - tem di - ci - mus___ ti - bi per o - mni - a,___ te

be - ne - di - ci - mus:___ Sal - ve per se - - cu - la.___

The 'Spring Song' is based on a plainsong hymn, *Urbs beate Jerusalem*, and is probably a medieval 'teaching-song', with some of the magic of later classical Dorian. The second (a Pilgrim's Hymn to Rome) was originally a secular love-song of neo-classic Greek origin. It spans the major hexachord—it has a Mixolydian lower seventh in its Vatican variant—and seems to be related to French *caroles* in its repetitive, rhyming lines and its jaunty, iambic flow, so characteristic of troubadour music. Yet it is not troubadour music: it stems from another source that showed itself, now hidden, now openly, in sequences and *lais*,[19] German *Minnesang* and *Meistergesang*, and later in 15th-century Flemish classicism and 16th-century choral polyphony. It was no longer a clear Mediterranean sound, but the slowly awakening sound of Northern and Western Europe—the voice of the new Europe.

1. *Cf.* E. Werner's article in *Hebrew Union College Annual*. XIX, Cincinnati, 1945—1946, pp. 333—335.
2. Sources: The Mongolian tune was published by P. Berlinsky: *Mongolski pyevez i musy kant Uldsuy—Lubsan—Khurtshi*. Moscow, 1933, p. 51; the Cheremissian (Mari) tune by R. Lach: *Gesänge russischer Kriegsgef. Tscheremissische Ges.* 1929, No. 200, given here with Kodály's corrections; Var. Koukal—Chetkarev—Rubkov: *Mary kalük muro.* Leningrad—Moscow, 1951, p. 219. The Hungarian tune was quoted by Dénes Bartha: "Untersuchungen zur ungarischen Volksmusik," I, *Archiv für Musikforschung* VI, 1941, p. 13. All five-note tunes have been transposed into the same pentatonic system.
3. Henning Haslund-Christensen: *Zajagan, Menschen und Götter in der Mongolei.* Stuttgart—Berlin—Leipzig, about 1940, p. 264.
4. M. Béclard—d'Harcourt: *Mélodies populaires indiennes.* Milano, 1928, p. 119. Although it only has 3 lines, there is an Abyssinian flute-tune which is a related pentatonic version (line-endings in our system, f^2—f^2—c^2, characteristic progressions g^2—f^2—d^2—c^2), published by E. W. Ewald, *Sovietski Folklor.* Moscow—Leningrad, 1936, p. 462.
5. W. B. Seabrook: *Geheimnisvolles Haiti. Rätsel und Symbolik des Wodu-Kultes.* Berlin, 1931, p. 30. The tune invokes the god Legba: it was performed by a native negro of Orblanche and noted by the West Indian composer Elie.
6. C. Sharp: *English Folk-Songs from the Southern Appalachians.* I, London, 1932, No. 8/D.
7. See the tune contributed by E. Felber : " Die indische Musik der vedischen und der klassischen Zeit." *Sitzungsberichte der Kais. Akademie der Wissenschaften in Wien,* 170. Bd., 7. Abhandl., Wien, 1912, Music Appendix No. 462. One part is as follows (transposed into our common tonal system):

Cf. ibid. No. 418 and No. 451; another equally primitive Indian tune-type (the *karma* melody of the Gond tribe) shows clearly how the 3-note pattern has been extended to a four- and five-note scheme (see W. Kaufmann's publ. in *The Musical Quarterly* XXVII, New York, 1941, p. 284):

Cf. the melody quoted by the present author in his article entitled "A Jewish Musical Document of the Middle Ages: the Most Ancient Noted Biblical Melody." *Semitic Studies in Memory of Immanuel Löw.* Budapest, 1947, pp. 131—133. Another form of the Hebrew *tonus peregrinus, cf.* No. 11/a:

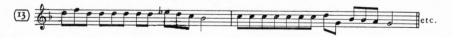

had a direct influence upon some Gregorian (*Magnificat*) tune-types as well as on some Hungarian folk-song forms (see Bartók—Kodály: *Transylvanian Folk-Songs*. 1923, No. 61 and *Kodály Memorial Volume*. 1943, p. 310, both in Hungarian). *Cf.* also E. Gerson—Kiwi: "Religious Chant, a Pan-Asiatic Conception of Music." *Journal of the International Folk-Music Council* XIII, 1961, pp. 64—67.

8. *Cf.* E. Werner: "Preliminary Notes for a Comparative Study of Catholic and Jewish Musical Punctuation." *Hebrew Union College Annual* XV, Cincinnati, 1940, pp. 335—366. By the same author: *The Sacred Bridge*. London—New York, 1960, pp. 419, 466.

9. R. Lach: *Gesänge russischer Kriegsgefangener*. Vol. 1, part 4 *(Tschuwaschische Gesänge)*. Wien—Leipzig, 1940, p. 11; Zoltán Kodály: "Characteristic Melody Structure in Mari Folk Music." 1935; B. Szabolcsi: "Data on the Diffusion of Central Asiatic Melody-Types." *Ethnogr*. LI, 1940. (These two articles in Hungarian.)

10. W. Steinitz: *Ostjakische Volksdichtung u. Erzählungen*. II, Stockholm, 1941, Melodies Nos. 41 and 27.

11. Ottó Gombosi: "Studien zur Tonartenlehre des frühen Mittelalters." *Acta Musicologica* 1938—1940. The bracketed variants of our melody examples Nos. 12 and 17 give the new version as quoted by Gombosi. See: *Papers Read at the International Congress of Musicology, held at New York 1939*. New York, 1944, p. 182.

12. Zoltán Kodály: *Folk Music of Hungary*. Eng. ed., London, 1960, examples Nos. 45, 56. For Bartók's quoted statement see "Ungarische Volksmusik," *Schweizerische Sängerzeitung*, 1933, and *Ethnogr*. LIII, p. 174. On the changing pentatonic final see also present author's study: *Elements of the Great Migration Period in Hungarian Folk Music*. Budapest, 1935, pp. 12—13 (in Hungarian). In reference to Peruvian instruments, C. Vega writes: "The series is relative and the scale can begin on any of the five notes." *Acta Musicologica* IX, 1937, p. 43.

13. P. Wagner: *Einführung in die gregorianischen Melodien*. I, Leipzig, 1910, pp. 214, 109—110, 141. For the oldest modes see: "Die Koloratur im mittelalterlichen Kirchengehang." *Peters Jahrbuch*, 1918, p. 14, by the same author. The development of European rhymes is probably related to the idea of the final: *cf.* J. Maróthy's study: "The Birth of European Folk-Song." *Zenetudományi Tanulmányok* VI, Budapest, 1957 (in Hungarian).

14. For the *patet* system, see Mantle Hood: *The Nuclear Theme as a Determinant of Patet in Javanese Music*. Groningen—Jakarta, 1954.

15. P. Wagner: *Einführung in die gregorianischen Melodien*. I, Leipzig, 1910, p. 214.

16. *Ibid.*, pp. 54—55. Views of Morin and Cagin.

17. P. Wagner: *Eigenheiten der deutschen Choraltradition*. (*Einf. in die gregor. Melodien*. II, 1912, pp. 443—448), further: *Elemente des gregorianischen Gesanges*. 1917, pp. 101, 104. For further studies by the same author on the subject, *cf.* "Germanisches im mittelalterlichen Kirchengesang." *Leipziger Kongressbericht*, 1925; *Das Leipziger Thomas-Graduale*. 1930—1934. Introduction.

18. Contributed by F. Ludwig in the chapter on the Middle Ages in G. Adler's *Handbuch der Musikgeschichte*. 2nd ed., 1930, I. pp. 162, 161. For variants of the Pilgrim's Hymn, *cf.* P. Wagner: "O Roma nobilis." *Kirchenmusikalisches Jahrbuch* XXII, 1909, 1 et seq. Also *Einf. in die greg. Melodien*. II, 1912, pp. 304—305 (the neumatic Vatican variant, the authority for completing the 10th bar of the Ludwig transcription); further: H. Besseler: *Die Musik des Mittelalters und der Renaissance*. Potsdam, 1931 (1934), p. 72 (with the original text of the melody and a Syrian variant) and W. Danckert: *Das europäische Volkslied*. Berlin, 1939, p. 307; also Dénes Bartha: *Anthology of Musical History*. Budapest, 1948, No. 7 (in Hungarian). Originally the melody was a setting of a 10th-century secular lyric from Verona, beginning "*O admirabile Veneris idolum*"; for both texts *cf.* F. Brittain: *The Medieval*

Latin and Romance Lyric to A.D. 1300. Cambridge, 1937, pp. 88—89. Related also to a Hungarian (Transylvanian and Moldavian) ballad, *cf.* P. P. Domokos: *The Hungarians of Moldavia.* Kolozsvár, 1941, p. 381, No. 110 (in Hungarian); and Bartók: *Hungarian Folk Music.* London, 1931, No. 165.

19. See e.g. melodies with Latin texts published by F. Gennrich from mss. of Paris and Evreux *Grundriss einer Formenlehre des mittelalterlichen Liedes.* Halle, 1932, pp. 217, 218.

No -vus an - nus di - es ma - gnus as - sit in lae - ti - ti a

In - ve - sti - gans se - mi - tas no - strae re - dem - pti - o - nis

THE BEGINNINGS OF MAJOR MELODY IN EUROPE

The year 1100, the turn of the 11th and 12th centuries, from many points of view was a dividing-line in the history of European music, particularly where Western melody-style was concerned. There were many more records of church music in existence after that time, but as Peter Wagner has shown, the richer and subtler meanings of musical notation had already been lost (i.e. the rhythm of neums, particularly as it effected semitones and ornaments). Gregorian chant was becoming diatonic by a process which was parallel to, and completed by, the new staff-notation of Guido d'Arezzo. At the same time, attempts to write polyphony were becoming increasingly frequent, in a huge semicircle that embraced England, France and Spain, so that the old technique of *organum* was left further and further behind. Most important of all, secular vocal and dance-music began to well up unexpectedly in Western Europe in the form of *trouvère* and *jongleur* music, sometimes disguised as sequences. Southern France seemed to take the lead, followed after 1200 by Northern France and Southern England, and later by Umbria and Tuscany with the *laude* of the Franciscan movement. The last wave came after 1300, already linked to other trends; but the epoch from the 11th to the 13th century was like a huge shared breath of awakening Western music.

So far as its precursors and background were concerned, much about this music was quite new. To start with, the sound, the 'intonation' was new; the change might seem gradual in comparison with traditional forms, but it was sudden in relation to the more advanced. The rhythms were new too, and introduced into the melody the rise and fall of trochees and iambs (chiefly three-and-a-half, six-and-a-half, and four trochaic feet), perhaps in recollection of folk-like *caroles*, ancient Mediterranean traditions, or even Celtic rites. According to Jean Beck, this famous 'modal' rhythm often completely overrode the claims of speech accents. In fact the melody became metrical, while the text had no metre at all. *Debemus habere respectum ad syllabae accentum, non ad tempus* (we must respect the syllable-stress and not the musical rhythm), ran the 13th-century rule of the English Goliard poet Gottfreed of Winesauf. The scale was also new, and frequently abandoned the pure diatonic church modes[1] in search of a new mode known as the major. Finally there was a new way of constructing melodies, which linked up strophic, chain and refrain-type dances in elegant closed forms, or more often in casually-improvised structures. All this amounted to a very characteristic world of melody, dominated by the major mode.

Were major sound and scale really so new? The major scale had a past of at least a thousand years if it was considered as a purely mechanical series of sounds, without reference to the vital inner functioning which produced note and mode, melody and music out of rows of notes. It was one of the theoretical scales of ancient Greece, and figured as 'Hypo-Mixolydian' in the early medieval system of Byzantine *Octoechos*, that is, as a derived form and a related mode. In those days it had but a shadowy existence; it was still undiscovered, and its pungent, dry sound went unrecognised. Nobody knew as yet that because of a quirk of writing, or a curiously apt mistake, it would come to be known as the 'dur' or hard scale (*B* natural = Gothic *B* or German *H*, standing for Hexachordum Durum). It must have shown itself truly major in character and have become much more Western European than Mediterranean by the time that Hucbald and Guido d'Arezzo adopted it as the basis of their hexachordal system[2]—presumably because of the tuning of the six-stringed instruments of the period, and particularly the organ. It must have had a challenging and strongly secular sound to make official defenders of classical diatonicism in the late Middle Ages call it the *tonus lascivus* (though at that time this meant 'sweet' as well as 'lascivious'!). Aribo felt that the major tetrachord had a rustic sound *(rustica sonoritas)*, and perhaps that is why theoreticians preferred the 'more pleasant' sound of the minor tetrachord, with a semitone interval in the middle. As yet it was probably not identified with the serene and triumphant mode which joined the hierarchy of recognised modes as 'Ionian' in Glareanus' 16th-century *Dodekachordon*—to become the chief idiom of Viennese classical music some two hundred years later. The new music was still at the very beginning of its career; it breathed a hint of fresh morning magic, the sound of awakening Western Europe, and was still hardly more than a *hexachordum naturale*.

What then was so problematical about this distinctive mode? Diatonic scales normally favoured whole tones—acoustically speaking this includes both large and small whole tones—yet they all had to include two semitonal intervals. Every mode placed its semitones differently, but always at a weak and sensitive point within the scale. The major mode was the only one to make one of its semitones into a leading-note, placing it at the highest point to introduce and support the final of the mode—a *subsemitonium modi* below the starting-note. This only affected the more exposed semitone, and served to identify the scale; as in the related Mixolydian, the other semitone sheltered between the third and fourth. The major differed from Mixolydian by its sharpened seventh or leading-note, though in other respects the two scales were the same. Both Mixolydian and Lydian had a major third, which today is considered a typical characteristic of the major scale.

Guido d'Arezzo's *Micrologus* emphasised that all but semitone intervals were to be avoided, the overbearing leading-note in particular. Medieval melody was not concerned with semitones and chromaticism in general: these were features of the Near East, and later of the High Renaissance. Wherever possible, it avoided the instrumental and pagan associations of such *musica falsa*, and made it its business to weaken the leading-note and challenge its function. If the final of the mode were approached from below, the mode did not resolve directly from the seventh degree, but slid down to the sixth, and from there passed to the final. This dodge characterised the whole epoch; so deeply was it rooted in the melodic feeling of the time that it was considered a commonplace and normal formula, even in the early part of the Middle Ages. It had its own ecphonetic sign among the early Latin neums, and was called *punctus elevatus*. A most characteristic cadence came into being (*c-b-a-c*, or *f-e-d-f* in the standard mode of the following examples). This was later attributed to Landino, and rightly so in the sense that it was Landino who elaborated and developed it into a richer melodic form:

20

Landino: a) Non ara ma pietà

etc.

b) El mie dolce sospir

etc.

Thus protected by 'Landino's cadence', the disguised major mode became one of the most familiar features of medieval melody, and a form which was intended to deny the leading-note ended up by establishing major sound. Its impetus was sufficiently strong to break through the convention, and give the lie to its own form.

But conventions do not always yield, particularly not in the direction of major tonality. For centuries, the semitones were the two weak points in the new scale (even today, the French call the leading-note 'note sensible'). Covering one semitone made the scale Lydian, covering the other made it Mixolydian. These two older relatives did not leave its side till the Middle Ages were over.

48

The Byzantine Court. The Emperor Justinian and his attendants
(6th century mosaic from Ravenna).

They were constantly at its side, tempting it to return—"you can still come back to us!" It seems, indeed, that only with great difficulty did major tonality extricate itself from church modality, and this it did by slow degrees, and by constantly colliding with Lydian or Mixolydian. If the conclusions reached by Machabey and Liuzzi can be trusted,[3] it proved to be of decisive importance that the modes started on definite notes: the major mode on *C* arrived at its modern version because its fourth 'tamed' the Lydian fourth, and the minor mode on *A* similarly influenced the Dorian sixth by its own sixth. To the musician of a later period, major sensibility in the Middle Ages was as uncertain and easily upset as later in the *frottola* or even in Bach. Yet patterns already existed which served as anchors for insecure motives: there were the sequences, which cropped up again and again in *trouvère* and *jongleur* music,[4] and the *ouvert-clos* system of line-endings (the use of first and second time endings as a means of varied repetition—known as 'periods' in the formal language of the 18th century[5]). Johannes Wolf's[6] transcriptions of English medieval dance-tunes show this formal principle very plainly:

21

English dance-tunes

etc.

But was this form of melody really so unsure of itself? It is difficult to be sure, for many melodies show no trace of it. They jumped their hurdles by luck and ignored the obstacles. It seems that the major hexachord must first have been mastered and prepared for the melody, if only by cautious movement in seconds. A dance-tune by Tannhäuser has recently come to light from the first half of the 13th century,[7] and both this and Adam de la Hale's pastoral-play (about 1260) seem completely at home in the style, and manoeuvre it with inherited assurance:

a) Tannhäuser: Leich

Ich lo - be ein wip

b) Adam de la Hale: Pastourelle (Jeu de Robin et de Marion)

J'ay encore i tel pasté

Gennrich's reading:

J'ai encore un tel pas-té

Sometimes neither sequential treatment nor the elementary pattern provided by first and second time endings helped a melody over its narrow compass. Moniot de Paris's folk-like *Vadurie* is a typical example. The compass visibly expands to no more than a Lydian pentachord, or rather a Mixolydian tetrachord with a lower seventh added. It is a major melody which has 'misfired'!

23

Moniot de Paris: Vadurie

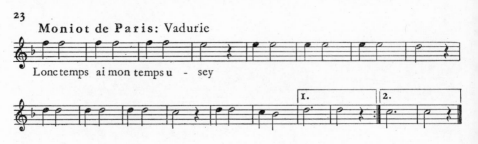

Lonc temps ai mon temps u - sey

1.   2.

The danger was even greater where a wider compass was concerned, as is evident in the dance-songs of Provence. (Perhaps Provence at this time preferred the diatonic church modes with their Mediterranean quality. *Kalenda maya,* one of the most valuable documents of the new major style, was characteristically brought to the Court of Montferrat about 1200 by French jongleurs— that is to say, by wanderers from the North.) The weak points of the mode still constituted a problem, and many an early major melody went astray by identifying itself with a related church mode: it changed its perspective, took on a plagal meaning, and vanished as a secondary scale. The next example comes from F. Gennrich[8]: from the thirteenth bar onward, a seemingly more correct Latin version from a Florentine manuscript *(Veris ad imperia)* is followed (the original drops a whole tone):

24

Provençal dance tune

A l'entra-da del tens clar   E - y - a

To turn to one of the loveliest of medieval melodies. Several eminent scholars (such as Aubry, Restori, Ludwig and Gennrich) consider that *Kalenda maya,* an *estampida* by Rambaut de Vaqueiras, is not a major melody at all, but Mixolydian or Hypolydian (i.e. with a lower seventh). The autograph in the Paris Bibliothèque Nationale (Nos 22, 543) apparently gives it as Mixolydian, without coming to any decision about the sharpened seventh. Pujol published a Catalan folk-variant which provides no further solution. As to the melody see H. Anglès: *La música a Catalunya fins al sigle XIII.* (Barcelona, 1935, p. 393); there is a new rhythmical interpretation in *Acta Musicologica* XXV, 1953, pp. 18—19 (H. Husmann):

25

Rambaut de Vaqueiras: Estampida

Ka - len-da ma-ya   etc.

Major tonality established itself all the more surely when it operated within a clearly defined compass. Some of the *virelay*-melodies transcribed by Gennrich,[9] which drop down from the fifth, turn confidently to the major cadence, and avoid the 'temptation' of the Mixolydian. Even so, they cautiously avail themselves of the leap of the third provided by the *punctus elevatus:*

26

Virelay melody

Or   la   truix trop   du - re   -   te,   voir,   voir.

da Capo al Fine.

A dance-tune sliding down from a fifth could afford to be more daring. The melody of *Aucassin et Nicolette*, for instance, touches lightly on the lower leading-note:

27

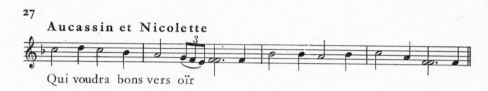

The first awkward attempts to grapple with the major might well have retreated within the bounds provided by a limited compass—but this was not what happened. It is true that the short-lined *Pastourelles* tended to adopt the major more than the more extensive *chansons*, but this period saw no limitation of range. Quite the contrary: of the 330 tunes in the *Chansonnier Cangé*, for example, only 69 melodies are less than an octave in range, and 261 have an octave or more. Although this includes church modal melodies (frequent even in the *Cangé* manuscript), there are almost as many major melodies as there are other types. Due to the fact that European taste rediscovered them some seven hundred years later, many 12th- and 13th-century melodies seem curiously 'modern' anticipations of 18th- and 19th-century melodies! Typical examples include the English canon *Sumer is icumen in*, Neidhart's tunes (generally melodic fragments, since few of his melodies belong here in *extenso*) from the same period, and 13th-century *laude*. Here and there in the *laude*, snatches of Hungarian folk-song idiom are discernible—perhaps a faint echo of the influence of the Franciscan movement in Eastern Europe.[10]

28

c) Lauda

A-ve ver-ge - ne gau-den - te

etc.

d) Lauda

Che vol lo mondo des-preg-ga - re

etc.

e) Lauda

Si- a la-u-da- to san France-sco

etc.

f) Lauda

Ogn' om can-ti no-vel can - to

etc.

Further examples are the small romantic masterpieces of major melody composed by Moniot d'Arras and the Duc de Brabant, some of them broadly conceived, and others warm and intimate:

29

a) Moniot d'Arras: Ce fut en mai

Ce fut en mai au douz tems gai

I. 2.

etc.

b) Duc de Brabant: Chanson

I.

Ma dou - ce da - me, on ne me croit

Here the compass is the result of a chance discovery, and has nothing to do with unhampered melodic invention. They are worth comparing with more experimental examples, where the simplest motive can be seen struggling towards a freer form of expression (e.g. the *lai*). It is strange how by groping about with the aid of sequences, they sometimes light upon the Oriental principle of transposition, which then encompasses the entire range as a series of variations. This is not only true of French *lais*, but also of Italian *laude*:

30.

a) **Anon.** Lai

Qui porroit un guier - re-don   Avoir de lonc tens a-mer

b) **Lauda** (13th century)

Spi-ri-to san-cto   da ser-vi - re   dann'al co - re   de te senti - re

Cp. A. Banchieri: Capriciata from "Festino nella sera del giovedì grasso," 1608

No-bi-li spet-ta - to - ri   etc.

So between 1200 and 1300 the new-born, undeveloped fledgling of European major melody came to try the strength of its wings. Had it come too soon? It may be that the Middle Ages constituted its great hour, or it may, indeed, have been too early, if such an idea is historically permissible. It slipped into the background, and was forgotten all through the great art music of modal diatonicism from the 14th—16th centuries. After the Baroque era it emerged again, to fill the whole of European music with new colour and life.

NOTES

1. According to the calculations of Jean Beck about 75 per cent of *trouvère* melodies are modally diatonic. One of the loveliest and most typical is Giraut de Borneilh's *aubade, Reis glorios* (see Jeanroy-Gérold: *Le Jeu de St. Agnès*. Paris, 1931, p. 61; G. Reese: *Music in the Middle Ages*. New York, 1940, p. 215). This Dorian type (with Gregorian opening phrase *d—d—a—a—b—c¹—b—a—[b]—g*) may later be traced in German chorales *(Erschienen ist der herrlich Tag)* and Hungarian folk-songs *(Ungarische Jahrbücher*, Berlin, 1938, p. 212).

2. For other instrumental relationships with medieval major melodies *(Alphorn-Juchzer, Jodler, Kuhreigen)*, see R. Lach's study: "Die Tonkunst in den Alpen," in H. Leitmeier's *Die Österreichischen Alpen*. Leipzig—Wien, 1928, pp. 340—343. Interesting data are given here about the stylistic influence of the Alpine horn's high fourth ('Alphorn-Fa').

3. A. Machabey: *Histoire et évolution des formules musicales du Ier au XVe siècle de l'ère chrétienne*. Paris, 1928, pp. 106—113, 132—161; F. Liuzzi: *La lauda e i primordi della melodia italiana*. Roma, 1935, I, p. 187.

4. J. Beck: *Les Chansonniers des Troubadours et des Trouvères*. II *(Transcription des chansons du Chansonnier Cangé)*. Philadelphia, 1927, p. 32. (Beck considers that Gregorian chant may have served as a model for the transposed sequences of troubadour songs.) My examples Nos. 23, 29b and 30a are quoted from this source (where they are numbered 200, 208 and 299), but they are given in the same key (F major) as the other quotations, and their note-values are doubled so as to be rhythmically consistent. The variant quoted at No. 22b comes from Gennrich's *Rondeaux, Virelais und Balladen aus dem Ende des XII., dem XIII. und dem ersten Drittel des XIV. Jh.-s mit den überlieferten Melodien*. II, Göttingen, 1927, p. 88, No. 15. Of the 198 melodies of this important publication (vol. I) 56 are major tunes, 23 are Lydian, and 23 are between the two. A high proportion of the transcriptions in vol. II can be read with or without B flat, i.e., as major or Lydian melodies. At p. 13 of vol. II there is a slightly different variant of melody No. 23—an example of ambiguous major-Lydian tonality *(op. cit.*, vol. I, pp. 77 and 117—118; vol. II, pp. 92 and 111) :

More than 20 per cent of the melodies quoted in F. Liuzzi's *La lauda e i primordi della melodia italiana*, Roma, 1935 are in the major (29 out of 135, including variants). The melodic aesthetics of the period clearly considered that major and Lydian were closely related, and even variants of each other. Aribo Scholasticus describes the major tetrachord as *rustica sonoritas*, while Guido d'Arezzo calls the Lydian mode *agricolae dictus*. They both clearly consider them countrified, folkish, and pagan. The tritone (augmented fourth) of the Lydian mode is particularly pagan, the *diabolus in musica*. (*Cp.* W. Danckert: *Das europäische Volkslied*. Berlin, 1939, pp. 195—196.) Even Glareanus in 1547 thought that the major scale was primarily for folk-songs and dances. This folk character does not seem to be connected with any one nation, though recent scholars have seen it as a Welsh or English peculiarity (G. Hayes: *King's Music*. London, 1937, p. 39; E. H. Meyer: *English Chamber Music*. London, 1946, pp. 43—45). They mention that the English theoretician J. Cotton (fl. 1100) was the first to find beauty in a major melody (Gerbert: *Scriptores* II, p. 254), and that more than 70 per cent of Dunstable's works at the turn of the 14th—15th century can be thought of as being in the major (from J. Stainer's list, *Sammelb. der Intern. Musikgesellschaft*. II, pp. 1—16).

5. One example is the *Benedicamus Domino* of Perotinus in the *Magnus Liber Organi* (c. 1180—1200).

6. Joh. Wolf: "Die Tänze des Mittelalters." *Archiv f. Musikwissenschaft* I, 1918.

7. See H. Spanke's article, *Zeitschrift für Musikwissenschaft* XIV, 1932, pp. 391—397.

8. F. Gennrich: *Grundriss einer Formenlehre des mittelalterlichen Liedes*. Halle, 1932, pp. 85—88. For text see A. Cavaliere: *Cento Liriche Provenzali*. Bologna, 1938, pp. 491—492. New rhythmic version by H. Husmann, *Acta Musicologica* XXV, 1953, p. 16.

9. Gennrich: *op. cit.*, p. 72; in Lydian form (i.e. without b *flat*) in Gennrich: *Rondeaux, Virelais und Balladen*. I, Dresden, 1921, pp. 137—138 and II, Göttingen, 1927, pp. 120—121.

10. F. Liuzzi: *op. cit.* Vol. I: Examples Nos. XIII, XXXV, XXXVII, XLIII. My example No. 30b is here No. XXX. Both this and No. XXXVII have been transposed. Apart from No. XXX, they all occur with variants in Liuzzi's volumes, in the *Laudarie* of Cortona and Florence; Nos. XXXI of Vol. I. and LXXVIII of Vol. II are the variants of No. XXXVII, and the No. LXIV of Vol. II is the variant of No. XIII. For Banchieri's cited work see the new edition in the series *Capolavori Polifonici del secolo XVI*. Ed. B. Somma, Roma, 1939 ; the melody quoted here comes at p. 38 of this work. Apparently it is linked with the *lauda* above through a common Gregorian ancestor—the *Deo gratias* of the second Mass of the Gradual:

(Transposed as before.)

The transposing of phrases a fourth or fifth up or down is not at all uncommon in ancient Italian folk music. See for instance A. Favara: *Canti della terra e del mare di Sicilia*. Milano, 1921, Nos. 9—11. For an interesting example of pentatonic repetition at the fifth see No. LXXXV in Vol. II of Liuzzi's cited work:

Cf. B. Szabolcsi: "Sui rapporti delle melodie ungheresi con le laudi medioevali." *Janus Pannonius* I, Roma, 1947, pp. 730—732; B. Rajeczky: "Deszendenzmelodik im Choral und unsere absteigenden Perioden." *Acta Ethnographica*, Budapest, 1958.

THE GREAT DIATONIC STYLE

LATE MIDDLE AGES AND RENAISSANCE

Nothing gives a clearer indication of the musical feeling of a period than the claims it makes on its own melodies. Deliberate concealment is impossible, for it emerges in the postulates and criticisms of theoretical works no less than in chance comments in essays and philosophical works. Opinions about melodic theory from the 14th to the 16th century were so unanimous that the period may be regarded as a single continuous unit. Known as the late Middle Ages and Renaissance, it seems to have admired melodies which were powerful, sweet, and expressive. If these adjectives are compared with authentic descriptions of the time, they are seen at once to explain and complete each other's meaning:

> *Le roi de ce moult se merveille*
> *Et dist que'oncques mais en sa vie*
> *Ne vist si très grant mélodie—*

wrote Guillaume de Machaut in one of his poems about the middle of the 14th century. By 'grant' (grand), he intended the penetrating power of the melody no less than the hero's astonishment. 'Grant' generally meant 'loud', 'penetrating' and 'vigorous': this was how Jean de Roye intended it when he described Louis XI's entry into Paris in 1461, and the attendant pageantry in the streets. The procession included singing sirens . . . *et prè d'eulx jouoient plusieurs bas instrumens* (i.e., low accompanying instruments) *qui rendoient de grandes melodies*[1]; obviously meaning that the instruments were playing resonant, 'penetrating' melodies. But the period plainly meant more by 'grant' than the word implied: a melody merited this adjective when it was moving and expressive. That was how Thomas More used it in *Utopia* to describe the church music of his wonderful kingdom: "the fashion of the melody doth so represent the meaning of the thing, that it doth wonderfully move, stir, pierce and inflame the hearers' minds." (*Ita rei sensum quendam melodiae forma repraesentat, ut*

58

animum auditorium mirum adficiat, penetrat, incendat.) In other words, the ideal melody of this period was 'powerful' and 'expressive'. That it also had to be 'sweet' is clear from Fra Salimbene's description (about 1230) of the singing youth in Pisa. Castiglione, Ronsard and Shakespeare all spoke of 'sweet melodies' too. F. Villani used the expression *melodiae dulcedo* when writing of Landino, and about 1360 Jean Lefèvre was enthusiastic about *douce melodie*.[2] Such descriptions as these penetrated literary consciousness: expressions such as *artificiosissima melodia*[3] also appeared, but less often. The ideal melody also had to be singable and tuneful. Johannes de Muris attacked chromaticism for being unsingable, and hence against the natural inclinations of the human voice *(contra naturalem inclinationem vocum humanorum)*. In any period, chromaticism has always kept pace with instrumental technique, and there is something in it which is alien to classical and particularly Mediterranean melody. That was why it was found in the music of 'decadent' Parisian composers about 1400 (Cesaris, Carmen, Tapissier), why it developed about 1550 in the Italian madrigal, and triumphed in the high romantic era of Spohr and Wagner's *Tristan* . . . it was strange that there was to be a period that realised the sweetness of chromatic melody. The late Middle Ages and the greater part of the Renaissance had different ideas: for them, a powerful, sweet and expressive melody-style meant diatonicism, and indeed these centuries represent the flowering of diatonic music in Western European culture.

*

It was as though the seed of Gregorian chant had taken root as a melody-style related to, and resembling, plainchant, but allowed to grow up in a purely European way as a diatonic plant. That was how it had come to flourish on French, Flemish-Burgundian, English, German and Italian soil during the late Middle Ages and Renaissance. Were there important national differences? If so, they are only a matter for conjecture: much more striking is the instinctive acceptance of ideas as a benefit conferred on humanity, a world-acquisition, to be studied and diffused from place to place. It was as if the new melody had been discovered by some court or city, from there to spread all over Europe with local variants, 'sown' along every European highway by wandering minstrels and scholar-poets.[4] Characteristically, the first signs of this new but age-old form of melody appeared at the same time and in the same way all over Europe— in Germany as in England, in Parisian as in Florentine manuscripts. Every type of music was equally affected: it was as unmistakable in German folk-hymns as in *Minnesang*, or the erudite collections of sequences. The great melodies of Western and Southern Germany date back to the high Middle Ages: *Victimae paschali laudes, Media vita, Christ ist erstanden,* Walther von der Vogelweide's *Jerusalemlied,* and many of Neidhart's melodies are all conceived in a broad diatonic vein. They are the new-born Northern offspring of Gregorian chant, coming to life in the spirit of Western and Central Europe:

31

a) Wipo: Easter Sequence

b) German Easter-song

Although merged into the main German tradition, they all stemmed from the outer edge of German cultural territory, and count as peripheral phenomena. Notker, who composed *Media vita,* was Swiss: Wipo, who wrote *Victimae paschali laudes,* was Burgundian. *Christ ist erstanden* and *Nun bitten wir den heiligen Geist*—the loveliest of 11th- and 12th-century German folk-hymns—probably originated in Southern Germany as adaptations of Latin sequences for Easter and Whitsun. Their pentatonic idioms

32

e) (Neidhart)

Mai - en - zît   â - ne   nît

may point to some hidden pentatonic tradition in Central Europe, or be imitations of pentatonic idioms in plain-song. It is not important: what matters is that the melodic texture is of the finest, and that in their final form they are models of classical balance. (Note, for instance, the scrupulously careful alignment of registers in *Victimae paschali laudes* and *Christ ist erstanden*.)

That such melody may stem from a peripheral tradition is borne out by the great flowering of melody in the following period. In musical history, borderline territories that have long been unknown quantities may suddenly—though not altogether unexpectedly—assume importance as focal points of melodic evolution. The great diatonic style of the 14th to 16th century began in Flanders, Burgundy, Northern France, Southern Germany, Northern Italy, and, to some extent, in England. The rich output of art- and folk-song culminated in two periods of classic achievement—the Burgundian Renaissance in the 15th century (till about 1520) and the Italian Renaissance in the second half of the 16th (1540—1600). The first stream clearly stemmed from Dufay, and reached Josquin by way of Binchois, Okeghem and Obrecht. The 15th-century *chanson* and the Italian *villota* were also connected with it. When Besseler describes (in *Bourdon und Fauxbourdon*. Leipzig, 1950), how the cramped and restless melody of the late Middle Ages yielded about 1430 to the tranquil, song-like, flowing style of Dufay and his successors, he was stating a basic fact about the history of Renaissance melody.

In broad outline this was how the story went in North-West Europe, but in the South it was more complicated. Palestrina represented the melody of mass and motet from 1550 onwards, as Luca Marenzio and Andrea Gabrieli represented the madrigal and all other secular melody from 1580. The Italian madrigal of 1580 absorbed the lighter-weight *frottola, canzonetta* and *villota* in the same way that Obrecht and Josquin had taken over the French—Burgundian *chanson ;* the folk-element was continually submerged and identified with art-music and academic styles. The folk-styles had taken over with irresistible force about 1500, and now it was the turn of the academic forms, which about

61

1600 seemed just as firmly entrenched, and even more so for having absorbed all the revolutionary novelty of the popular forms. Their strength was renewed at the expense of their foster-brothers, and this in the service of an ideal which was far more reticent and exclusive—that of *musica reservata*.

The first diatonic melodies of 'modern' type probably appeared about 1350 in Machaut's ballades: they were still of minor importance, and figured here and there in the polyphonic texture like a chance digression of the part-writing. A hundred years later, Dufay handled melody in a much more definite and assured way, so that in its rise and fall it formed its own symmetrical curves. Here is the opening to Dufay's famous *Lamentatio Sanctae Matris Ecclesiae Constantinopolitanae*—a celebrated composition, which was presented in 1454 at the Pheasant Festival at Lille to celebrate the inauguration of the last Crusade. An urgent necessity because of the fall of Constantinople.[5]

33

Dufay: Lamentatio

Tenor

An even newer style appeared in Binchois' melodies (mid-15th century). His chansons are full of unconstrained, secular gaiety: it was not surprising that his contemporaries called him *le père de joyeuseté* (father of joyousness). They show real *bel canto*, or rather they anticipate certain basic types of European melody centuries before they actually appeared. The chanson *De plus en plus*, for instance, opens with the same melody that appeared in Mozart's *Divertimento in E flat* three hundred years later; *Triste plaisir* reveals a melody-type that is familiar from Bach's works (e.g., the short *Organ Fugue in G minor* : in Binchois' melody the fifth is still missing):

34

a) **Binchois:** Chansons

De   plus   en plus   se   re-nou - vel   -   le

Mozart: Divertimento in E flat major, 1788

b)

Tris - te   plai - sir   et   dou - lou-reu-se   joi   -   e

62

Bach: Organ Fugue in G minor

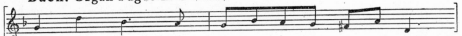

But at the turn of 1500, melody showed an even more important feature, which came to dominate Burgundian classicism, and in particular the music of Josquin. This was the almost unarticulated, broad surge of melody, from which the texture of choral polyphony was always woven. It was still a vocal line and not a solo melody, and it came and went in loosely built, asymmetrical patterns. It flowed like a wave or a stream, and it could also be described as 'runner-melody'. Of the Flemish masters, it was Okeghem who gave it its most characteristic shape. Okeghem's complicated melodies probably represented a special Flemish type of which the origin is unknown. They have little in common with the works of contemporary French and Italian composers, they rather suggest a link with contemporary English style. The upper part of *Alma Redemptoris* is an example: Bach wrote such endless, long-winded, floating melodies some two hundred years later, and his conception was naturally more chromatic and instrumental:

35

Okeghem: Alma Redemptoris

Yet there was clearly an Italian influence at work in the music of the Flemish–Burgundian school, simultaneously with the almost abstract, North-Western art of Okeghem. Obrecht and Josquin were both saturated in Southern melody, and transplanted its clear symmetrical outlines into the classical Flemish forms as well as into the milder French *chanson*. Italian influence pervades them all: compare Okeghem's *chansons* (e.g., *Ma bouche rit*) with Obrecht's, Isaac's or Josquin's—not to mention those of Lasso. Sooner or later the new spirit of the Italian Renaissance was bound to enter mass and motet. Was it chance that melodies like Josquin's *Adieu mes amours* play such an important part in a Venetian *villota* manuscript?[26] There was nothing fortuitous about the pure lyricism of Josquin's famous *Ave Maria :* this popular song-type survived into Schubert's day in the crystal-clear symmetry and stepwise gradation of its melodic shape:

63

36

Josquin: Ave Maria

Such a melody was the result of Josquin's wide European culture, but it was also a conscious and far-seeing synthesis of the national trends about the year 1500. After this synthesis the great choral themes in Palestrina's masses (about 1560) bring the only essential newness by combining Okeghem's 'runner-melodies' and floating lines with Josquin's song-like lyricism and solid proportions. Take, for instance, the broadly flowing *Agnus Dei* in the *Missa Papae Marcelli*, a melody which shows very convincingly how Palestrina's works summed up the dynamic principles of European choral melody by what amounted to an application of the 'laws of gravity'. The familiar stylistic principles have still not lost their validity. Repetition, chromaticism, the altering of intervals, sequential development and too much symmetry are all avoided in favour of stepwise progressions, falling lines, limited compass and pure intervals. Leaps to the lowest extreme of the compass are balanced up against a stepwise return, and wider intervals most carefully prepared and followed, often appearing in the lower register in slow *tempi*. Such melodies begin on their final, and return to it stepwise once they have touched their top note, etc.[7]

37

Palestrina: From 'Missa Papae Marcelli'

The great masses of Josquin, though later in date, already incorporate the same principles, as may be seen in the mass *Fortuna desperata :*

Exeter Cathedral. A typical architectural example of the 'flamboyant Gothic art' of the
Late Middle Ages (13th to 14th centuries).

38

Josquin: From the Mass 'Fortuna desperata'
Qui tollis

Agnus II

The significance of this music is not wholly revealed unless it is considered in relation to the popular music of the period. The popular trend of the Renaissance constituted a great change in taste, and needs a passing comment. The simplest and clearest form of popular art was the Italian *frottola*, which flourished about 1500. It had been preceded by the 15th-century *villota*, which many modern Italian scholars consider as the herald of the second *ars nova*, although it is only a beginning. Some of the popular tunes by Philippus de Lurano, Rosino Mantovano and Tromboncino (from Books IV, VIII and XI of Petrucci's *frottola* collection, dated 1505, 1508 and 1514 respectively[8]) show a dance-like rhythmical balance: their swaying lilt is sufficiently pronounced to exert a decisive influence on the song-writers of the following period. They adopt the age-old principle of motive-repetition and transposition with the same ease as certain medieval melodies (see above). It is more and more probable that the principle of question-and-answer, which was originally entirely monodic in conception, entered polyphony by way of popular melody, giving rise to the practice of imitation, from the *rota* (or round) to the fugue. The theoreticians of the late Middle Ages (e.g. Garlandia, Paumann, and Tinctoris) had already formulated the rules for *repetitio* and *similitudo-dissimilitudo* on the basis of what was commonly practised at the time.

39
a) Lurano 1505

Don - na contr'   a   la   mia   vo - glia

b) Mantovano 1508

(Tenor - Cantusfirmus)

A pe - de la mon - ta - gna

c) Tromboncino 1514

A - qua non e l'hu - mor che ver - sa gli oc - chi

Although there was a gulf between this and 'learned' music, the two worlds met in the *chanson*, which acted as a mediator. The loveliest of them served to stimulate the great (and greatest) forms. The Italian song *Fortuna desperata*,[9] for instance, was used as a *cantus firmus* in masses by Obrecht, Josquin, Isaac, Senffl, Breitengraser and others. The chanson *Je suis deshéritée*[10] appeared in masses by Palestrina, Lasso, Gombert and Goudimel. The first is quoted as it appeared in Josquin's mass, as no authentic, contemporary version of the song exists; the second is given as published by Attaignant in 1539, from where it found its way into later publications:

40

a) Josquin: From the Mass 'Fortuna desperata'

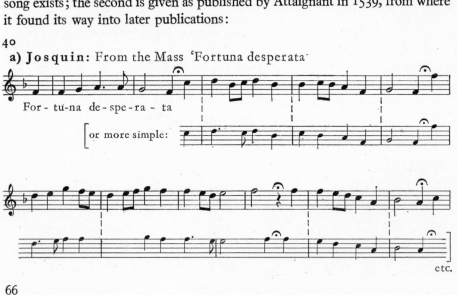

For - tu-na de - spe - ra - ta

[or more simple:

etc.

b) 15th century chanson

Je suis des-hé-ri - té - e   Puis-que j'ay per-du mon a - my

These melodies are not folk-songs, maybe not even popular types. The dreamy, elegiac voice of the court-poet mingles in them with that of the wandering scholar, and they are permeated with self-conscious, town-cultivated humanist poetry. This relates them very closely to Isaac's masterly *Innsbruck* which has since become the classic type of old German folk-song *(Nun ruhen alle Wälder...)*. It is in fact clear that they must have had some sort of folk-flavour, a feeling for land and nature, which was recognised by the community at large. They must have satisfied the country needs of the early 16th century, otherwise they would have never become favourite songs (not folk-songs), accepted and sung by entire communities at the turn of 1500—virtually the whole of Western society.

A closer look at the text of *Fortuna desperata* shows the melody to have seven lines (there seem to be eleven because the first four are repeated). The syllabic count is $4 \times 7 / 4 \times 7 / 7$—$7$—$11$, the rhyme-scheme is ABBAACCADEE and the structure is iambic. The melody-rhymes are ABBA://CCB or AA_1A_1A://BBA_1—A_1 denoting a melodic line akin to A but different in length, with an added melisma unrelated to the text. The melodic structure is complicated and cleverly thought-out—observe the linked line-endings, the careful balancing of registers, the inventive but economical way that the phrases have been made to rise, fall and finish. It would need special study to relate this song to French *chansons* and German court-songs and chorales between 1460 and 1590.[11]

The major melody of *Fortuna desperata* contrasts with the minor quality of *Je suis deshéritée*, which has a more antique flavour. The latter is an Aeolian or Hypo-Dorian melody without the sixth, pronouncedly plagal in character (moving about and below its final, rather than above it). Its archaism is constantly in evidence: the opening leap to the minor third and fourth, for instance, is typical of the 15th-century *chanson*,[12] but it is also related to old

German models, such as *Hildebrandslied (Ich will zu Land ausreiten)*. The melody shows many 'modern' features as well, such as a careful balance of line and register. Masculine and feminine rhymes are most economically arranged: line-rhythms and line-endings in the second half carefully correspond to those of the first half. If B denotes lines of four complete iambs, A those of three-and-a-half and C those of four-and-a-half, the melodic scheme can be represented as ABAB/BCBC. Palestrina, Lasso, Gombert and Goudimel would not have used it in their masses without being well aware of its masterly structure.

The revolutionary new 'church songs' of the period should also be mentioned, that is to say the many great psalms and chorales. The most obvious is *Ein feste Burg*, but there is also the 36th (68th) Huguenot psalm. Both have such a mighty melodic span that they could be called 16th-century Marseillaises. There are also a quantity of 15th-century Hussite melodies, known from the collections of Zdeněk Nejedlý and others *(Dějiny Husitského Zpěvu* III. *Jan Hus*, Prague, 1955, p. 134, and others):

41
a) **Marot and Greiter:** Huguenot psalm

Du ma-lin les faits vi-ci – eux

b) **Hussite chant**

Je – sus Chri – stus no-stra sa – – lus

c) **Hussite chant**

etc.

Ktož jsů bo- ži bo – jo-vni – ci

etc.

In addition to these main lines of development, diatonic melody also developed along branch-lines which in many respects mirrored or extended the main trends. Some merely confirmed it, but others influenced the actual development of the classical melody. Two of these merit special attention. One was formed of the popular-style major melodies which spread under diatonic influence, constructed in the same broad way. The most obvious are the melodies of the Mastersingers, at the historical turning-point when they began to merge with the growing flood of Protestant choral music. Hans Sachs' *Silberweise* (1513) belongs to this category, and so, even more obviously, does Nachtigall's *Abendton*. The text, beginning *Wiltu erkennen Regen*[13] was contributed by Sachs:

42

Nachtigall: Abendton
(Approximate rhythm)

The whole melody is steeped in German folk-feeling, even though it only consists of the free repetition of two folk-like phrases. The way the opening sweeps up to the octave, as well as the half-close at the fifth, reflect the carefully balanced and calculated technique of classical diatonic melody, characteristic of humanistic literature too. The educated citizens of old Nuremberg obviously felt the influence of court-poetry bearing in on them from all directions (particularly from beyond Germany's southern and western frontiers) and this coloured and refined their own music and poetry. The lower middle class interpreted both these arts in a narrower and more realistic way, and added a strong folk-element. The humanism of courts and scholar-poets became more earthy and close to life, inheriting from its earlier existence an instinctive feeling for proportion rather than aristocratic forms and ideas. It acquired something that was missing in aristocratic art—the uncomplicated realism of life in small town or country, which expressed itself in easily understood folk-idioms. So do spheres of life replace one another almost undetected—the aristocratic, secular Renaissance slowly giving way to that of town and country. Historically, it is the familiar process by which cultural acquisitions 'sink downwards', to be completed and counterbalanced by the even more abundant supply of raw material, forcing its way up from underneath. This was particularly true of the Renaissance.

The change of feeling and level can be seen best in the second branch-line of diatonic music—humanist songs in the strictest sense. These were the metrical melodies which became popular in German schools between 1490 and 1550 as a result of the linguistic studies of Konrad Celtis, Peter Tritonius-Traybenreiff, and others. The movement, preceded by the poems and songs *all'antica*, written by Italian humanists from 1480 onwards, later reached a still higher level in the works of the French Pléïade and the *chansons mesurées*. This was how Horace, Virgil and even Homer—not to mention their humanist imitators—came to be known throughout Italy, Germany, England and France during the 16th century.

This literature of humanistic 'odes' was not confined to academic or literary circles, but soon reached a wider public. In England, France, Holland, Germany and Hungary, it gave rise to the Protestant hymn-psalm, which included the London metrical psalter, the metrical chansons by Du Caurroy and Lasso, Honterus' Transylvanian collection of odes, the Flemish *Souterliedekens*, and Calvinist 'hymns of praise' by Bourgeois, Le Jeune and Olthovius. They all proclaim the glorious marriage of classical Greek and Roman metres with Europe's new sensibility. In most cases, the melodies were little more than academic experiment, a mechanical marking and churning out of some metrical pattern. Some, however, were really valuable finds, being clearcut, shapely melodies, which served to inspire others. They showed with great clarity the 'declassing' process which characterised the new European melody. Whether in Holland, France, England, Italy or Germany, learned and aristocratic poetry had become food for the masses. A subjectively conceived melody became a rallying-song, a psalm-chant, a chorale, a badge of either Reformation or Counter-Reformation, until finally it became a folk-song. The melody lost its learned or subjective origin, and was moulded to the popular taste.

Sooner or later, the wheel turned full circle, and in a new sense the melody became 'classical' again. For it was not merely a process of 'sinking' and diffusion, but rather an adjusting to the 'growing claims of reality', as described by art-historians in connection with this period. Whatever the reasons, it appeared all over Europe at the same time. About 1900 Courajod considered that the movement originated in Flanders, but it now seems clear that it arose in the North as in the South within a period of some thirty to forty years, to be summed up in the work of the Van Eyck brothers and Klaus Sluter, in Masolino, Ghiberti and Brunelleschi, in unknown Rhenish masters, in anonymous Flemish, German, Italian and English composers. First came the realisation, the moment of truth, followed by a new perception and process of revaluation on the part of a new social group or generation. This in its turn was followed by an attempt to shape the concepts into a fixed form. The search to find labels and forms to fit the new outlook was carried on simultaneously by a great many people, with varying degrees of intensity.

There are two masterly examples of the humanistic movement in music: one is an Alcaic melody in Dorian mode, appearing in Honterus' collection of odes (Corona-Brashov, 1548), the other is known as *Modulisemus omnes*, which in origin was obviously a humanist text. It became sufficiently popular to be sung on Czech and Hungarian territory as a Protestant chorale, with independent texts. Initially, it may have been Hussite (there are traces of it in Hungary during the first half of the 16th century in the shape of a printed document of 1514 or 1554 in the Archiepiscopal Library at Esztergom). A song-text which appeared in the song-book of Várad (1566) and in one published by Gergely Szegedi (1569): *Jer, mi dicsérjük, áldjuk* (Come, let us praise and bless), alluded to this melody in the directions for singing. Finally it made its appearance—with Hungarian text by this time—in *Cantus Catholici* (1651) and Ferenc Lénárt Szegedi's song-book (1674).[14] The Czech version had previously appeared in the great *Kancionál* (1576), and is worth comparing with the Hungarian variant. The Czech has ABCD/EFBCD in contrast with the Hungarian ABCD/EEBCD. They differ in line C and lines E—F. The Czech version adds line F which makes it more elaborate than the Hungarian, but the latter is more economical in line C, deferring the final until the end, and remaining on the dominant.

The Horatian melody in Honterus' collection is a most lovely melody of antique type, yet it never achieved wide popularity. It seems to be a composition of the Swiss Glareanus (H. Loris), in whose *Dodekachordon* (1547), Bk. II, chap. 39 it occurs in a slightly different (Asklepiadic) form, as a Dorian setting of Horace's first ode:

43

From **Honterus'** Collection of Odes
(the rhythm has been adapted to the metre)

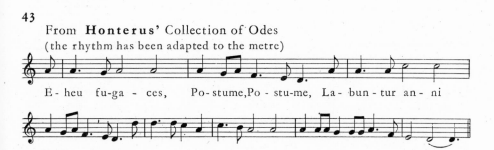

E - heu fu-ga - ces,   Po - stume, Po - stu-me, La - bun - tur an - ni

Modulisemus omnes is given below in both Czech and Hungarian versions: the third line (C) is an approximation of what is likely to have been the rhythm:

44

Modulisemus omnes
a) Czech version 1576

b) Hungarian version 1651

Jer mi di-csír-jük, áld - gyuk, és fel-ma - gasz - tal - lyuk, min-de-

c) Approximate rhythm

nek-nek Te-rem-tő - jét, A-tya Is-ten ne - vét

A gay company amusing itself outdoors — from the series by the Limbourg Brothers; each picture represents different months of the year of which this is April (*Les très riches heures du Duc de Berry*, around 1410).

The third line reveals that the fundamental form is a re-working of the primitive Latin Saturnian metre. It becomes more obvious if Naevius' famous epitaph *Immortales mortales* is set to it:

> *Immortales mortáles*
> *Sí forét fas flére,*
> *Flérent divae Caménae*
> *Naévium poétam . . . . . etc.*

The melody consists of two verses, with different starting-lines (ABCD—EBCD); the first line of the second verse is repeated, so that the text has nine lines, contrasting with the strophic unity achieved by Naevius' eight. We do not know, in Latin literature, of any other example where from lines of such type closed strophic form has been built. The metre of the two verses is exactly the same, and forms two identical four-lined structures. The melodic curve represents one of the most important achievements of diatonic song-construction; ascending and descending arches alternate with each other, whilst in the second verse, the high range of the opening line is replaced by a lower one, only to return to it unchanged. Yet the return is satisfying because it gives the effect of a necessary solution. The finished product is well worth-while: a classical form, worked on by humanist melodic invention, is transformed into a classic folk-form by dint of being worked over by the folk-feeling of two nations.

*

Mingling and separation formed the essence of a century rich in contrasts, and applied just as much to the melodies of the period, which 'sank', merged, and re-emerged. The process is seen at work even more clearly in the controversial but important branch of European melody known as ornamentation ('melody in miniature'). Naturally, the melodic style of ornamentation differed from region to region, and from nation to nation. In the South, what mattered was a melodic line that was constantly being reborn, in the West, ornamentation had a motor function; in the North, the constructive and building energies prevailed in the ornamentation too, whilst in the East, it gathered up all the dynamic energy of the monodic line in the form of arabesque.[15] The process of separation served to accentuate national trends, whilst the spirit of the Renaissance simultaneously encouraged a process of amalgamation and integration. Language split up into national 'dialects', but the main vocabulary was clarified and condensed. From the decorative and ornamental emerged the organic, from a mass of detail a unified conception. The Renaissance was in process of emerging from the 'autumn' of the Middle Ages, and the atmosphere of the 16th century from that of the 14th and 15th.

Yet by the end of the century, the humanist love of proportion was losing its hold. Other ideas of form were dimly shaping themselves in the efforts of rising generations: even the 'matter' of music was in process of change. The ideal of pure choral music was disappearing, together with the strenuous search for balance. The dramatic implications of word and text were becoming as insistent as the clamour for instrumental music. The noble reticence and symmetry of Renaissance vocal-writing was yielding to a new struggle for proportion and balance, a new sense of time, a new restlessness, known from the second half of the period as the Baroque.

NOTES

1. Quoted by Huizinga: *Herbst des Mittelalters*. 5th ed., Stuttgart, 1939, p. 459.
2. F. Gennrich, *Zeitschrift f. Musikwiss.* IX, 1927, p. 515. *Cp*. also Sigismond von Luxemburg's complimentary description when he visited England in 1414: "Blessid Inglond, full of melody." (A. Pirro: *Histoire de la musique aux XVe et XVIe siècles*. Paris, 1940, p. 96.) For the Burgundian use of the word see J. Marix: *Histoire de la musique de la cour de Bourgogne (1420—1467)*. 1939, pp. 37, 40, 99, 183, and *Acta Musicologica* XXIII, 1951, p. 108 (R. v. Ficker.)
3. *Cp*. A. Schering: *Stud. zur Musikgesch. der Frührenaissance*. 1914, p. 70.
4. *Cp*. F. Gennrich: "Internat. mittelalt. Melodien." *Zeitschr. f. MW*. 1929.
5. Published by H. Besseler, *Zeitschr. f. MW*. XI, 1928, p. 12.
6. F. Torrefranca: *Il segreto del Quattrocento*. Milano, 1939, p. 540. Torrefranca dates the manuscript as 15th century, whereas Jeppesen gives it, probably more correctly, as 1520, though its material may well be much older.
7. Musical theory at this time distinguished between intervals the notes of which progressed in contrary motion. This is shown most interestingly in V. Galilei's *Dialogo*. 1581, new edition, ed. by F. Fano, Milano, 1947, p. 76.
8. *Cp*. articles by Ferand, Jeppesen and Einstein, *Musical Quarterly* XXVII, 1941, p. 322; *Kodály-Emlékkönyv* [Kodály Memorial Volume]. 1943, p. 269 and *Zeitschr. f. MW*. X, 1928, p. 620.
9. *Cp*. W. Danckert (*Das europ. Volkslied*. 1939, p. 310). The latter has a list of the adaptations of its descant and tenor lines. Its text was published by Torrefranca (*op. cit.*, p. 297) from Parisian and Perugian sources. See also E. Lowinsky: M. Greiter's "Fortuna" in *Musical Quarterly*, 1956, pp. 518—519. A Phrygian version of the melody by H. Isaac is to be found in Kotter's *Tabulaturbuch*, 1513: *cp. Denkm. der Tonkunst in Öst.* XIV, p. 144, and W. Merian: *Der Tanz in den deutschen Tabulaturbüchern*. Leipzig, 1927, pp. 68—69.
10. *Cp*. Th. Gerold: *Chansons populaires des XVe et XVIe siècles avec leurs mélodies*. Strasbourg, undated (1913), XVIII.
11. Its Italian origin is also confirmed by a related *villota (L'ultimo dì di mazo)*, *cp*. Torrefranca: *op. cit.* p. 486. There is also a French *chanson* with a similar opening (*Une petite feste*. 1599, Gerold: *op. cit.* No. XXXVII). Konrad Paumann's *Weiblich Figur* is also related (did it precede or follow it?), in Schedel's *Liederbuch*, c. 1465, published by Eitner in *Das deutsche Lied des XV. und XVI. Jh.-s* (Beilage zu den *Monatsheften f. Musikgesch.* 1880).

Quoted more recently by B. A. Wallner, in the appendix to an article on K. Paumann, published in A.-H. Bolongaro Crevenna's *Münchner Charakterköpfe der Gotik*. München, 1938, pp. 33—36. The two compositions are related in an unusual way: of the seven melody-lines, line 1 is closely related to Paumann's *contra*, lines 2—5 to Paumann's *descant*, and lines 6—7 to Paumann's *tenor*. Paumann's is a three-part madrigal, and its text is a court poem, perhaps translated. The second half of the *Fortuna*-melody occurs in a slightly altered form in the German chorale *Es ist das Heil uns kommen her* (1523).

12. *Cp.* Gerold: *op. cit.* Introduction, pp. XLIV—XLVII.

13. *Cp.* R. Genée: *Hans Sachs und seine Zeit*. Leipzig, 1902, p. 404.

14. *Cp.* Géza Papp: *A magyar kat. egyházi népének kezdetei* [The Beginnings of Hungarian Catholic Folk-Chant]. Budapest, 1942, pp. 27 and 33, melody No. 3 (in Hungarian). The author is indebted to G. Papp for the Czech melody.

15. *Cp.* the author's study "Über Kulturkreise der musikalischen Ornamentik in Europa." *Zeitschr. f. MW*. 1935, also in the Appendix to the present volume (p. 244).

THE BAROQUE MELODY

In the spring of 1611, a new play was presented at the Globe Theatre, London. The spectators were treated to a surprise at the beginning of Act IV, when the 'Chorus', who had appeared in many guises, now came on as Time, and began to speak of his power:

> "*I that please some, try all, both joy and terror*
> *Of good and bad, that makes and unfolds error,*
> *Now take upon me, in the name of Time,*
> *To use my wings. Impute it not a crime*
> *To me or my swift passage, that I slide*
> *O'er sixteen years, and leave the growth untried*
> *Of that wide gap, since it is in my power*
> *To o'erthrow law and in one self-born hour*
> *To plant and o'erwhelm custom. Let me pass*
> *The same I am, ere ancient'st order was*
> *Or what is now received : I witness to*
> *The times that brought them in ; so shall I do*
> *To the freshest things now reigning, and make stale*
> *The glistering of this present, as my tale*
> *Now seems to it. Your patience this allowing,*
> *I turn my glass and give my scene such growing*
> *As you had slept between . . .*"

This was to explain the sixteen years which had elapsed between the two parts of *The Winter's Tale*. But neither the actor nor the aging Shakespeare could have addressed the audience in this way had they not been aware of their own uncertainties in this affecting confession—and with them perhaps a whole generation. For Time had long been the source of all uncertainty, the focal point of worry, the core of every discontent. About 1590, Bacon gave one of his early works the distinctive title of *The Birth of Time*. The might of Time was a common 17th-century theme: it turns up in lyrical poetry from Milton to Gryphius and the Hungarian poet Miklós Zrínyi, in plays from Calderon to Dryden, in epic poetry, prose and philosophy. As for painting, Ortega y Gasset commented not long ago: "Up to the time of Velazquez, the representation of Time had been in favour of a timeless world ... But Velazquez paints Time itself, at the moment when it starts to lose its existence in transition." It was as if an entire generation had had a sudden violent shock, as if even the best of them had been attacked by sudden dizziness. The inner causes of the crisis were plain to see: the security of the Old was giving way to the unformed character of the New; the feudal world was tottering, but the bourgeois world was slow in coming to birth.

The real content of a moment or a year, of sleeping or waking, depends on what is experienced in them. In *As You Like It*, Shakespeare makes Rosalind say to Orlando: "Time travels in divers paces with divers persons." Paul Fleming wrote in 1635:

"*Die Zeit, die stirbt in sich und zeugt sich auch aus sich.*
Dies kommt aus mir und dir, von dem du bist und ich.
Der Mensch ist in der Zeit, sie ist in ihm desgleichen,
Doch aber muss der Mensch, wenn sie noch bleibet, weichen ..."

(*"Time dies of itself, and generates itself.*
This springs from you and me, because of what we are.
Man is in Time, and Time in him,
But though Time still stays, Man has to give way ...")

These were current ideas in the 17th century, when Time had become an unknown quantity.

*

Since the middle of the 16th century, the chromaticism inspired by instruments had begun to act on the purely diatonic structure of vocal music, like some terrifyingly beautiful will-o'-the-wisp. It had begun as a hidden process, but continued quite openly. Even as early as 1555, Cipriano de Rore had opened his famous Catullan ode *Calami sonum ferentes* with a sinuous chromatic melody, and the madrigals of Caimo, Orso, Marenzio, and Gesualdo confirmed the revolutionary trend. With its feverish semitonal melody and freely roaming harmony, Marenzio's *Solo e pensoso* is a kind of chromatic fire-trap, while the flurry of sliding chords in Gesualdo's *Moro lasso* is musical anarchy personified. Even the most daring modulations of Wagner lack the freshness of these earlier attempts, which sip the sweet poison of chromaticism for the first time, and all the more eagerly for that very reason. From 1580, the crisis in tonality and melody was even further intensified by another upheaval, i.e. the crisis in the sense of Time.

The melodies of the Golden Age of choral polyphony are often irregular and asymmetrical if judged by the rhythmical standards of a later period. But asymmetry was perfectly possible so long as it was covered over by the ever-changing and polymetrical patterns of sound so essential to polyphony. The following melodies by Josquin and Lasso, for instance, hold their own in the choral texture by never being heard alone, but always with other, accompanying melodies:

45
a) Josquin de Près: From the "L'homme armé" Mass

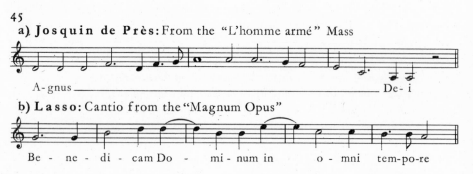

b) Lasso: Cantio from the "Magnum Opus"

They never become so dominant and self-assertive that they upset the variable balance of the other parts. About 1590 the revolutionary growth of monody brought a sudden change. By wishing to dominate the other parts, and make them subsidiary, the melody becomes responsible for the metrical shape of the work. If it is erratic and irregular, uncertainly balanced and full of sudden changes, it can upset the whole musical texture. Movement in any form is the equivalent of Time. It is the impatience of the new music which chiefly distinguishes it from what has gone before. If uneasy melodies can indicate the nervous state of a generation, there has seldom been a more edgy one than that which lived about 1600! Giovanni Battista Doni, conscientious chronicler of Florentine monody, published in 1635 a treatise on the problems of perfecting melody (*Discorso sopra la perfettione della melodia*) in which he declared that the chief merit of the new monody was its new refinement of expression. For him, it was expression which mattered, but a different idea of Time also brought with it a new sense of outer proportion. The new art of expression could not be mistaken for the old, even in its external shape.

The difference was patently obvious, for it broke out on the surface of music like a feverish rash. In 1614, Caccini wrote that he was putting down the whole life of the melody, its delivery as well as its melodic idea: *io scrivo giu-*

stamente come si canta. The notation shows exactly how the vocal line works out from the singing point of view; notes are lengthened, joined, left out or shortened, nuances are shown or suggested, even though they may complicate a clear understanding of the melody and make the piece less plastic. Rubato, fluctuations in speed, or actual changes in tempo are indicated, but longer notes are used instead of writing 'slower', and a crowded line of short notes appears instead of the word 'quicker'. Such a method is not reliable enough for a musician of the present day: the bar-divisions are not systematic, and indications of pulse-changes, upbeats and intricate rhythmical relationships are too few and too imprecise. But at that time a musician had different ideas and needs. It was a new style, needing to make itself clear to those who had never heard it; it had first to persuade society to make its acquaintance, to show whatever was unusual and irregular, and from this to formulate the rule.

Irregular, unusual, asymmetrical, fantastic, exuberant, impatient—all these adjectives typify the feeling of the new period. Caccini did not set out the new principles of notation until 1614, but in 1590 and 1600 passages such as the following were already appearing in manuscripts and printed books (Cavalieri, Corsi, Viadana):

46

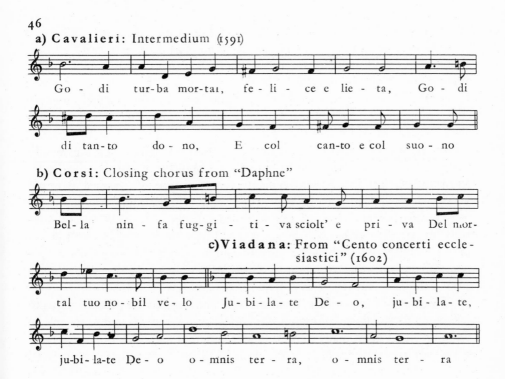

a) **Cavalieri**: Intermedium (1591)

Go - di tur-ba mor-tai, fe - li - ce e lie - ta, Go - di di tan-to do - no, E col can-to e col suo - no

b) **Corsi**: Closing chorus from "Daphne"

Bel-la nin - fa fug-gi - ti - va sciolt' e pri - va Del mor-

c) **Viadana**: From "Cento concerti ecclesiastici" (1602)

tal tuo no - bil ve - lo Ju - bi - la - te De - o, ju - bi - la - te, ju-bi - la-te De - o o - mnis ter - ra, o - mnis ter - ra

It is clear that a struggle was going on. Time had suddenly become so problematical and transient that it had to be caught and set down in writing. Whilst Caccini was battling for this new idea, Frescobaldi in the Preface to his *Toccatas* (1614—1616) was declaring in theory that tempo could be both free and relative, that it depended on melody and expression, and on the performer's sensibility: *. . . rimettendosi a bon gusto e fino giudizio del sonatore il guidar il tempo : nel qual consisti lo spirito.* (". . . leaving the tempo to the good taste and judgment of the performer, for tempo brings the music to life.") Indeed, already in the middle of the 16th century Vicentino demanded *(L'antica musica ridotta alla moderna prattica,* 1555) that the tempo of music, like that of good oratory, should slow down or speed up according to the sense of the words. Others felt the same: in the Preface to the *Nuove Musiche* (1602), Caccini wanted verbal rhythm to prevail over strict tempo, and Horatio Modiana (1623) even asked for "the suppression of bars." In 1638, Monteverdi requested "the excited tempo of the soul, not of the hand," and in 1642, Giovanni Bonachelli talked of tempo being determined by momentary feelings *(conform all'affetto guidare la battuta ricercandosi hor presta hor tarda*—"suit the bar to the feeling, making it slower or faster as needed"). Music was finding its way in Time, and Melody, ever more deeply concerned with the last phrase, went on stretching and shrinking like an elastic garment, without any fundamental change in texture. The same melodic pattern could grow or shrink in time and space. It could become a giant melody or a dwarf, shrink to an ornament, or expand into an endless *cantus firmus.* One of the basic laws of Baroque melody is its freedom from the claims of 'matter'. The claims of voice and instrument only affected its general outline. If it was not under the direct pressure of an actual sound, it could be indifferent both to pitch and register, and equally at home in any sphere, or in none. It was not the slave of an absolute norm of time, but created its own, as has been seen. The beginning of the 17th century saw a generally accepted form of suite in which the same theme would appear in different—even contrasting—guises in every movement. And the type of classical Baroque melody which appeared at the end of the same century could be adapted to voices or instruments, be restricted or extended in form, move briskly or sluggishly, in fast or slow tempo—in fact it could only function amid such a plethora of possibility. Bach's melodies merely completed what Monteverdi's generation had begun—the "conquest of Time." There seemed to be many routes to this conquest, and the various Baroque generations tried them all.

The first way led through anarchy. The uniform flow of melody began to be exposed to declamatory rhythm, for composers of 1600 longed to be able to talk in music. A great many musicians with different and often opposing views began working for the same artistic ideal, in the same way that certain facial types come to characterise a generation, in spite of the laws of heredity manifestly at work in certain families. A generation which is acutely aware of the transitoriness of things, generally possesses a strong dramatic instinct. Opera is nothing more than the completed form of this drama, just as the single voice is the mouthpiece of human destiny in intensified stage form. That is why from 1590 onwards the need for monody and opera became ever more imperative. Vincenzo Galilei and Jacopo Peri insisted upon the declamatory melody, the setting of inflection, for they realised that this was the closest point of contact with the ancient Greek ideal. Bardi considered that the song should follow the verse as obediently as a servant his master, or the child its father. Agazzari claimed (in *Del suonare sopra il basso*, 1607) that music must express the sense of the word: *lo stile moderno di cantar recitativo . . . il vero stile d'esprimere le parole, imitando lo stesso ragionare nel miglior modo possibile* ("the modern style of declamation—the true way of expressing the words by imitating their thought in the best way possible"). This claim becomes ever more peremptory and dogmatic. Writing at the same time as Agazzari, Giulio Cesare Monteverdi, Claudio's brother, set out his brother's well-known confession of faith in the splendid, forward-looking manifesto he called his *Dichiaratione: L'orazione sia padrone dell'armonia e non serva* (declamation should be the master and not the servant of music). This formula echoed far and wide: in 1647, the German musician and writer, Christoph Bernhard, was still distinguishing between *stylus gravis* (or *antiquus*), *stylus luxurians* (or *modernus*) and *stylus theatralis*. In the first, he declared, *harmonia orationis domina* (harmony dominates the speech); in the second, harmony and speech are of equal importance, whilst in the third *oratio harmoniae domina absolutissima*[1] (speech completely dominates the harmony). Had Monteverdi been able to realise the literary ambition of his old age, the *Melodia, overo Seconda Pratica Musicale* (Melody, or the new Practice of Music), it is more than likely that he would have taken the new-style declamatory melody as the dividing-line between past and present.

But in practice where did all this lead? The first operas and solo madrigals steered a careful middle course between the claims of pure declamation, and the need for flights of virtuosity. The balance was not easy to find:

47

Luzzaschi: Madrigal (1601)

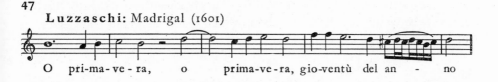

O pri-ma-ve-ra, o prima-ve-ra, gio-ventù del an - no

Even later on, it was always hanging by a thread. Word-accents and pure melody could no longer live together, once Luzzaschi and Caccini had begun to emphasise the virtuoso side of solo singing, and the art of coloratura had begun to flourish alongside dramatic declamation. By the time of Monteverdi's *Orfeo* they were already used in different forms, and in the great works of his old age (*Il Ritorno di Ulisse* and *L'Incoronazione di Poppea*), Monteverdi had created an entirely new arioso operatic style by merging the two. Before reaching this, however, he had followed every conceivable line of development to the bitter end, developing free dramatic declamation to the point of writing *senza battuta* (unbarred) above the monodic *Lettera amorosa* of 1614 (*sans observer aucune mesure*, as Froberger put at the beginning of a lament forty years later).

48

Monteverdi: Lettera amorosa (1614)

In Monteverdi's train came a whole group of composers in search of the last wild freedoms of declamation, which they contorted to the point of nervous eccentricity. The boldest were Claudio Saracini and Domenico Belli: their melodic lines are descriptive, illustrative and explanatory, with ever more numerous slides, modulations, abrupt transitions and dissonances. They supplied all the fervent detours which Lomazzo's aesthetic theories had proclaimed as essential for the representation of feeling. The dissonant melody is just another form of the dissonant, chromatic chord, which flashes up behind it at moments of great emotional tension:

49
a) Saracini: Madrigale in stile recitativo (Musiche, 1614)

b) *Ibid.*

c) *Idem:* Seconde Musiche (1620)   d) *Ibid.*

e) From a Florentine manuscript (Sigismondo d'India?)

f) **Belli**: Orfeo dolente, 1616   g) *Ibid.*

There was still another way to break with tradition and break up the texture of music. In 16th-century music, popular and court dance-rhythms had already played an important part. *Frottola, gagliarda, brando, bassadanza* and *passamezzo* had paved the way for the whole body of instrumental music, and the stylised series of dances, or music of the suite, was ready to emerge. The 17th-century composer began to realise that he could develop these rhythms still further by linking them, drawing them out, or mixing them together, thereby providing music with vital new energy. Here too Monteverdi was a pioneer, and was joined by a group of extremists, we might say 'mannerists'. Anacreontic verse, which was obviously an ancient Mediterranean dance-rhythm, was taken over by the Renaissance mostly in the form of incidental dance-tunes, *balletti, villanellas,* and *morescas.*

6*

83

B. Donati: Canzonetta (1551)

Vi - va sempre o - gni - e - ta - te con la gra - zia d'o - gni stel - la

This form also appears in the operas of Peri and Caccini, but it is Monteverdi who was chiefly fascinated by it: it appears among the 'French' *canzonettas* of the *Scherzi Musicali,* and entire scenes in *Orfeo* grow out of it *(Ecco pur ch'a voi ritorno, Vi ricorda o boschi ombrosi),* a *ritornello* with fantastic rhythmical variations and orchestral interludes.[2] Later, in the second half of the century, echoes of these metrical schemes pervaded the music of Lully and especially that of Francesco Provenzale; Anacreontic verse was also revived amongst others.[3] Fifty years later it was to become the favourite form of Neapolitan *opera buffa* and the chief verse-form of Pergolesi's *Serva padrona.* It also recurs in Mozart's *Figaro* (Cherubino's first aria) and even in Beethoven's *Hammerklavier Sonata.* Provenzale's generation inherited the problem of rhythmical shapes almost as a convention; Monteverdi had traced them right back to Plato (witness his preface to the *Combattimento),* and if not always to Plato, at any rate to Renaissance dance-forms and any other sources in which he caught a whiff of antiquity or ancient traditions. Somewhere, far in the background, gleamed the asymmetrical forms of ancient Greece. Who could more fitly discover them than the Baroque generation, so disillusioned by symmetry? In one part of his *Orfeo dolente* (1616) Domenico Belli arrived at a five-beat rhythm, interestingly set out in the unusual way found in the *Kalevala:*[4]

Belli: Orfeo dolente (1616)

O fe - li - ce se - mi - de - o Fre - na mai l'a - cer-bo duo - lo

It seems that this passionate craving for rhythmical complexity could not be stilled so long as other ways of constructing the bar and interpreting its flux remained unplumbed in the depths of rhythmical sensibility. All the same, things grew somewhat calmer about the middle of the century, and indeed even earlier, about 1640: tension eased off before extreme conclusions were reached. On the one hand there was a growing sense of structure and the assertion of purely musical values, on the other a new surge of popular melody (this period saw the earliest type of *opera buffa*). This counterbalanced the excesses of the mannerists. The results of all this appeared during Monteverdi's last years,

84

at the time of Carissimi, Cavalli and Legrenzi: one single achievement, the art of spinning melodies, was transferred from the workshop of revolution into the musical practice of the High Baroque.

Repetition is the natural way to prolong and preserve the life of a melodic idea, and this is as true of primitive society as it is of highly developed cultures. But, at a certain stage, melodic feeling forsakes mere repetition and craves variation, without undergoing any fundamental change. Baroque composers realised that certain parts of the melody could be heard again with emphasis and at different pitches, thereby saying the same thing in a different way. Although it appeared to stay in the same place, the melody had in fact advanced, so that by a stealthy stratagem it had won a rearguard action over Time. Such was the sequence, the chief melody-spinning technique of the Baroque. Although the idea is simple, its realisation is varied and subtle. That is why its form and feeling can change so much from one generation to another. In the music of the first opera composers it was almost a mechanical device, a simple means of extending and developing the melody. Its dramatic significance seemed to start with Monteverdi. Compare the first ritornello of Cavalieri's *Rappresentazione* (1600) with the famous basic theme of *Orfeo*: in each case, they open their respective works as the first ritornello:

52

C a v a l i e r i : Rappresentazione (1600)

Both are pure sequences, but the spirit that informs them is quite different. Monteverdi does not think of the sequence as an easy way of fabricating music, but a magnificent way of representing reality. Human emotion, pain, anger and joy mount up until they burst out in a cry, a scream, a jubilant shout. He generally uses sequences at dramatic climaxes—as when Orpheus sobbingly asks that Euridice be allowed to return from Hades:

53

M o n t e v e r d i : Orfeo, Act III (1607)

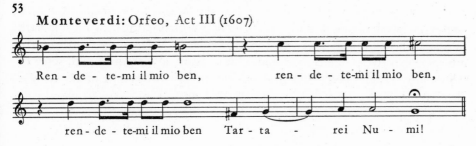

Ren - de - te-mi il mio ben,   ren - de - te-mi il mio ben,

ren - de - te-mi il mio ben   Tar - ta - rei Nu - - mi!

or when Esperanza reads Dante's motto on the Gates of Hell: *Lasciate ogni speranza ...*, when Odysseus and Telemachos embrace each other in ecstasy: *O padre sospirato ...*, or when Seneca goes to his death in proud self-awareness in Act II of *Poppea*:

54

Monteverdi: L'incoronazione di Poppea, Act II (1642)

O, o me fe - li - ce, fe - li - ce me,
o me fe - li - ce, fe - li - ce me.

He can also use the sequence in a playful melody, such as that sung by the page in the same opera:

55

Ibid.

Sen-to un cer - to, non sò che, Che mi piz - zi -
ca e di - let - ta Dim-mi tu che cosa egli è

This opens up a whole series of possibilities. Orpheus' cry is still hardly a melody, it is both less and more. Little by little, his others lead up to the broad span of the constructed sequence, which lets the melody swell up or die away as it will, and repeat or recapitulate on a large scale rather than a small one. Later generations of the 17th century also tended to develop the 'large' type. The sequence was primarily concerned with openings, climaxes, development and *melisma*, and came into its full glory in the middle and second half of the 17th century. (Two hundred years later, at the height of Romanticism, it came back in a similar way in the 'grand gesture' melodies of Wagner and Verdi.) Here are some examples from Stradella and Purcell, and also from Corelli, some of whose *largo* themes even influence classical melody at the time of Haydn and Beethoven:

a) Stradella: Cantata

Che non sa-tio Del-lo stra-tio Nè con-ten-to Del tor-men-to

b) *Idem:* Duet

En-tro tranquil - la pa - ce, en-tro tranquil - la pa - ce

c) Purcell: Golden Sonata (1683)

d) *Idem:* Dido and Aeneas, Act II (1689)

So fair the game, so rich the sport

e) *Ibid.*, Act III

E - li-sa bleeds to - night

f) Corelli: Largo from the First Concerto

There are some remarkable examples in Corelli and Bononcini (as in Vitali, Purcell, and others) where as a result of the sequence the melodic phrase is repeated a fifth lower or a fourth higher, reminiscent of typical Asiatic (Hungarian) melody-structure:

87

57

a) Corelli: Sarabanda

b) Giov. Bononcini: Lungi da te (aria, 1721)

E pur la speme io sen - to Dir-mi: Sa - rai con - ten - to

Se tor-ni a ri - ve - der Sull'a - li del pen - sier

Finally, there are sequences in the form of *melisma :* they show even more clearly how displacement of the motive can also unobtrusively change the proportions of the melody. A certain ambiguity results: there is unity of motive and rhythm within the group, but no obvious repetition, in order to allow the form to shape itself from the asymmetry of such irregular repetition. In this period everything seems to encourage this kind of asymmetry. Many a capricious melody seems to prefer meandering. Irregular phrases appear, such as themes with seven beats to a bar, still favoured by d'Astorga. Legrenzi and Stradella stretch, shorten or combine their themes. Certain classical metres, such as the trochaic tetrameter, the septenary, crop up again in new guises (the septenary traces its descent from Archilochos and the great tragedians via late-Latin folk-songs to the troubadours and Ronsard).[5]

58

Melani: Il Girello (1670)

Bion-da chiome e bel sem-bian-te la for-tu-nae il ciel ci

da; Ma d'e - leg-ger-si un a - man-te, las - cia al cor la li-ber - tà

The classical *incipit*—called a 'motto' or 'device' by Riemann and a 'prolepsis' by Della Corte—is a favourite of Legrenzi, Lonati, and Scarlatti.

Giuseppe Galli-Bibbiena : Stage-Design (1740). Highly characteristic of the theatrical style of the Late Baroque, this masterly design 'plays with infinity' in the amazing manner dear to Baroque architecture.

The sequence is the most common of all. The chains of sequences occurring in *melismas* are really reductions of huge melodies, and their working principles reflect the melodic development of the whole century. J. S. Bach enters at this point, alongside Michelangelo Rossi, Luigi Rossi and Alessandro Scarlatti, since his style developed and surmounted all these complex trends:

59

a) Michelangelo Rossi: Erminia sul Giordano (1637)

a   sa- lu - ta - re   il   gior   -   -   -   -   -   -   -

-   -   -   -   -   -   -   -   no

b) Luigi Rossi: Passage from an aria

di-fen   -   -   -   -   -   di-ti A-mo   -   re, A-mo   -   re

c) A. Scarlatti: Arietta

On - da   per   on   -   -   -   -   -   -   -

da,   per   on   -   -   -   -   -   -   da

d) Bach: Cantata No. 3 ("Ach Gott, wie manches Herzeleid")

ein   rech - ter   Freu   -   -   -   -   -

-   -   -   -   -   -   - den - him - mel   sein

This is Bach's melodic workshop, as it were. When he came to it, the Baroque melody all over Europe was either at its height or already in decline, for at its culmination it was already slightly out of date. The greatest melodies of the period were written about 1700, and nearly all of them were couched in the 'motive-spinning' idiom. Corelli, Scarlatti, Steffani, and especially Vivaldi, unfurl them in their concertos, operas and cantatas as a sailing-boat unfurls its sail at sea. One of the typical melody-types of the Italian High Baroque is the warmly lyrical minor form, which rises and falls on the tonic-dominant-tonic-subdominant pattern. It abounds in many of the *Siciliano*-fantasies of Scarlatti and Vivaldi:

60

a) Vivaldi: From the Concerto for 2 Violins in A minor, Op. 3, No. 8

b) *Ibid.:* Larghetto

c) Vivaldi: Violin Concerto in G minor, Op.6, No. 1 (Grave)

d) *Idem:* Flute Concerto in F major, Op.10, No.5 (Largo)

e) Steffani: Duet

Già non cer - co far ven-det-ta, vin-to ce - do al

vostro fu - ror _____ vin-to ce-do

f) A. S c a r l a t t i : Siciliana   **g)** *Idem:* Siciliana

Bel - la, se vuoi per te   Giammai la lon-tanan- za

But Bach's melodies are different, and although they gather up much of the 17th-century heritage, they cannot be thought of as a recapitulation of Italian Baroque melody. They fulfil older, more Nordic trends, and sum up all that is complex, abstract and constructed in Baroque: they bring to the surface a message from a remote and hidden past. Bach's melodies seem to come from four directions. One is the world of the *sequence :* this technique shapes most of his melodies, spinning them out almost for entire works with incomparable flexibility and inventive skill in variation. Bach's melodic material has almost unlimited elasticity, and can be endlessly worked and developed. With the help of the sequence he builds small forms which by variation are turned into large or cyclic forms. The figure or outline in his sequences takes precedence over the single note.[6] This accounts for the casual indifference with which single notes are altered round, the middle part of a fugal theme fantastically 'derailed', or its intervals contorted. Hence his sequences are often the messengers of medieval diatonicism, which breaks through the major-minor tonality (this being often a means of modulation)[7]. It always makes Bach's sequences seem unexpected and even disconcerting in their functioning, in spite of their apparent formal logic and predictability. Their note-by-note expansion, like a coiled spring, or a tense play of muscles and nerves, is best seen in themes in which every turn of the sequence winds round some recurrent or slowly-shifting pivot:

61

B a c h : Fughetta

His sequences have structural importance as well. They are accompanied along their circuitous course by an ever-wakeful dynamic pulse, which constantly goads them on to greater heights, altering, varying and consolidating the form by ever-renewed efforts.*

* H. Besseler recently showed ("Bach als Wegbereiter," *Archiv f. Musikwissenschaft* , 1955, pp. 1—39) that round about 1720 Bach had already developed a type of contrasting, question-and-

Bach: **a)** Little Preludes, No. 6

b) St. Matthew Passion

c) Well-Tempered Clavier I, No. 4

d) *Ibid.* II, No. 7

e) *Ibid.* II, No. 24

answer 'character theme', which decisively influenced the music of a later period through
C. P. E. Bach and Haydn.

92

f) Piano Concerto in D minor, 2nd movt.

g) *Ibid.*, 3rd movt.

Declamatory melody is another of Bach's melody-types. It too has its roots in the 17th century, and perhaps even earlier, in the 'expressive' and 'text-describing' movement of the 16th century (i.e. *musica reservata*), which had given rise to a whole series of rhetorical 'figures' in music.[8] The strenuous efforts of the Florentine *camerata* to achieve the *stile rappresentativo*, with its radically new sung declamation, seems to have been realised in Bach. No longer was it formless, exuberant, or wild; there was no need for it to be marked *senza battuta*, for it had calmed down. It had retained as much of its youthful turbulence as was consistent with the more dignified and self-controlled art of the high Baroque—the broad perspectives, the dramatic impact of speech-inflection, the big passionate gestures, the declamatory pathos. In this form it fitted the style of recitative of the second half of the 17th century. Word and movement had a determining part to play in the musical thought of the period: aestheticians around 1700—from Bartoldi to Duval and Mattheson—discussed and even classified the various types of speech inflection and movement possible in music. For all these figures were considered to express definite types of feeling and to be based on the laws of nature. This was how *parlando* made its appearance in Heinrich Schütz:

63

Schütz: "Geistliche Chormusik" (1648)

Ich bin ei-ne ru-fende Stim-me in der Wüs - ten

and persisted in Rameau:

Rameau: Dardanus (1739)

.Nos cris ont pé-né-tré jusqu'au som-bre sé - jour

how it occurred in Froberger's laments and Della Ciaja's toccatas, in Reinhard Keiser's cantatas and passions, and the great vocal and instrumental *ariosos* of Handel. In Handel, inner intensity and rhetorical eloquence were combined in a rare way—a musical equivalent of Baroque sculpture with its demonstrative display of pain and passion:

65

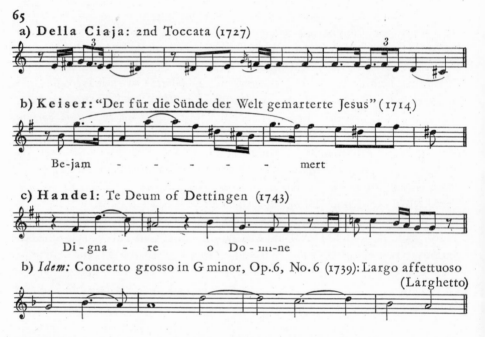

a) **Della Ciaja**: 2nd Toccata (1727)

b) **Keiser**: "Der für die Sünde der Welt gemarterte Jesus" (1714)

Be-jam - - - - - mert

c) **Handel**: Te Deum of Dettingen (1743)

Di - gna - re o Do - mi-ne

b) *Idem:* Concerto grosso in G minor, Op.6, No.6 (1739): Largo affettuoso
(Larghetto)

Finally, there were the great passion melodies of Bach (*Erbarme dich, mein Gott, Ach Golgotha, Am Abend, da es kühle war* from the *St. Matthew Passion* and other works). Here melodic line is so concentrated that it could not endure expansion into a larger form. That is why it is generally contained within a straight *arioso,* for it is an outburst which suffices to itself. A few of the great prelude-melodies of the *Well-Tempered Clavier* (e.g., Bk. I, in E flat minor, Bk. II, in G minor) transplant this type of tragic monologue to an instrument; for Bach makes no marked distinction between the melodic style used for instruments and that used for the human voice.

The 'runner'-melody, so characteristic of the late Baroque, occurs in Bach as a cross between the sequential and the declamatory melody. It is a speech-phrase set to music, and generally unfolds over an ostinato bass (e.g., in the middle movements of the *Italian Concerto*, the *D minor Piano Concerto* and the *E major Violin Concerto*). Bach himself would probably have called it *fantasia*, *aria* or *recitativo*, since he described a similar form in the *D major Suite* as an 'air' and in the *Goldberg Variations* as an 'aria.' Handel uses the same expression (in the *3rd Piano Suite*) and so does Telemann *(Air italien* in the *A minor Flute Suite)*. The Italian Baroque would have described it in the same way: some of Vivaldi's slow movements and instrumental recitatives, for example, are closely related to Bach's 'runner'-melodies:

66

a) **Bach**: Italian Concerto, 2nd movt.

b) **Vivaldi(?)—Bach**: Adagio from the Organ Concerto in C major (originally Concerto in D major for strings)

The same form persists in some of the minor adagios and 'arias' of Zipoli, Porpora, and Martini (1716, 1741), in the very different musical atmosphere of Italian Rococo. Inspired by the tone of violin and gamba, these instrumental songs produce the richest melodic harvest of Western Baroque. Debussy called it

95

'musical arabesque', the art of ornamentation, which is the foundation of every kind of music.

The insistent *'throbbing'* melody is yet another universal type; a uniform rhythm-pattern shapes the melody and encloses it in a rigid frame with a regular beat. Every eminent composer of the late Baroque, from Vivaldi to Leclair and Reinken, from Muffat to Handel has recourse to it. Handel gives it a floating, dance-like quality, but in Bach it turns into an impatient obstinate rumble: a rhythmical *ostinato*, a sharp, fierce rattling, alternately broadening out or closing in.

67

a) Joh. Ernst, Duke of Weimar — Bach: From the Concerto in G major

b) Handel: "Scipio," Duet (1726)

Si fug-ga - noi tor - men - ti   Si ven-ga - noi con -

ten - ti *etc.*

c) *Idem:* Andante larghetto from the Concerto Grosso in F major, Op. 6, No. 2

d) *Idem:* Andante from the Trio Sonata in B minor (= Largo of the Flute Sonata in C minor)

e) Bach: Cantata No. 56 ("Ich will den Kreuzstab")

96

f) *Idem:* Cantata No. 26 ("Ach wie flüchtig")

An ir - di - sche Schä - tze das Her - ze zu hän - gen ist

ei - ne Ver - füh - rung der tö - rich - ten Welt

g) *Idem:* Brandenburg Concerto No. 3

The *'thesis'* melody, principal subject of fugues and fugatos, is formed in another way. It is built round some clearly defined basic figure, generally an important interval, which has a decisive effect on the thematic discourse, and calls forth a long winding figure to restore the balance:

68

B a c h : 4th Piano Duet

These themes have great importance in Bach, and their derivation is mostly very distant; some are Flemish in origin, whilst others stem from plainchant. Themes which start on the fifth and rise to the sixth were already very significant at the time of Josquin, Gombert, and Arcadelt, and form the most substantial of his organ and piano themes. (*Well-Tempered Clavier*, Bk. I, in G minor and *E flat* minor: Bk. II, Fugues in *E flat* major, F minor, etc.) The themes of the *Musical Offering* and the *Art of Fugue* are also formed in this way; of the organ works, the themes of the *Passacaglia* and the small *G minor Fugue;* of themes borrowed from other composers, there is the organ *Canzone*, borrowed from Frescobaldi, the *C minor Organ Fugue* from Legrenzi, the *B minor Organ Fugue* from Corelli, and the *B minor Piano Fugue* from Albinoni. Consciously or unconsciously, Bach chose the same type of theme even in his borrowings. They are also important because they show how Bach's thematic construction is independent of substance and tempo. This is also true of Bach in other instances: he has even more chance to make his themes grow or diminish here:

69
Bach: a) "Bist du bei mir"

b) Brandenburg Concerto No. 3

The chief requirement for a fugal theme is that it can be contracted or expanded, reversed or mirrored. It is the essence of fugue-spinning, and Bach's skill was always increasing (as far as the *Art of Fugue*) because from the very beginning his imagination had been stimulated by the idea of elasticity.

He was understandably less drawn to other types of theme. In contrast to Handel or Vivaldi, he makes less use of flamboyant, galloping fanfare themes based on common chords, which form the raw material of much concert-music (a motive such as *Der Held aus Juda* from the *St. John Passion* probably comes closest to Handel's approach). The Baroque excitements of such themes were fundamentally alien to Bach's love of clambering, which tolerated the existence of wider intervals only in some 'thesis' melodies:

70
J. H. Schmelzer: Fantasia (about 1670).

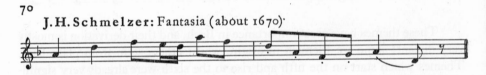

In any case, fanfare melodies emphasised major-minor quality so strongly that they were bound to be alien to a composer who was the last prophet of medieval diatonicism. Although the major and minor triad would later become vitally important in Viennese classical melody, it only occurred in a rare, dissolved melody-type of Bach, and was generally confined to serving the figurative design.

*

This entire development came to an end with Bach's generation. The near future was being prepared in quite a different quarter, worlds away from Bach and the last great men of his generation. It came from a distant past, and ignored Bach's existence.

Popular music reasserted itself soon after the Italian reformers and extremists, as if music's life-urge had had enough excitement and high tension, and needed to return to simpler foundations. It was not just a case of Italy and Italian popular music. It could be heard in the same general form throughout Western Europe, in English, French, German, Hungarian, Polish and Spanish folk-music, but it was naturally adapted to the stylistic idiom of the composer who was using it. Italian folk-music had already broken through here and there, in 16th-century *frottole* and *balletti*. It showed itself in monodic *canzonettas* and operatic *arias*, even though Caccini and his followers had rigorously excluded all popular tendencies. Stefano Landi, with the exception of Monteverdi the greatest of early 17th-century operatic composers, gave popular music a new twist when a page appeared in the first act of his *Santo Alessio*:

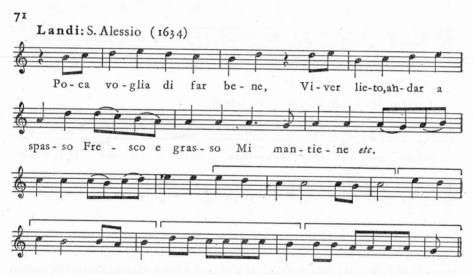

71

Landi: S. Alessio (1634)

Po - ca   vo - glia   di   far   be - ne,   Vi - ver   lie-to,an-dar   a

spas - so   Fre - sco   e   gras - so   Mi   man - tie - ne   *etc.*

and in *La Tancia* (1657), one of the first comic operas, Jacopo Melani already used it as the spontaneous mother tongue of *opera buffa,* evoking memories of the *Commedia dell'Arte*:

72

Melani: La Tancia (1657)

S'io   mi - ro il vol - to   del   mio   bel   Cia - pi -

no,   par-mi ve - der   il   Ciel   d'A- mor   in   ter - ra

7*

The popular melodies tended to prefer small symmetrical forms and short, balanced miniature phrases, in contrast to the prevailing tendency for long-winded lines of melody. They too were full of sequences, but what a difference between these folk-like repetitions and the 'runner-melodies' of art-music! Melani's Italian *canzonetta* type, appearing in *La Tancia*, made itself felt even outside Italian borders, and its lilting rhythm was taken over into the Baroque dance melodies of Lully's ballets[9] (influenced by Spanish and Italian models just as the dramatic techniques of Corneille and Molière).

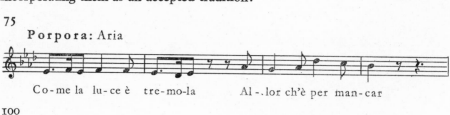

After the middle of the century, these tunes increased in number, side by side with the now totally victorious technique of melody-spinning, and the supremacy of Late and High Baroque. It was as if a form of democratic opposition was silently but tenaciously preparing to challenge Baroque hegemony. A fresher, simpler form of music was waiting for the moment when the star of Baroque music, with all its pathos and rhetorical solemnity, would begin to fade. The rhythms of the South Italian *siciliana* were developing apace, and from the time of Alessandro Scarlatti and Vivaldi were assuming more and more importance in vocal and symphonic music. It was not long before Porpora was incorporating them as an accepted tradition:

This tradition continued in Italian opera until the time of Donizetti (the love-potion in *l'Elisir d'Amore*) and even later (e.g., Verdi's *Otello*, Act II, Mascagni's *Cavalleria Rusticana*, etc.). The *gagliarda*[10] was revived, along with the *gavotte, courante, forlana* and *tambourine*. *Chaconnes, rigaudons,* and dance-music generally, came more and more to the fore. With its stylistic flair, the Baroque had elevated dance into an art-form in the suite, only to discover that it had nurtured a mortal enemy in its bosom. Foreign popular tunes had only to make their appearance to be unfailingly marked out as allies by the new movement.

Significantly, Italian collections of this period frequently contain foreign music from as early as 1620. It was as natural for Giovanni Stefani to use the *Vilanella spagnola* in his *Affetti amorosi* (1621) as for Giovanni Picchi to use the *Todesca,* or the Hungarian and Polish ballo in his *Balli d'arpicordo* (1620). Hungarian and Polish virginal books of the period vouch for the authenticity of these latter:

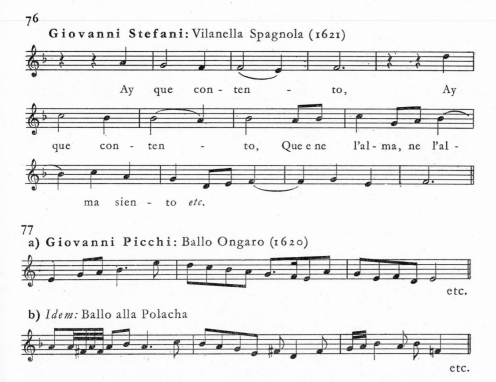

76

Giovanni Stefani: Vilanella Spagnola (1621)

Ay que con - ten - to, Ay que con - ten - to, Que e ne l'al - ma, ne l'al - ma sien - to *etc.*

77

a) Giovanni Picchi: Ballo Ongaro (1620)

etc.

b) *Idem:* Ballo alla Polacha

etc.

East European dance-motives described as *Ungarescas* and *Polonicas* sporadically appeared in Western collections from the 16th century onwards.[11] They took on new meaning because they were a direct source of stimulus to the Western musician. He was fascinated alike by their kinship and by their strangeness.

Picchi elaborated his Hungarian dances as devotedly as if they were old Italian melodies. Contemporaneously, typical East European elements (Hungarian, Slovak, etc.) were appearing in volumes by Saracini and Stefani, with Italian *canzonetta* texts:

78

a) **Saracini:** From Musiche II (1620)

Quest'a-mo-re quest'ar-su - ra *etc.*

b) *Idem:* From Musiche III (1620)

A-ma pur, a-ma pur Nin - fa gra - di - ta *etc.*

c) **Stefani:** Affetti amorosi (1621)

An-gio-let-ta tropp'in fret-ta *etc.*

(The latter melody appeared first in 1615 with Gagliano, under the title *Fanciuletta ritrosetta;* after 1630 the Dutch poet Vondel popularised it in the Netherlands as a children's dirge. See comments by V. Denis, Mélange Ernest Closson, Bruxelles, 1948, pp. 100—101.) Where such elements were encountered is anybody's guess. The answer may well lie in personal contacts during the wanderings of mercenary forces: it is known that Monteverdi visited Hungary in the suite of Prince Gonzaga, and he may have heard much to set him thinking. (This type of melody appeared much later in Hungarian publications [János Kájoni's litanies and Pál Esterházy's *Harmoniae Caelestis*] but many such examples occur in Hungarian and Slovak folk-music.) Composers such as Marenzio, Scacchi and Pacelli went as far as Poland; and it is not surprising that Heinrich Albert wrote *Proportio nach Art der Pohlen* (Proportions as in the Polish manner) above the customary variant in uneven rhythm of one of his dance-tunes in East European style:

79

H. A l b e r t: From the Arias (1640)

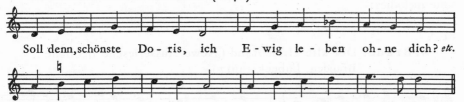

Soll denn, schönste Do - ris, ich E - wig le - ben oh - ne dich? *etc.*

That was how foreign elements infiltrated into Western music: Telemann even boasted about them. But 'new winds were blowing' not only from the East, but from the West too. The English Sailors' Song, the *Western Wind*, stayed within its national frontiers in spite of having been used in Masses by Taverner, Tye and Shepherd, after the style of *L'Homme armé*. But because of the speedier diffusion of piano and violin music, two such melodies served as models for instrumental composers on the Continent. *Walsingham*, published in the *Fitzwilliam Virginal Book*, displayed the art of variation of John Bull and his contemporaries: and the *Fit's come on me now* unexpectedly introduced genuine English (or maybe Scottish) pentatonicism into Playford's *English Dancing Master* in the mid-17th century:

80

a) J o h n B u l l: Walsingham (Fitzwilliam Virginal Book)

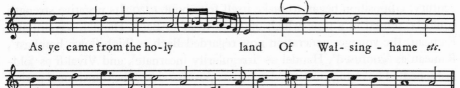

As ye came from the ho-ly land Of Wal- sing - hame *etc.*

b) "Fit's come on me now" (Playford, The English Dancing Master, 1650)

German folk-tunes also turned up, sometimes quite recognisably and sometimes camouflaged. Familiar in European music since the 14th century as folk-hymns, secular songs, or Protestant chorales, they began to assume instrumental form in this period. The basic melody was sometimes centuries old, often stemming from the Middle Ages, but as a dance-form it was decked with Baroque ornaments and tended to be asymmetrical in rhythm because sequential phrases were added. All the same, a much-disguised medieval form underlay Baroque suite-melodies:

81

W. Brade: Der alte Hildebrand (Newe Ausserlesene liebliche Branden, Lübeck, 1617)

All this added to the hidden ferment. Like every other period, the Baroque bore within itself its own antidote and future conqueror, which in its case was the 18th century. Opposition began to make itself felt about 1720. Its negative strength could be sensed in a taste which opposed itself to Bach, Handel, Vivaldi and Rameau; the younger generation now regarded Bach as 'high-flown bombast', Rameau as 'confused', Handel as 'irregularity incarnate', and Vivaldi as 'old-fashioned'. The change in taste also had its positive side. The transitional period produced composers who looked both ways, such as Telemann—or even more strongly and more significantly—Domenico Scarlatti, one of the most daring pioneers of the new language. In this mysterious composer, arduous Baroque structure and playful glimpses of Rococo charm would suddenly give way to romantic depths. Were the exact chronology of his piano works known, it would probably make it easier to see how he slowly crossed from one world to the other. Instead, one can only guess at his bridge-function, and ponder about the stylistic diversity and change of outlook evinced in his works. The three types of form recently recognised in his works by Scarlatti experts[12] are far from being conclusive pointers to their chronology. It is probable that the greater part of his melodies continued to reflect Baroque ideas and forms of expression. Melody-spinning and sequences form their normal method of construction, in larger as in smaller forms, but at a certain stage (or perhaps at the same time?) the principle of the 'smallest cells' begins to make itself felt. Scarlatti may well have taken it over from 17th-century folk-tunes:

82

D. Scarlatti: Pastorale

The theme may start like this straight away, or break up later into playful little motives, with here and there a glimpse of Pergolesi's coquettish and sprightly Neapolitan sweetness. The idea is rounded off as it breaks up, and a new idea presented in a contrasting key, the whole process generally taking place in transparent two-part texture. This is the same playful dualism that appears in Pergolesi's works, soon to lead to the creation of the classical sonata:

83

a). Scarlatti: Sonata No. 96 (Kirkpatrick's Cat.)

b) Idem: Sonata No. 159

c) Idem: Sonata No. 531

d) *Idem:* Sonata No. 13

And so the Baroque flame burnt itself out, perhaps because it had at last contrived to catch up with Time, its ardour and precipitous restlessness all spent. In the quiet calm that is only possible after great battles, the Rococo came to rediscover the delights of balance and the containment of Time. Burckhardt's assertion that "styles usually expire after having reached their climax" may not be valid for every period, but it is certainly true of the Baroque, which at its height gave way to a new stylistic trend, one that "wanted to live off its own flowers, its ornaments."

But the Baroque earthquake was not finished for all time. It was making no first appearance in 1600, and was far from complete in 1720. It had come from afar, from the submerged Gothic, and was off once again, on a secret journey to Romanticism.

NOTES

1. R. Haas: *Musik des Barocks*. Potsdam, 1928, p. 4.
2. *Cp.* for the latter Riemann: *Handb. d. Musikgeschichte.* II, 2. Leipzig, 1912, pp. 197—198. In the madrigal cycle *Festino nella sera del giovedì grasso*, 1608, new edition, Rome, 1939, A. Banchieri characteristically captions the performance of a variant of this rhythm: *morescano cantando il Spagnoletto*, i.e. in Spanish-Arabic style. It is known that the *moresca* was a masked, pantomimic dance of the late Middle Ages. The 15th-century chronicler Molinet once described the sound of the tambourine as being *a manière de moresque.*
3. L. Landshoff: *Alte Meister des Belcanto*. Peters. p. 79; Riemann: *op. cit.*, p. 388. For a relevant melody by Lully see Ex. No. 84 of the present work.
4. For its rhythmical interpretation see Riemann: *op. cit.*, p. 292.
5. W. Christ: *Metrik der Griechen und Römer*. Leipzig, 1879, 2nd edition, pp. 294—303; Klotz: *Grundzüge der altrömischen Metrik*. Leipzig, 1890, p. 385 and following pages; P. Verrier: *Le vers français*. I, Paris, 1931, pp. 19, 257, II, 1932, pp. 276—278. Beethoven's setting of Schiller's *An die Freude* belongs here too, like its many antecedents, from Rousseau (see No. 106) to the final ensemble of Mozart's *Schauspieldirektor* and Beethoven's *Chorphantasie*. The link with classical metres is indirectly confirmed by the fact that Bürger (whose *Gegenliebe* was the original inspiration for the melodic content of the *Chorphantasie*)

used the same metre for his translation of the late classical *Pervigilium Veneris*, i.e. he conserved the rhythm. In its 1796 form, Bürger's poem *Die Nachtfeier der Venus* may perhaps have inspired the *Chorphantasie* even more directly than the actual text, written by Christian Kuffner when the composition was nearly completed. Three relevant melodies have been published by Dénes Bartha in *Hungarian Songs of the 18th century*. Budapest, 1935, Nos. 37–40. It is possible that the East European *kolomeika* type was derived from this ancient Mediterranean song-form by way of Middle-Latin songs *(Omni die dic Marie, Omnis mundus jucundetur . . .)* and Renaissance dance-tunes; but it is more likely that an identical song-form developed independently as 'vagrant' verse in the West, and as *kolomeika*, or the Arabic *ramal*, in the East. Incorporated in Italian dance-tunes, the septenary may well have symbolised the vitality of Southern Rococo for Northern Romanticism, Robert Browning used this metre in the three-lined verses of *A Toccata of Galuppi's* ("O Galuppi, Baldassaro, this is very sad to find"), possibly under the direct inspiration of Galuppi's music.

6. Although elsewhere his sequences show themselves highly sensitive to the quality of the interval. The best example of the melodic significance of the inverted interval is to be found in the secondary theme of Bach's *F major Organ Fugue*, in its first form (a) and reprise form (b):

(Here there are two contrasting shapes, one hopefully reaching up, the other graciously bending down.)

7. In contrast to Handel's 'more modern' melodies, which instinctively emphasize the major tonality and the relationship of third and fifth. Take the famous *Largo*, for example, or the slow movements of concertos and violin sonatas. They are much more rooted in harmony than Bach's melodies. The beginning of the *D major Violin Sonata* is a typical example, leaping upwards with the double strength of two major fifths (d^1—F^1 *sharp*—a^1—e^2). As an older but more 'modern' contemporary of Bach and Handel, Rameau on the other hand affects major tonality most clearly where it is practically expected by the musette-basses of courtly and popular dance-tunes. He uses the elegant, ingratiating idioms of the *dolce stil nuovo* as in the famous dance melodies of *Platée* (a) and *Les Indes galantes* (b):

8. See H.-H. Unger: *Die Beziehungen zwischen Musik und Rhetorik im 16.—18. Jahrhundert.* Würzburg, 1941, pp. 26—33, 120—144; C. V. Palisca: "A Clarification of 'Musica Reservata' in Jean Taisnier's 'Astrologiae', 1559." *Acta Musicologica* XXXI, 1959, pp. 133—161.
9. This melody of Lully became a church chant in Denmark during the 17th century, and figures in Buxtehude's piano studies under the name of *Rofilis*. See D. Buxtehude: *Klaver-vaerker.* Ed. E. Bangert, Koebenhavn—Oslo—Stockholm, 1944, XIII. A German-

Jewish variant of the *Rofilis* melody was published by A. Z. Idelsohn from a source of 1727: *Hebr.-orientalischer Melodienschatz*. VI, Leipzig, 1932, p. 234, No. 9.

10. See note on p. 130.; see also 17th-century operas (generally choruses); H. Goldschmidt: *Studien zur Geschichte der italienischen Oper im 17. Jh.* Leipzig, 1901, I, pp. 163, 170, 174, 178, 201, 212, 216, 232, 242, 261, 264, 270, 281, 301 (extracts from works by Mazzochi, F. Caccini, Landi, M. and L. Rossi, and Loreto); and Riemann: *op. cit.*, p. 239 (Cavalli).

11. See Ottó Gombosi's article on the *Ungaresca* in the *Hungarian Music Lexicon* (1930), and the author's study, *Hungarian Dance Music of the 16th Century*, in *Centuries of Hungarian Music*. Vol. I, Budapest, 1959 (in Hungarian).

12. W. Gerstenberg: *Die Klavierkompositionen D. Scarlattis*. Regensburg, 1933, p. 76 ff. As early as 1912, Sándor Kovács pointed out in a study on Scarlatti (*Posthumous Musical Writings*. Budapest, 1926, pp. 372—373) that the repetition of small sections was a formal principle of the late Baroque, and a substitute for polyphony; *cp.* also C. Valabrega: *D. Scarlatti, il suo secolo e la sua opera*. Modena, 1937, 2nd ed., 1956, and the important monograph by R. Kirkpatrick, Princeton—London, 1953.

THE EMERGENCE OF ROCOCO

DANCE-RHYTHM AND BEL CANTO

"We danced . . . " or: "then the company danced on the lawn till the early hours of the morning," or "then the members of the Ballet appeared, and the whole assembly began to dance with them." Dancing was constantly being mentioned in 18th-century memoirs, particularly from 1720 to 1750. The entire aristocracy seemed to be filled with the joy of dancing; apparently it had come to represent the essence of the radiant and carefree new life which the ruling class cultivated as an ideal. It was as if the bright new sound of European Rococo had come to life in the swing of one immense dance, from Paris to far-off Hungarian country-houses. The Goncourt Brothers were quite right to call the 18th century the 'dancing century'; people instinctively thought in terms of poised, rhythmical movements and flowing lines.[1] Dance-theorists such as Cahuzac, author of *La danse ancienne et moderne* (1754) considered that Life, Nature and Art found their ideal point of encounter in the rhythmical movements of the human body. Plays, and particularly operas, tended to form a background for dance-suites, and even straight actors came to the foot-lights with carefully studied gait. Painting seemed to be intoxicated with dance-movement, so in 1725 even as stern a moralist as Hogarth produced a series of this kind. The longing for dance was insatiable: everything manifested the same deep-seated thirst—the hundred different forms of the same dance, the endless variations on the same theme, the countless names for the same step. In a book entitled *Répertoire du bal ou Théorie pratique des contredanses* (1762), the dancing-master De la Cuisse listed thirty-three different kinds of contredanse, all with different names, not to mention the German contredanses just then coming into favour.[2] They were quite obviously only variants of the same kind of dance—but how such variations were enjoyed! There was Handel, for example, who wrote sixty-two, or the young Moffat, who produced thirty-eight variations for a single Chaconne-melody, or Bach, whose *Chaconne for Violin* is made up of sixty-three variations; or his *Goldberg Variations*. A dance-tune involves continual repetition, and so round about 1720 the stylised dances of operas, ballets, suites and chamber concertos are full of refrains and repetitive themes. The Chaconne, which served to bring an opera to a close—once described by Despréaux as a concerto in its own right—provided a suitably festive finish with its long repetitive festoons of melody. Similar 'festoons' were formed by other dance-tunes, too, and appeared in various guises such as *musette en rondeau, passepied en rondeau, tambourin en rondeau*, or something of the sort. Generally speaking, the name of the dance was more important than has been realised; it is clear from Mme Campan's *Mémoires* how deeply the Court was affected when the capricious Princess Adelaide changed the 'Rose Ballet' into a 'Blue Minuet'.[3] There was dancing everywhere, and all the time: *on danse*, or at the very least, *on dansait*.

How deeply the love of stylised movement had taken root in this period would not have been realised but for the evidence of contemporary paintings. They are the clearest mirror of social customs at the turn of the century. Aristocratic society was pining for the open air: the gardens were full of dreamy, light-hearted groups. It was a strange new delight to walk along romantic garden alleys, sit in neatly clipped or profusely flowering bowers, lie on the lawns and listen to guitars from the balconies. All the characters of society's new fashion moved out into the fresh air for the space of one long summer: the gallant in search of a flirtation, the singer, the adventurer, the dancing-girl, the musician, the masked comedian.

Watteau, the greatest painter of the period, saw it all in terms of a visionary dream. Yet the ideal was not new. In the 17th century there had been the 'Venus bowers', or Baroque garden-scenes of love and revelry. A contemporary looking at the pictures of Rubens, Weenix or Palamedes might well have thought he had already reached the Islands of the Blest, or Cytherea's enchanted world—or, at the very least, the green sward of some Flemish May-Festival. Watteau was able to evoke it all both as a native tradition, and as a direct recollection of his life in Flanders. Yet in his art there was something quite new, not to be found in any of his forbears. His brush removed all the warm-blooded Flemish crudity, the clumsy, gaudy finery. The landscape became suffused with golden afternoon light, the human figure became delicate and slender, responsive and poised; an all-pervading musicality lent lightness and translucence to every movement. Music in fact penetrated the very pores of the picture—for Watteau was the most musical of painters. He took every opportunity of painting music-making, and wherever possible showed instruments and performing groups, with flutes, guitars and violins playing almost incessantly. Yet all this was merely the outer symbol for what was going on in the hearts and minds of his figures. Almost all of them moved with dance-steps, which emphasised their link with ballet and opera even more strongly than did their fantastic, variegated costumes. Many of Watteau's pictures obviously referred to actual operatic scenes. *Festes Vénitiennes*, with its unusual title and wonderful atmosphere, was probably connected with Campra's opera by the same name (1710). But the picture en-titled *l'Indifférent* had no connection of this sort, although it was plainly an apo-theosis of dancing and dance-steps; the many versions of *Fêtes champêtres* were not inspired by any specific musical occasion, any more than were the paintings, with their lilting, swirling groups of comedians and musicians. Dance-rhythm was clearly becoming an integral part of the composition, perhaps even the whole. This was an entirely new factor; the art of painting was turning musical, and flooding music with a new look. Although it was never to be superseded, it was still only a prelude for what was to follow. The style which Watteau initiat-ed about 1715 was continued in France about 1730 by Watteau's followers, Lancret and Pater, and by Tiepolo in Italy from 1740 to 1750. They took over Watteau's instruments and dance-rhythms. They even kept his famous dance-step, the *pas des pavanes* (so described by one of Watteau's biographers because of its resemblance to the old step[4]); it made no difference that the background scenery was different, or that Tiepolo was rooted in quite another tradition. The *pas des pavanes* turned up as much in Lancret's pastoral idylls as in Tie-polo's Venetian carnival scenes.

It was not just France, but a whole continent which adopted these dance-rhythms. They stimulated a new kind of music, with a rhythmic pulse which was deeper and more pervasive, and more universal in its appeal. Like one of Watteau's operatic heroes stepping out of Arcadia, or the belle of the ball from a flurry of masks in Tiepolo's carnival scenes, Rococo between 1720 and 1730 skipped lightly on to the European stage out of its Baroque background. It tripped on unannounced, but its dreamy, winning gestures showed it to be already most accomplished.

*

The fact that dance-rhythm was definitely established in European con-sciousness at this time was bound to make a tremendous impact on music, and particularly on melody.

What are the essentials of dance-rhythm? Clear structure, above all, a sort of geometrical regularity, and the repetition of certain sections: symmetry, in other words. 17th-century melody, and in particular the melody of late Baroque, was complex in its structure, and asymmetrical in its phrasing; it indulged in 'motive-spinning', bridging over too obviously matching phrases with broad-spanning, interweaving arches of melody. It was natural that French recitative, the very embodiment of asymmetry, began to develop in that period. Fidelity to the spoken inflections of the text meant that the rhythm altered almost from bar to bar. Even great melodies of the period, such as those by Legrenzi, Lully or

Steffani, all show the same longing to extend the line in 'tendril'-fashion—regardless of whether the rhythmic pulse be slow and dignified, or gay and jaunty. The aim is to expand into a larger form, and so more and more 'tendrils' are put out until the whole structure is filled. If the line is shaped for dancing (as is often the case in Lully) small regular caesuras have to be suppressed, and the dance fitted to a complex, shifting design which ignores small symmetrical shapes. This is equally true of melodies by Campra and Destouches, written at the time of transition. A melody such as Juno's aria in Lully's *Isis* (1677)[5] is a splendid illustration. The phrasing is made up of one nine-bar section and two seven-bar ones. The rhyme-scheme forms itself into *aab/abba*, and both sections are repeated:

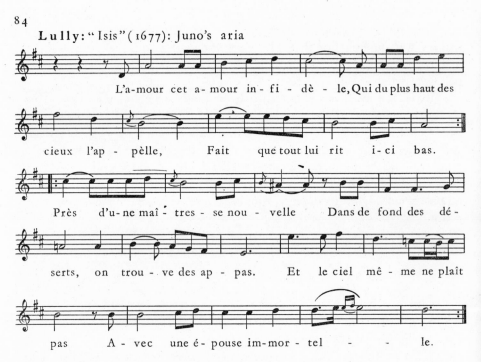

Lully is very fond of this kind of repetitive refrain, and also spins out his melodies without regard for their texts. His dance-forms are nearly always shaped in such a way that the corresponding *abab* and *abba* sections alternate or interlock. This studied use of melody-rhyme gives his asymmetrical rhythms balance and greater poise. It is even more noticeable in Campra, a Rococo composer who faces both ways. Mention has already been made of his great ballet-opera, *Les Festes Vénitiennes* (1710). Dances abound in this colourful work, and even the March in the fourth *entrée* is made up of 'irregular sections'. Seven, nine and eleven-bar sections follow on each other's heels, and even in melodies which begin in the most regular and song-like way Campra manages to add asymmetrical details and cover up simple caesuras:

85

Campra: Les Festes Vénitiennes (1710), 5th entrée

La Far - fal - la in - tor - no ai fio - ri, Va vo-lan - - - - - - - do, non po - sa mai

Many similar examples occur in Destouches, Lalande, and other French composers of the transitional period. The new tendency to symmetrical melody was of course getting stronger and stronger, and melodies of folk-type with small, symmetrical song-phrases were already to be seen in Destouches' pastoral-play *Issé*:

86

Destouches: Issé — Shepherds' Chorus (1697)

Les doux plai - sirs ha - bi - tent ce bo - ca - ge,
Des plus longs jours il nous font des mo - ments

But irregularity was still the rule. It was very hard for the new change in taste to break through the complexity of Baroque. Couperin was perhaps the first who confidently followed the signs of the times and his own instincts; his harpsichord and concerto melodies took the decisive step which led into the altered world of 1720, into the 18th century. German examples show the whole process even more clearly; let us turn to one of Bach's most typical instrumental melodies, from the *First Brandenburg Concerto*. This expansive giant-melody is the very embodiment of Baroque musical architecture—it forms one mighty span, one long continuous line; it is too irregular to admit caesuras, and is totally asymmetrical.

87

Bach: Brandenburg Concerto No. 1, Adagio (1721)

What the composers of 1720 disliked so much in the music of their elders suddenly becomes plain—its 'shapelessness' and 'lack of melody', its ponderousness, its sudden rushes, its lack of grace, and its 'high-minded disorder'. Younger composers were on the look-out for something quite different.

*

What did they want? Sharply defined melody, above all, and a symmetry that affected the smallest notes, a bright, secular sound, a free and springy rhythm—whatever was right for dancing. Batteux' chief claim was that music be comprehensible to the ordinary listener; Dittersdorf maintained that the most important pieces in a comic opera were those which were "immediately understood and easily memorised." But who could sing a Bach melody after a single hearing? Even the subject-matter of melody had changed. "My melodies are concerned with what is agreeable, charming, droll, trifling, amorous and gay," wrote Valentin Görner in 1752, in the Preface to the Third Part of his *Neue Oden und Lieder*.[6] Domenico Scarlatti, too, asked his audience to look for playful invention in his music, and not deep meaning *(non il profondo intendimento, ma lo scherzo ingegnoso dell'arte)*. The ideal melody of the period was full of playful, charming coquetry. "We hate melancholy," said one young composer in Tosi's treatise on singing (1723). "We wish to sing!" exclaimed Telemann. They even passed sentence on the older masters in the name of this ideal, claiming that they had exhausted their inventive faculties in old-fashioned counterpoint and artificial devices; the new generation needed to find in melody "the only real source of music," and to abandon all high-sounding conundrums. "We conceal great art," Mattheson claimed in 1739, and Doles, Bach's successor as Cantor at the Thomaskirche in Leipzig, boldly asserted that "the fugue is considered chaotic by everyone but the specialists." Thus Telemann found "no melody in the music of older composers, even with the help of Diogenes' lamp," and young composers unanimously accused their elders of having no idea of real melody. And so it was that their melody was intricate, well-contrasted, tuneful and transparent—just like dance.

This involved a fresh look at the past. Whenever this process takes place, a rebel generation always searches for its own traditions in the period it reviews. In this case there were certainly traditions to justify such a search, but they needed reexamining. So it was, for instance, that the dance-rhythms of folk-music suddenly acquired new meaning. These had never taken kindly to the unnecessary complexity of Baroque, and had continued to emphasise clear matching phrases and simple, symmetrical designs. Sensitive composers in Paris, Naples, London, Leipzig or Vienna began to lend an ear to the respective folk-songs and street-cries of France, Italy, England, Germany and Austria: in Paris there was Lesage, in Naples Pergolesi, Pepusch in London, Standfuss and Hiller in Leipzig, Wagenseil, Umlauff and Haydn in Vienna. But something else emerged from the recent past as well as the folk-motives: anything which encouraged a more shapely and closely articulated song-shape. The only 17th-century Baroque dances to survive were the few which had clear structure. The Gavotte, Allemande, Pavane, Sarabande and Courants fell more and more out of favour. On the other hand, the Minuet, which had been able to maintain its clear and simple symmetry even in Lully and Campra *(Les Festes Vénitiennes)* now began to come to the fore. So did the *Rigaudon, Bourrée,* and *Musette,* with their preference for minutely articulated phrases. The strong attraction of dance, and the power of a rhythmic pulse, came to influence purely vocal music too, causing

8*

words to be set to dance-tunes. The fashion for sung dance-tunes spread from Paris to the farthest borders of Hungary. *Parodies bacchiques* had been popular in France from as early as 1690, and Lesage's theatres in the market-place, or *théâtres de la foire*, became all the rage in Parisian suburbs between 1710 and 1725. It was a fashion which had been spreading for twenty or thirty years, as a result of Sperontes-Scholze's song collection in Leipzig *(Singende Muse an der Pleisse)*, and Rathgeber's *Tafelkonfekt* in Augsburg. Even as late as 1780 the Viennese enjoyed setting texts to minuets and Ländlers—and all over Hungary occasional verses were set to popular minuet-tunes, and later to recruiting-dances too. Anything owning even a distant connection with dance-rhythm was sure to prosper and occupy the centre of attention. That was why pastoral tunes became so popular. The pastoral scenes of that highly Arcadian ideal which was Rococo are close to the idyllic visions of Sicilian dance-festivals of Theocritus.

But more basic elements of the new style were already beginning to show in the wake of fashion. Baroque asymmetry and its complex giant-melodies had everywhere been associated with monothematic construction. A single motive would inspire virtually an entire form with its prodigious energy. It would appear in ever different perspective, transform itself by renewal or repetition, and then throw off sequences, which it would wrap round itself like waves or draperies. In its search for small, clear symmetries, the new type of melody abandoned the monothematic construction of the 'giant' type, and pursued balance and contrast instead. Similar or contrasting themes were set side by side, so that a kind of dualism was created. Melodies that complemented or contrasted with each other were linked with similar or contrasting types of rhythm. The dualism of the dance-form paved the way for the sonata, just as surely as monothematic construction led the way to the fugue. The opposite is also true: were monothematic construction to appear again, it would inevitably still be connected with asymmetry and polyphony.

The new way of thinking about 1720 favoured polyphony as little as 'formless complexity'. Since this was closely allied to diatonicism and the old church modes, the new composers turned to the major mode, that old ally of folk-rhythms, dance-melody and the homophonic way of thinking. It seemed as if major music had been connected with straightforward, simple shapes from the very beginning: had they not appeared together in troubadour music? The new style took up the major mode and made it familiar throughout Europe. *Le style galant*, the characteristic style of Rococo, was predominantly major in character.

To study the melodies of the 'new' or 'transitional' period is to be immediately struck by the importance these composers attached to major tonality and dance-rhythms, considered essential elements of the *style galant*. So far as the taste of the older composers was concerned, the lilting rhythms of *pastorale* and *siciliano* served to ease the way for the new sound. Take Telemann's and Couperin's melodies for example. They are already real major melodies, but the connection is more obvious if they are compared with their Italian counterparts, e.g., Tartini's huge and passionate melodies in the minor (*Devil's Trill*, etc.). These minor melodies naturally sound closer to Baroque tradition. Telemann's and Couperin's melodies, on the other hand, are distinguished by the sharp brightness of their major sound, and the more finely articulated small phrases. Here Telemann is more directly and deeply rooted in the past: some of his melodies could have been written by Handel. He was actually a few years older than Handel and Bach, and outstripped his own generation by being able to keep pace with every new advance, renewing his youth by contact with youth. Hence he encountered the *avant-garde* movement of his century almost without realising it.

88

a) Telemann: Aria from a cantata — Largo (probably about 1720)

Bin ich denn so gar ver-las - sen, sind mir Glück und Him-mel feind?

b) Telemann: Pastorell (Sing-, Spiel- und Generalbassübungen, 1733)

Schal - le nur, du mun - tre Flö - te, da die hol-de Morgen-rö - te noch mit tau - send Far - ben spielt

Couperin was much less closely connected with the polyphony of the past; no inherited German tradition held him back, so that he was able to step over spontaneously and easily into the new world. Some of his dreamy major melodies achieve complete 'modernity', and the swaying 6/8 rhythms of his Pastorale themes are constantly underpinned by minutely calculated supports. His melody-openings acquire a definite shape by use of the characteristic *ouvert-clos* (1st and 2nd time) formula. Nearly all his Rondo melodies—light and lilting *Régence* melodies in two and three parts—descend from French opera and ballet music around 1700:

a) C o u p e r i n : La Pastorelle (1713) with ornaments as originally intended

b) *Idem:* Sœur Monique (1722) with ornaments written out

The younger composers, on the other hand, have quite another sound, for they were immersed in an entirely new environment. The *vaudeville* at the end of Lesage's *Temple de Mémoire* (1725) quite clearly stems from Parisian street-traditions; old though the tradition may be, the melody has all the ease of youth. It is not conceivable in any other rhythm, or in a minor variant; its mockery is explosive, jaunty, and gay. Even when it stops short for a moment in an irregular short line, this is merely to gather strength for a triumphant pointing of the refrain. In origin was it a *gavotte* or a *bourrée*? Nothing courtly or ceremonious remains—and all that is left of its dance-inheritance is an impelling, life-loving vigour:

90

L e s a g e : Le Temple de Mémoire (1725), Vaudeville (Théâtre choisi de Lesage, II, Paris, 1821, p. 232 [text] resp. Appendix No. 219 [melody])

Mes - sieurs,   à   la piè-ce nou - vel - le   Ac - cor-dez

un   peu   de   fa - veur; Quoi que vous puis-siez   pen - ser

d'el - le, Ne chan-tez pas d'un ton mo - queur: Hé, vrai - ment

voi - re! Zis - te, zes - te, et lon - lan - la, Vo - yez

comme on re - vien - dra A leur tem-ple de mé-moi - re.

Dance was also responsible for transforming and clarifying the instrumental themes of Pergolesi. It also inspired the wonderful 'singing Allegros' of Rococo, which frisk and jest in a lilting by-play of turns, points and ornaments while contriving to bask in their own loveliness. Pergolesi's music was as unequivocally major as the new French and German tunes, and showed it unmistakably in its bright scale and common chords. It was also secular, only one step removed from dance-music. Yet it was not popular street-music so much as the work of a conscious creator, conserving his energies and instinctively aiming at a closer unity between melody and dance:

91

Pergolesi: Trio Sonata (1732): Molto moderato

Yet what was happening here was ultimately to lead away from Rococo. It can be seen clearly enough in French, German and Italian examples of the new style: from 1720 onwards, the catchy, dance type of major melody held sway, and the art of the *style galant* was enclosed in a symmetrical structure, closely worked and self-contained. These melodies depended for their courtly elegance and charm on short phrases and miniature forms.[7] They appealed to a generation which had wearied of the longwindedness, the vastness, the range and foresight of Bach, Handel, Rameau and Vivaldi. When a composer lets his gaze wander far afield, he has no time to polish the single small turn, and make the melody a model of melodiousness and grace: no time, in fact, to be a miniaturist, such as were all Rococo artists. To outgrow miniature forms and the *style galant*

119

meant outgrowing Rococo as well. 18th-century performance indications show this very clearly. General markings were *dolce, grazioso* and *teneramente*. Round about 1700, *doux* in French scores took the place of *piano*—as in the works of Lully and Campra. These were reinforced wherever possible. Couperin would write *tendrement*, whilst Rameau added *tendre et gracieux*. Telemann and Mattheson asked for *singend*, and must have quickly realised that they were behind the times. In 1721, Bononcini requested *dolce e con grazia, cantabile*, whilst Pergolesi, Scarlatti, Sarri, Handel, Piccini, Hasse, Monsigny, Boccherini and C.P.E. Bach all wrote *amoroso*. From 1756, when Algarotti had raised *melodia espressiva* to ideal heights, *espressivo* appeared with increasing frequency, in Paisiello, for instance. The list probably ends with Mozart, who still reflected Rococo sensibility in the markings of his early works:—in a *Menuetto galante*, for example, or the *dolce* of some *Andante cantabile* (middle movement of the *Piano Sonata*, K.V. 330).

The art of interpretation now assumed more importance than ever before. But at this point the Rococo encountered one of its great precursors, particularly in the over-ripe art of ornamentation.

*

During the second half of the 17th century, the art of 'beautiful singing', or Italian *bel canto*, had been developing in the singing schools, choir-schools and opera-houses of Naples, Bologna, Rome and Venice. It linked the ideal of impeccable singing to the strictest and most systematic form of training; anyone wanting to sing had to devote his whole life to the art. Singing determined the manner of life, the practice and interpretation of a work, every detail of performance and delivery, and even artistic behaviour. It became a way of life, and its technical demands brought a special social caste into existence, in the shape of the *castrati*—eunuchs of music, condemned to endless singing and perpetual childhood. The great singing virtuosi, *primo uomo* and *prima donna*, combined with the *castrati* to form a unique and privileged social phenomenon. The heroes and pioneers of this movement were Italian singers, who appeared as representatives of the new style in the courts and opera-houses of all large cities. Operatic music from 1660 onwards meant Italian music and *bel canto*. Italian opera was still considered the only authentic model, even in places where a national tradition was beginning to form, as in Paris and, for a while, in London and Hamburg. Other types of opera were known as *tragédie lyrique, pastorale héroïque, Pastoral-Tragikomödie*, or something of the kind. 'Opera' in the full sense was Italian opera, and especially Italian singing. In the way in which it appeared after 1700, *bel canto* was the most highly developed art of melody

Watteau : "L'indifférent" (around 1710). One of the most beautiful representations of the rococo dance-movement in art, with complete harmony of rhythm, figure and background.

that music has ever known. In a way it was almost over-developed. The style was definitely elaborated by Alessandro Scarlatti and his followers in Naples; Porpora championed it in Vienna and Dresden, and Farinelli, the most famous *castrato* of his time, conquered London and Madrid. The schools of Pistocchi and Bernacchi flourished in Bologna in a state of emulation and rivalry; by 1750—1760 their somewhat reserved and restricted outlook had merged with the schools of Naples and Rome. Burney relates how in their thirst for new sensations the Neapolitan and Roman schools quickly exhausted what their virtuosity had gained. An Italian singer such as Marchesi, who began his career in the second half of the century, summed up in himself the findings of the various schools, yet this did not mean that he was superior to his predecessors in every respect.

The chief significance of *bel canto* was that it provided European music with a rich supply of ultra-refined melody. It has since remained the unsurpassed model of trained brilliance, smooth and studied technique, and shapely phrasing. Securely founded on a century-old technique, *bel canto* spelt not merely control, but total freedom, beyond the imagination of present-day singers and instrumentalists. This freedom combined strength and flexibility, and showed itself mainly in ornamentation and the allied art of improvisation.

Voices and instruments had for centuries been applying and developing the skill of melodic ornamentation, of *fioriture*. Detailed manuals of instruction for the embellishment of organ music had existed from the 15th century, and for flute and viol from the middle of the 16th century. Special manuals dealing with *canto figurato* and *passaggi*—apparently the earliest of all vocal ornaments— had appeared at the end of the 16th century. These important books covered the entire field, demonstrating by hundreds of examples both the easy and more complex type of ornament. They detailed whole legions of *esclamazioni, ribattute, gruppi, trilli, messanze, tirate*, from the simplest shake or note-change to complete re-writing of the melody. Professional musicians were expected to practise them daily, a hundred times over, as though this were the most natural thing in the world. Each interval, melodic turn and embellishment had its own special rule, which had to be memorised in essentials by singer or player, so that when its practice had become second-nature, he could improvise something similar. The types were rooted in tradition, but the performance was always different. That was the crux of the matter, for every great melody-style is basically an art of *types*. It represents the sum total of the related turns and ornaments, and allows several versions of every formula, so long as these fit into the collective vocabulary of the tradition. (In this respect, although itself a typical product of art-music, *bel canto* adheres to the general principles of folk-music.)

Let us look for a moment at these manuals of instruction. The instrumental ones are every bit as interesting as those on singing. In 1553, Diego Ortiz was advising the viol-player to "take the part you wish to ornament, and write it anew." Agazzari in 1609 and Praetorius in 1620 both considered that "to ornament is the same as re-writing the part." Or as Zacconi put it in 1622, *formarsi un canto a suo modo*, create a new melody for oneself. "In this consists the science of improvised ornaments," wrote Giambattista Mancini in his *Riflessioni pratiche sul canto figurato* (Milano, 1774); the singer must adorn *(abbellire)* the composition with complete freedom, the play of his creative fantasy being reflected in new and unexpected ideas. This very unexpectedness was important. According to J.A. Hiller *(Anweisung zum musikalisch-zierlichen Gesang*, Leipzig, 1780), the singer must endeavour to give the listener a pleasant surprise; even though he does not imitate those older singers, who never left a single note unornamented, he will at least never perform anything twice in the same way. A great deal about these legendary great singers emerges from Pier Francesco Tosi's manual *(Opinioni de' cantori antichi e moderni*, Bologna, 1723); "They felt it to be their duty to sing all the serious and some of the gay arias of an opera in a different fashion every evening." It was essential that the singer always *varied when he repeated*, and "whoever does not vary and beautify what he sings is no great artist" *(chi non varia migliorando tutto quello che canta, non è grand'uomo)*. Ornamentation tended to concentrate on the *da capo* section of an aria, or in instrumental music on the cadence. This was what Josse de Villeneuve meant in 1756 when he said that arias could not be recognised when they were repeated, and that "at every performance even the very form is changed." Could such an art be formulated into teachable rules? In his *l'Art de bien chanter*, 1668 and 1679, De Bacilly reluctantly decided that it could not. Although ornaments were "as important in music as colours to a painter," they could hardly ever be written down. Yet Tosi's manual mentions eight different types of trill, and Jean Rousseau's viol-tutor *(Traité de la viole*, Paris, 1687) points out that the old French singing-school included six different *agréments*, and a further three to be learned by the viol-player ... Hiller, what is more, had no qualms about formulating rules for 'optional variations' *(willkürliche Veränderung)*. "Variations can be formed in three ways: the first way adds more notes to few, the second replaces many notes by few, whilst the third substitutes a certain number of notes for the same number of others." Anyone examining or hearing the variations of these belcantist virtuosi, as written down at the time—Farinelli's *fioriture*, for instance, or Marchesi's elaboration of an aria by Cherubini (1784)[8]—may well ask himself whether their chief virtue lay in the prudently accumulated stock of knowledge, or in the daring individual flights of fancy.

Vocal and instrumental music presented much the same picture. In the 1750's, four basic manuals on the teaching of contemporary music appeared in German—Quantz on the principles of flute-playing in 1752, Philipp Emanuel

Bach on keyboard-playing in 1753, Leopold Mozart on violin-playing in 1756, and Agricola in 1757; the latter formulated the new singing theories into a teaching method, on the basis of Tosi's book. They all dealt with the technique of improvised ornaments, and since the performer in this period was primarily concerned with free improvisation, it is true to say that this was almost all they minded about. Quantz expressed the Italian point of view; a performer "improves the melody" with new and surprising ideas through the use of free variation, because "the only themes to be varied should be those which in themselves make no great effect." C.P.E. Bach was already uttering words of warning about excessive ornamentation, although he added that a performer "likes almost any idea to be varied when it is repeated." Leopold Mozart inveighed against those who "bedeck the uncomplicated notes of an *Adagio cantabile*, and form two dozen notes out of a simple note." Yet in his keyboard-tutor towards the end of the century (1789), Daniel Türk pressed the claims again, even more strongly. The improvised ornament improved the piece, made it "more eloquent," gave it "light and shade." For him it could never be sufficiently beautiful or varied. "The variations," he said, "must be . . . at least as good as the original melody." Jean Rousseau's claim in his viol-tutor of 1687 still in fact held good: the player takes an unadorned melody and "works on these few notes as on a canvas, sometimes filling his subject with chords in an infinity of ways, and using diminution after diminution; sometimes discovering most tender airs and a thousand other diversities furnished by his genius; and all without seeming to be premeditated . . ."*

The performer's new-found urge to create in such rich profusion was reflected in these instrumental compositions, which caught and held the improvisational practice of the time almost by chance, as it came into being. It can be seen at work in some of the violin sonatas of Corelli, Telemann and Benda, and in Handel's keyboard suites . . . it is easy to deduce from them the dismay of a progressively minded musician some few decades later, faced with the remains of this prolific Golden Age in the form of decadent and slovenly mannerisms. In 1813, a musician called Mosel was shocked that "not a single bar of the original melody (in the arias) can often be recognised" because of the "performer's embellishments." Another (Spohr) was amazed and vexed that Roman orchestral players ornamented so freely "that it has become second nature, and they cannot rid themselves of the habit." Admittedly, this was now 1816, and the opinion came from a North European composer from Germany, home of the new art of the symphony. Ornamentation which sounded so strange to a Ger-

---

* "*sur ce peu de notes, comme sur un canevast,* . . . *travaille remplissant quelquefois son sujet d'accords en une infinité des manières & allant de diminution en diminution; tantost y faisant trouver des airs fort tendres, & mille autres diversitez que son genie luy fournit; & cela sans avoir rien premedité . . .*"

man was still for Mancini in 1770 "the adornment, the life and the preserver" of the melody. It had clearly lost its attraction and its significance in the interval. ("The art of singing is in decline," Metastasio complained to Burney as an old man, and Haydn thought that singing ought "to be classified amongst the lost arts.")

But as long as the art of singing was flourishing, it was able to concentrate into itself the entire life of the music. The *bel canto* ideal started by being vocal, but soon spread to instrumental music. Rococo music on the other hand had developed from dance-rhythms and instrumental music, but soon affected vocal music, and emerged with *bel canto*. Both these two Latin-derived forms were soon cultivating the ornamented melody of the *style galant*. Because the sources of melody lie so deep, it seems as though ornamental traditions have from the outset shown certain basic differences, according to the areas where they occurred. The Italians instinctively fostered the shape of the melody, the French stressed the flexibility of the line, and the Germans the way it was constructed. Hence there had long been a fruitful interchange of lyric, dynamic and structural ornaments in West European culture. These differences disappeared during the course of the 18th century, and ornamentation became at once more united and more uniform. The difference which remained—the fact that voices and instruments used different types of ornament—was slowly diminishing in importance at this time. Writers at the turn of the century—J. Rousseau for instance— stress this strongly: others, such as Telemann and Quantz, emphasised the tendency of ornamentation to show national characteristics. Yet all these differences were obviously vanishing before the new claims of ornamentation, which seem to have manifested themselves everywhere in the same way. The greater part of Baroque ornamentation sprang from the need: to create movement, and gave the century's old instruments—lute and harpsichord, for example—a natural answer for their most pressing need: to prolong the ephemeral life of the sound. Here and there this frenzy of activity now began to subside. The new type of ornament aimed chiefly at adornment, and was actually described as 'gracing' or 'embellishing' *(agrément* and *embellissement)*. Its task was to make the melody more lyrical (hence Mancini's *cantabile sia la cantilena*), more definite and flowing (C.P.E. Bach and Türk), create a definite impression on the receptive listener (Couperin). It was soon systematically arranged in groups. In a key attached to his keyboard works (1713–1730), Couperin explained twenty-three types of ornament *(pincé simple, double, continu, diésé* [sharpened], *bémolisé* [flattened]: *port de voix simple, coulée* and *double : tremblement appuyé, lié, ouvert, fermé, continu* and *détaché : accent : arpègement, en montant* and *en descendant, coulés, tierce coulée, en montant* and *en descendant, aspiration, suspension, double*—with *unisson* added for good measure as the twenty-fourth). He became thoroughly vexed if the player did not observe them all. In 1722, he

wrote in the Preface to the Third Book of his keyboard works, "It always aston-
ishes me that although I have carefully explained in a clear, intelligible manner
how my keyboard tutor should be interpreted, many players perform these
works without observing these instructions. This is unpardonable carelessness,
since it is not for the performer to decide which ornaments to apply. I declare
that my works are to be performed as I have myself indicated … " In addition to
Couperin's twenty-three *agréments*, there were Tosi's eight types of trill,
Rousseau's nine ornaments for viol, Hiller's three types of improvised ornament, and Türk's ten cadence-rules. (J. S. Bach set out a further thirteen in the
explanatory table of the *Klavierbüchlein*, prepared for Friedemann in 1720.)
In his later keyboard sonatas, C.P.E. Bach refused to allow the player to
improvise freely, and wrote out every indication. Yet *bel canto* and its free improvisation still continued to flourish like an eternal protest within the framework of
attempted control. The profusion of ornamentation and free variation took
advantage of every unguarded moment to produce an endless series of melodic
turns. So long as the creative urge and spontaneous outpouring of melody were
unexhausted, the restrictive veto had no real effect. Regulation only won its
cause when ornamentation began to show signs of impoverishment and decay,
by which time it was proper and possible to combat it. But by that time both
Rococo and *bel canto* were in decline, and the "Golden Age of the 18th century"
had come to an end. Until then, this exuberant and insatiable form of melody
had still to reach an important new phase of its existence.

★

As was frequently stressed at the time, the new melodic idiom in process
of development between 1730 and 1750 was more colourful, more minutely articulated and more flexible than what had gone before—and in particular it was
much more regular. "At last we can both sing and dance!" The passion for
dance-rhythms sometimes threatened to overpower the more tranquil rhythms
of vocal music. "Out with it, you singers!" exclaimed Tosi, representing the
older generation, "tell the composer you wish to sing, not to dance"! There
was general complaint about rhythms in fast tempi: the chief criticism levelled
at Sammartini in Milan was that he drove his orchestra at an excessive pace
(Burney), and the strict and academically-minded critics of Vienna saw nothing
but undignified antics in the lilting dance-rhythm of Haydn's symphonic movements. Yet it was precisely at this point that the melody of the day began to part
company with dance-rhythm.

Melody and dance had been linked in a long, significant alliance, but it
was based on a community of interests, not on a permanent bond. Dance-

rhythm helped to liberate melody and give it rhythmical impetus, but melody only carried dance as long as it needed it, until it had utterly absorbed it for its own purposes, mastering with its help the new type of articulation. Definite results were soon to follow. Two-part and then three-part sonata form began to appear, first in Domenico Scarlatti's sonatas, and then in Tartini's. The stage-forms of dance were established, to be used by Rameau, Grétry and even Gluck as basic elements of dramatic construction. Dance also appeared in the movements of symphonies, chiefly as Minuet and Rondo. The new 18th-century symphony, this classical or rather pre-classical form, was profoundly indebted to dance. Once it had been established, dance and melody had achieved their object, and their alliance could be broken up.

Italian, German and French melody about 1750 was quite extraordinarily agile. Sammartini in Milan, Monn and Wagenseil in Vienna, C.P.E. Bach in Berlin, Stamitz in Mannheim and Mondonville's group in Paris had polished and refined it as well as rendering it flexible. And making use of this new agility received from dance-rhythm, it gradually began to detach itself from the dance. It then fell into the hands of composers who knew much less about pure dance symmetry than in Pergolesi's day, and who in fact set up considerable resistance to it. It was not just coincidence that in Germany this generation was that of the *Sturm und Drang* period, and that its leader in France was Jean-Jacques Rousseau, who in his *Devin du Village* had made an exemplary collection of light popular dance-tunes. As early as 1763, he was writing from Motiers to the chief dancing-master, Marcel, at Gotha: "The company would probably find it less tedious if there were more variety in the dances. The unending series of minuets with their constant repetitions, which are used to open and form the substance of the ball, have never in my own observation represented attractive entertainment for the assembly. Is this not also true of the flat symmetry of the *contredanses*? Why not introduce some reasonable irregularity into them, such as appears in a good design, or contrast of the kind that is found in music?" These were telling words; and the awakening discontent found an echo in other fields, even to the point of taking over his own descriptions of 'flat symmetry' and 'reasonable irregularity'. Such a critical attitude was no longer entirely new, nor was it isolated. Scheibe was already writing in the 1740's: "We know how quickly all is turned to passion, which in itself is nought but agitation and unrest. A musician must therefore be able to play a hundred different roles, represent a thousand different characters . . ." 1760 saw the publication of Noverre's famous *Lettre sur la danse,* which championed the cause of dramatic mime instead of the symmetrical dance-steps, the costumes and masques of Rococo. It preached new methods of performance and a new art of movement. By a strange coincidence, William Chambers was creating an English counterpart of the widespread European ideal the very same year (1763) that

Rousseau was writing from Motiers. His Kew Gardens was a model of asymmetry, irregularity and 18th-century 'sentimentality'. So far as operatic music was concerned, contact between Germans and Italians in the 1760's was producing works that aimed at dramatic reform; Gluck's *Orpheus* and *Alceste*, Jommelli's *Fetonte* and *Vologeso*, Hasse's *Piramo e Tispe* were all *dramma per musica*, irregular, free and asymmetrical in their construction, with loosened arias and free-flowing recitative. Piccinni's *Cecchina* and Monsigny's *Déserteur* even managed to break through the framework of comic opera, proclaiming the advent of 'sentimental', flexible, impressionistic forms.[9] Unbeknown, the 'bourgeois anarchy of feeling' had set in, and with it a decisive change in ideas of European musical structure. 'Nature' was as much of a watchword for young people in this period as it had been for their elders some fifty years earlier; but the emphasis and meaning had changed. They no longer wandered in Watteau's groves but along Werther's paths. Surrounded by ruins, they walked in a 'sentimental'* daze along the moonlit shores of lakes. 1772, described in biographies of Haydn and Mozart as a year of 'romantic crisis', witnessed the publication of *Götz von Berlichingen* and *Werther*. This was no more of a coincidence than the joint appearance in the 1760's of Rousseau's *Nouvelle Héloïse* and Piccinni's *Buona Figliola*. Equally significant was Diderot's request that the 'cry of human passion' should rise from composers as well. Feeling was no longer mere tenderness, and melody involved turbulence as well as a regular pulse. It became irregular, and quivered with new anxiety. Works in the minor spread as if by magic in European music round about 1770.

Sturm und Drang showed itself in music earlier than in literature. The restless urgency of early Romanticism was apparent in the keyboard works of W. Friedemann and C.P.E. Bach, Platti and Schobert and in Stamitz's symphonies, long before it appeared in Rousseau's and Goethe's novels. (*Werther's* most direct links seem to have been Beck, Vanhal and other composers.) It was chiefly due to composers that the stylised dance-forms only made occasional appearances in the new instrumental forms after 1750. Schobert turned the minuet into more of a character-piece, whilst the North German school positively disliked it. In Vienna, from Wagenseil and Starzer onwards, it became more of a symphonic movement, and lost its dance-character in Haydn's later works. Mozart showed a rather similar tendency, in that both his *bel canto* style (deriving straight from J.C. Bach) and his dance-rhythms (plainly derived from Parisian sources) were gradually both set free in the full flood of his symphonic and dramatic evolution. J.C. Bach, Paisiello, Schobert and Grétry paled before Mozart's victorious star. Mozart was unconsciously fulfilling the law of the

---

* This word has been used in its 18th-century sense (cp. Sterne's *Sentimental Journey*) which refers to the 'feeling' side of life as opposed to the 'rational'. (Translators' note.)

period[10] and this meant the end of Rococo. It was absorbed into a new classicism, which both summed up what had gone before, and strove after a new synthesis.

What a remarkable paradox! Rococo music came into existence as a reaction to the massiveness of Baroque—a classical art-form—yet it spent itself by preparing for a classical Renaissance! But the paradox was an illusion. For the great classical music which emerged from the *style galant* was seldom *galant* and never ultra-refined, and could never be confused with Baroque classical music. Yet within itself it carried the Rococo heritage: its resources were richer, both in articulation and thematic ideas, its colours more varied, its rhythms more dance-like, its melodies more prolific and more eloquent in their detail; all qualities which emphasised that Rococo melody, far from 'blushing unseen', formed a most important constructive element in the new European music.

NOTES

1. *Cp.* Taine: *Les origines de la France contemporaine. L'ancien régime.* 19th ed., 1894, p. 177. (*Les moeurs et les caractères*, chap. II, 3): "*On peut dire avec vérité qu'en ce siècle la cheville ouvrière de l'éducation est le maître à danser. Avec lui, on pouvait se passer de tous les autres; sans lui, tous les autres ne servaient de rien. Car, sans lui, comment faire avec aisance, mesure et légèreté les mille actions les plus ordinaires de la vie courante, marcher, s'asseoir, se tenir debout, offrir le bras, relever l'éventail, écouter, sourire, sous des yeux si exercés et devant un public si délicat?*"
2. E. and J. de Goncourt: *La femme au dix-huitième siècle.* Paris, 1862, chap. II, p. 117. Note.
3. *Ibid.*, chap. I, p. 26. Note.
4. E. Pilon: *Watteau et son école.* Bruxelles—Paris, 1912, p. 102.
5. Act II, scene 5, Ed. Lajarte, pp. 154—155.
6. E. Bücken: *Die Musik des Rokoko und der Klassik.* Potsdam, 1928, p. 74.
7. Here are a few examples of the charm and elegance' of Rococo: in J.C. Bach: *Concertante in A major*, second theme of first movement:

In Mozart, first finale of *Don Giovanni*:

Second movement of the *D major String Quartet*, K.V. 575 (1789):

Figaro (Marcellina's aria):

J. C. Bach:

(*Alessandro nell' Indie*, 1762, *Zanaida*, 1763, *Adriano in Siria*, 1765, *Carattaco*, 1767, *Quintet for flute, oboe, violin, viola and 'cello*, op. 11, No. 4, *c.* 1775.)
Also Francesco di Majo (*Ipermestra*) :

It is clear that all these turns acquired very definite meaning in the 'sentimental' years of the 1760's. They became much-loved commonplaces, and if the music were 'feelingly performed', as Dittersdorf put it, would move an audience to tears.

8. R. Haas: *Aufführungspraxis der Musik.* Potsdam, 1931, pp. 185—186, 225—230.

9. For the onset of middle-class 'sentimentality' in French literature and fine arts, see the chronological summary in Taine: *L'Ancien régime.* Vol. II, chap. 3. (*Inconvénients de la vie de salon*) II, in the edition quoted, p. 209.

10. H. Abert: "J.Chr. Bachs italienische Opern und ihr Einfluss auf Mozart." *Zeitschrift für Musikwissenschaft*, 1919; *idem*: "Paisiellos Buffokunst und ihre Beziehungen zu Mozart." *Archiv für Musikwissenschaft*, 1919; Tóth—Szabolcsi: *Mozart.* Budapest, 1941, pp. 141—158. It hsould be added that Mozart borrowed innumerable stylistic devices and melody-types from the commøn stock of Rococo idioms in use amongst his predecessors and contemporaries, changing their emphasis quite considerably in the process. They acquired quite a different meaning in the course of his development. A typical example is the sharp, pointed rhythm of the *gagliard*. Stemming from the Italian Renaissance, it became one of the most popular Rococo 'joy-rhythms', an expression of festive gaiety. It summed up the joy of living shared by both Renaissance and Rococo, and aptly illustrates Huizinga's general observation that the *joie de vivre* and optimism of the Renaissance "did not achieve its final victory until the 18th century" (*Wege der Kulturgeschichte.* München, 1930, p. 135). There are traces of the *gagliard* in Lully, Campra, Destouches (see No. 86), and in Handel; in collections of 1720, in Galuppi and Piccinni (characteristically, Piccinni uses it to set the words *che vuol ballar*). (S. Abert: *Mozart.* I, pp. 421, 451, II, p. 546.) It also appears in the English national anthem, in J.C. Bach's *Piano Sonata in E flat major* (op. 17, 2nd

movt.), at the end of Haydn's *Lo Speziale* (1768), and in an aria of Sarti's opera *I due litiganti*, which Mozart quotes in the banquet scene in *Don Giovanni*. For Mozart, the *gagliard* represents the quintessence of dance-rhythm (e.g., Figaro's *gagliard*-like cavatina, *Se vuol ballare, Signor Contino*). Yet he ranged from the joyous fanfares of his youth (Finale of *Divertimento*, K.V. 131, and of the *Sinfonia* K.V. 182, Introduction to *La finta giardiniera*) to the wild outburst of sensuous passion in *Don Giovanni* (Finale of Act II, *Sostegno e gloria d'umanità*) and the playful dig at conceited pomposity in *Così fan tutte* (Finale of Act I, *Eccovi il medico*). As a formula, it is as much at home in Mozart's finales as it is in Piccinni's (e.g. *La Buona Figliola*): it seems to have been the typical rhythm for the 'happy ending' in 18th-century opera. (*Cf.* also its role in Rossini's *Barbiere*.) Goethe used the same form for his poem *Wechsellied zum Tanze*, as well as for many other dramatic passages and choruses. For him as for Mozart the *gagliard* obviously stood for festivity. Yet it can be strangely ambiguous: in Gluck's famous underworld scene in *Orpheus*, it turns into a roundelay of infernal spirits. In Hungary it was a familiar verse-form from the 16th century onwards, used in folk-hymns, drinking songs and nursery rhymes, and appeared in Rococo guise in the poetry of Amadé, Faludi and other lesser-known academic poets. See also R. Velten: *Das ältere deutsche Gesellschaftslied unter dem Einfluss der italienischen Musik.* Heidelberg, 1914, pp. 124 ff.; *Irodalomtörténeti Közlemények* (Contributions to Literary History), 1924, pp. 23—24 (J. Kastner: *The Italian Verse-Forms of Ferenc Faludi* [In Hungarian]; R. Gálos: *László Amadé.* Pécs, 1937, p. 129 [in Hungarian]; *Ung. Jahrbücher*, Berlin, XVIII, pp. 211—212). Here are some typical examples of Italian, German and Hungarian forms of *gagliard*:

Gipsy chorus from *La zingara*
(Rinaldo da Capua) *c.* 1740:

O dell'Egitto
Nume, custode,
La nostra frode
Proteggi ognor.
Opra è divina
Punir l'avaro
Cui solo è caro
L'argento e l'or.

Goethe: *Zum neuen Jahr* (1802)

Zwischen dem Alten,
Zwischen dem Neuen
Hier uns zu freuen
Schenkt uns das Glück;
Und das Vergangne
Heisst mit Vertrauen
Vorwärts zu schauen,
Schauen zurück.

Ferenc Faludi: *Clorinda* (*c.* 1760)

Gentle Clorinda
In the cool spring-tide
On the fair hillside
Wanders alone.
Hasten, Dorindo,
Her heart is pining,
Her eyes are shining,
For thee alone.

(Translated from the Hungarian)

This form plays a prominent role in Verdi's opera *Il Trovatore*.

THE CLASSICAL MELODY

The 18th century was the great century of European self-awareness, and in music too it engendered fresh ideas, and fostered their fulfilment. All at once there came into existence, quickly gaining ground, the idea that music was international, or rather supra-national. Faint hints of such a claim had been evident in the years of contact between Flanders and Italy about 1500, during the lifetimes of Josquin de Prés and Erasmus of Rotterdam, but all at once the problem showed up in sharp relief.

It took on the form of a rivalry and an amalgamation. A dispute about French and Italian music had been raging in France since the pamphlets of Abbé Raguenet and Lecerf de la Viéville had been published, respectively in 1702 and 1705. Which was the better music, the French or the Italian? Which language was more adapted to music? What was the real language of opera? These were the salient points. The rival points of view were intensified around the middle of the century as a result of the guest-performances of the "Bouffons". Public opinion was stirred up by the writings of Rousseau, d'Alembert, Grimm and Diderot, and split into two camps. The musical controversy spilled over into social and political discord, so that the original cause of contention was somewhat obscured. It emerged that there was no such thing as genuine French melody, that the French language was best used in declamation, whereas Italian was the hotbed of the *aria*. Hence genuine French comic opera was a contradiction in terms, and Rameau's music was fighting for a lost cause.

Yet in the meantime, almost by chance, a folkish type of *opéra comique* was showing itself in the works of Rousseau and others, a late offshoot of Lesage's initiative at the beginning of the century. Twenty-five years later, in 1774—1775, the dispute broke out again for the third time, and concentrated on the rivalry between Gluck and Piccinni. By this time French music was represented by Gluck—and especially by his literary supporters—and also by Rousseau himself, who was both the opponent and the reformer of French music. The outcome was of course still uncertain: the melodic styles of France and Italy—declamation and *bel canto*, the dramatic and the musical—existed quite happily side by side. Musicians who survived the dispute, and particularly those who

9*

saw beyond the complexity of the immediate issue, were well aware that solution involved not 'one or other', but a combination of both. Although the whole discussion seemed pointless, it did in fact serve to resolve and clarify a great many problems.

Yet the idea of an amalgamation had lain buried in the consciousness of the period since the end of the 17th century. In the Preface to his *Florilegium* (1695), the elder Muffat had in fact mooted an international merging of styles. A pupil of Lully and Pasquini, he had proposed a unification of three musical languages (French, German and Italian), in order to "prepare the peaceful harmony among the nations" (*préluder . . . à l'harmonie de tant des nations à l'aymable paix*). Couperin, too, in his *Apothéoses* and *Concerts royaux*, had been attempting to reconcile French and Italian music; Campra and Destouches were also working on the same idea at the same time. German composers were in a slightly easier position, in that they were followers of either the Western or Southern European schools, and willy-nilly their work could only be a parallel or a recapitulation. (Obvious examples are Keiser, Telemann, Graun, Hasse.) Necessity soon became a virtue: by 1752, the Berlin flautist and composer, Quantz, had the impression that German taste "exercises its judgement in selecting the best from whatever is preferred by other nations." The only composers required were such as could undertake the 'selection'. The challenge did not go unheeded, and a reply was forthcoming. By 1778, the young Mozart was writing proudly from Mannheim that he could absorb and imitate every style (. . . *ich kann so ziemlich . . . aller Art und Stil von Kompositions annehmen und nachahmen*). Only five years earlier, in 1773, a letter from Gluck had appeared in the *Mercure de Paris*, in which he explained that he was seeking "a noble, moving and natural melody, a declamation in keeping with the prosody of each language and the character of each people." He went on to explain his "great desire to produce a music which can speak to every nation, and eliminate the absurd distinctions between national forms of music." In 1776, the *Mercure de France* praised Grétry for music which "speaks an international language of all nations, a universally acceptable language of free nature, speech and feeling." So the plan was already in action, and its realisation apparent in Gluck, Haydn and Mozart, composers of Germanic stock whose music was intended for every nation. Yet the actual formulation of the principle was left to Frenchmen. Chabanon in 1785 exalted music as "the universal language of our continent" *(De la musique considérée en elle-même)*, and Lesueur rather pretentiously announced in the commentary to *La mort d'Adam* in 1798 that his work was not addressed to any one nation, but to the "common spirit of humanity." (This resembles the belief held by Novalis, Schlegel and Liszt, that music is the basic common language of man.) Classical music meanwhile was flourishing in the hands of German composers, and the French initiative carried a further decisive step forward, as far as the French Revolution. (Although German classicism was a world-language without need of translation, its listeners unconscously interpreted it in terms of their own language; the French understood it as declamation, the Italians as plastic shape, and Eastern Europe as national Romanticism.)

As far as the French Revolution, well and good: yet there was no revolution in progress so far as European music was concerned. Rather was there an amalgamation and fulfilment. It was a most unusual moment, awaited for centuries, and never to return again. Viennese classicism between Gluck and Schubert represented the sudden flowering of a whole city and culture.

★

But why was it Vienna, and not Paris, which became the capital of 18th century Europe? The answer is almost too simple. No other Rococo city could unite so many foreign influences, yet remain so strictly and organically within its own folk-culture. Vienna had been preparing for its great role as unifier o peoples since the reign of the Emperor Charles VI, at the beginning of the 18th century; as capital of Austria it was a natural metropolis for the countries bordering on its territories. With the new masterpiece of Fischer von Erlach, the Karlskirche, standing at its centre, the Vienna of 1730 had made it its business to become the capital of a renascent Empire. It gathered the music of the whole world within its walls without ever forgetting that it was the southernmost point of the Austro-Germanic countries. Sometimes Johann Joseph Fux would identify himself with the Palestrina tradition, sometimes with that of Cavalli. The younger Muffat vacillated between French, Italian and German trends. Italy was represented by composers such as Caldara, the two Conti, Bonno, Porpora, Metastasio and Salieri. A local school of symphonists was also growing up, thanks to Reutter, Monn, Starzer and Wagenseil. Although they depended on Italian models for their design, their music already had a definitely South German flavour. It is also important to remember that Stranitzky, Prehauser and Kurz were living in Vienna in these decades, that it was the city of the Austrian folk-play, and home of the immortal Augustin, Kasperl and Bernardon. There was music in the houses and the streets, serenades and folk-singers with harps and violins, music in the garden of every inn. Minuets abounded, to be converted in outlying districts into *ländlers* and *waltzes*. Vienna was as saturated with music as Venice, yet for this very reason it clung to its rather provincial character. It was a city in which potentially great music could be detected everywhere as it welled up from its source in folk- and street-music, only to collapse and flow back once again into the popular stream. The *Theater-*

Almanach of 1794 describes the summer evening serenades which young people would organise in the Vienna streets, generally on name-days. It was customary to perform operatic ensembles with wind and brass accompaniment, but sometimes larger symphonies were included too. In a trice the windows were *choc à bloc* with people, and the players "were surrounded in a matter of minutes by a crowd of listeners loudly applauding, and often demanding the repetition of some piece, just as if they were in the theatre; often they would flock to escort the Serenade to other parts of the town." In his *Memoirs*, Franz Gräffer comments that in 1800 the brass band of Augarten, some twenty strong, performed "nothing but symphonies, operatic selections and classical pieces by such great masters as Gluck, Handel and Mozart." A likely story is told of Haydn about 1760, how once out for a walk in Vienna, he recognised his own composition in a minuet that was being scratched out by some violin at the door of a suburban inn. The same city which berated him for his 'clownish' high spirits, was the first to call him "the darling of our nation" (*Liebling unserer Nation—Wiener Diarium*, 1766). J.F. Reichardt was soon to add: "Had we only Haydn and C.P.E. Bach, we Germans could boast of having a manner of our own, that our instrumental music is the most interesting in existence." National awareness was clearly awake and vigilant. Yet it did not and could not have realised how long and how eagerly the entire musical hive had been absorbing foreign musicians! As early as 1677, the Viennese court-organist, Poglietti, had composed a parade-like set of variations on the nations of the Monarchy. It included Bavarians, Czechs, Styrians, Hungarians, Moravians, Poles, and even French and Dutch, sometimes with their instruments and dances. From 1770 onwards, the music of janissaries and gipsies was no longer a rarity in Vienna. As many opportunities offered for *alla turca* as for *all'ongarese* and *zingarese*. (The first Viennese compositions to be written in the style of Hungarian recruiting dances began to appear between 1770 and 1775, about the same time as the Hungarian motives of Haydn, Dittersdorf and Mozart, and the barbaric Scythian dances in Gluck's *Iphigénie en Aulide*.) When George Reutter, for example, calls one of his piano pieces *Paisanne*, it is difficult to know whether he means countrified, 'rustic' music, or whether he is toying with the folk-rhythms of Italy, France or Germany. It is equally impossible to know whether Haydn's early chamber music is more indebted to Austrian, Czech or Italian folk-sources, and whether later in life Hungarian music meant more to him than, say, Scottish or Croatian. Again, did the pioneers of Viennese *singspiel*, Gassmann and Umlauff, succeed in discovering a German style that was based on Italian music, or was it vice versa? What mattered was that those who required it could always draw on a folk-source or other source of supply. It gave them the strength with which to mount up and scale the heights. The native stock of South German music flourished and grew strong on the rich 'humus' provided by multifarious foreign elements,[1] so that in time it could produce from its Viennese hothouse the peerless European bloom which was classical music.

★

The German folk-movement in music had been gathering strength since the middle of the 18th century, and had been given a fresh stimulus after 1770 by Herder and Schubart. What was art-music able to learn from it? Melody, above all, for German folk-idioms spoke from the heart, and were simple and direct. Joh. Peter Schulz maintained that a composition aiming at 'folk-feeling' *(Volkston)* was bound to be light and artless, well-shaped and 'seemingly familiar', and hence easily understood by all. Melody of this type was bound to be simple, clear-cut and unassuming, but what of Handel and Pergolesi, who half a century earlier had provided melodies which were just as simple, clearcut and 'seemingly familiar', yet at the same time intensely exacting? Their melodies were intended for stage and concert-platform, yet what had been learnt from folk-music was just as relevant in 1780 as it had been in 1730. Already at that time Handel and his Italian contemporaries were writing clearcut music in major keys, which would later be heard in minuets, *ländlers*, and in peasant- and student-songs. The 18th century followed on their lead, so that by 1780 composers were profiting from the earlier achievements. Haydn and his contemporaries were influenced by folk-song, and also, without realising it, by the new French and Italian styles of 1730; in this way they came upon the folk-like yet universally European beauty of the major triad and the common chord.

Yet folk-music was still the principal influence. Whether or not they were aware of it, it taught composers the meaning of bright, major sound, and matching, symmetrical phrases: it made them aware of the polyphony latent in melody, of the common chord, and the harmonic structure in thirds between tonic and dominant. The new types of German and Italian folk-music were generally well-supplied with all these elements, for they had been nourished on the art-music of the Settecento, but by 1780 so much interchange had taken place on all sides that no precedence could be established. To a similar extent, the new way of constructing chords in thirds had been furthered and stimulated since 1600 by means of the visible symbol of the figured bass; it now appeared reinforced, on the strength of Rameau's new theory of harmony. Rameau himself was convinced that the major common chord was of paramount importance (and this in spite of teaching that chords could be inverted, and that apparently dissimilar chords were in fact the same). Is it possible to conceive of anything clearer and more organic than these common-chord melodies with their even,

135

regular flow? They seem to have been created for a classical art. Take Ditters-dorf's famous settings (about 1785) of Ovid's *Metamorphoses*. Was it sheer chance which led him to describe the Golden Age by means of a gently curving melody on a common chord?[2] Most of the broad melodies by Gluck, Mozart and Beethoven—let alone Sammartini, Clementi, Paisiello and Cimarosa—open out spontaneously with the help of written-out ornaments and broken chords. It is characteristic that they are nearly all introductory themes:

92

a) G l u c k : Iphigénie en Tauride, Act II (also the earlier Clemenza di Tito, 1752)

b) M o z a r t : Le Nozze di Figaro, Act IV

c) B e e t h o v e n : Die Ruinen von Athen (chorus)

They are even more typical of Haydn, who felt entirely at home with the common chord, major triad and 'post-horn' style of melody. They form the basis of most of his ideas:

93

H a y d n : a)From Symphony No. 101   b)From Symphony No. 94

c)From Symphony No. 88   d)From Symphony No. 102

e) From the "Creation"

94

a) Sammartini: Flute Concertino (1750)

b) Stamitz: Trio Symphony in B flat major (around 1750)

c) J.C.Bach: Symphony in B flat major (1772)

d) Paisiello: Aria from "La bella molinara" (1788)

The many different forms of common-chord melody do in fact provide an elementary introduction to the various styles of classical melody. (These do not include themes which are obviously pastoral[3] or fanfare in type, although their constant increase is one of the features of the period.)

95

Types of common chord melody in the classical period

a)   **b)**   **c)**

d)   **e)**

This is not to say that classical melodies were produced to type after certain set patterns. They show important differences, otherwise they would never have been equally acceptable in the clearly differentiated forms of realistic comic opera, and the ever-expanding world of the symphony. Yet certain types tend to recur because composers in this century were drawing on a melodic supply which still clung to typical modes of expression. Both the Mannheim school of symphonists and Italian operatic composers still thought in generic terms. They use idioms which sigh, shoot up, move stepwise, leap or run; themes which modulate, or else form subsidiary themes or groups of themes; associations of key and sound, form and pace. (This profusion of formulae and combinations in 18th-century music and particularly in Mozart's stage works is directly reminiscent of Shakespeare.) Little by little the Viennese composers ceased to find it a universally applicable style,[4] and it was replaced by specific personal idioms, used on one occasion only. Slowly the style was transformed from the collective to the individual, although for the sake of general intelligibility the collective was never entirely abandoned. Mozart and Beethoven in their later works were the first to abandon it. (So far as Mozart's incomparably rich output is concerned, his supposed ten thousand melodies have been calculated to belong to some seventy melody-types. Typical formulae begin to disappear relatively late, in works of 1780 onwards.)

Up to that time, melody was trained to carry the weight of the new individual awareness. More and more was expected of it, it was flooded and saturated, impelled towards ever greater refinement and sensitivity until it was exhausted, broken and overstrained. Each composer had his own way of doing this. Gluck preferred concise, 'basic' melodies, and was rarely concerned with others; Haydn expected them to have a rocking rhythm, from which at a certain moment he would carve out his motive. Mozart's melodies underwent important changes in this respect, first in Italy and then, even more strongly, in Paris. Particularly towards the end of his career, he relaxed the exact symmetry which existed in the Rococo melodies of J.C. Bach, Paisiello and Grétry, and often introduced slight rhythmical displacements into a large, regular structure, choosing for his melodies mostly the brightest part of the compass. (Although Haydn and Mozart were both well aware of the sound of 'cello tone-colour as applied to the keyboard, it is significant that they seldom made any use of it. Beethoven's great melodies, on the other hand, were mostly written in the dark viola and cello registers, or else their harmonic accompaniments concentrate on these registers.) As for Mozart, he abandoned the idea of a larger compass so as to give his melodies the same clear, transparent colour all the way through. He never exceeds the octave or the tenth, and they always find their justification in expressive tension:

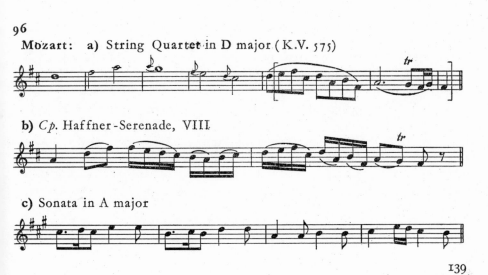

96
Mozart: a) String Quartet in D major (K.V. 575)

b) Cp. Haffner-Serenade, VIII

c) Sonata in A major

d) Clarinet Quintet, 2nd movt.

e) Magic Flute, Finale to Act II

It is at this point in Mozart's melody-style that the broken common chord plays such a vital role. His ornamentation almost always involves a re-writing of the common chord, or else a bridging across it in the manner of his Italian contemporaries. Sometimes—as in the *F minor Fantasia*—he makes his ornamentation take on a structural function in the old German sense, as Beethoven did, by subjecting it to the influence of Baroque polyphony. Mozart's ornamentation is 'melody-in-miniature', saturated through and through with *bel canto*, and appearing at its most colourful in the reprises of his slow movements. His romance-themes, with repeated notes, almost always develop round the common chord, and Mozart maintains a most careful balance by having their small intervals move fast and their larger ones more slowly. (Some of these movements are actually called 'Romances', as in the *D minor Piano Concerto* [K.V. 466] and *Eine kleine Nachtmusik* [K.V. 525], whilst others convey the same sort of feeling, e.g., the slow movement of the *C minor Piano Concerto*, the *String Quintet in E flat major* and Belmonte's B flat major aria.) The melody-type based on the common chord plainly belongs here too: it moves from the lower fifth via the tonic to the third, and is generally used by Mozart as an introductory theme (as in several operas). This is how it appears at the beginning of *Bastien et Bastienne*, *Il rè pastore*, *Entführung*, and in the development section of the first movement of the *F major Piano Sonata*, K.V. 332. (It is interesting that most are C major melodies, which would seem to indicate that the type is closely bound up with tonality.) Others, and these include the great *cantabile* melodies such as the Serenade and Canon in *Così fan tutte* and the canon's closely related forerunner in the finale of the *E flat major Piano Concerto* [K.V. 482], show the waves of energy alternately massing together and then spreading out in release. In all three themes, the spreading out process is represented by a broken descending 6/4 common chord [Ex. No. 97 (a)—(d)]. In other places, at the beginnings of melodies, it is the repeated dominant[5] which provides a springboard for the ascending broken chord [Ex. No. 97 (e)—(j)]:

Mozart: **a)** Così fan tutte, Act II   **b)** *Ibid.*: Act II, Finale

c) *Cp.*Violin Sonata in F major,   **d)** Piano Concerto in E flat major (K.V.
  1st movt. coda (K.V. 547)   482) 3rd movt. (Andantino cantabile)

e) Divertimento in   **f)** Piano Concerto (Coronation) in
  D major (K.V. 251)   D major (K.V. 537)

g) Piano Concerto in C minor   **h)** Quintet for Winds and Piano
  (K.V. 491)   (K.V. 452)

i) Piano Sonata in C major ·   **j)** Concert aria, "Non temer, amato bene"
  (K.V. 330)   (K.V. 505)

The elements involved in this alternating surge of ebb and flow, gathering and release, take on quite another aspect in Beethoven's conception of form and movement. Earlier on we noticed that Beethoven favoured two types of theme[6]: the first swings up in a broad sweep from the common chord (e.g., the chief themes of the *Appassionata* and the *Ninth Symphony*, the finale of the *E flat major Piano Concerto*); the second type is an *espressivo* melody which barely goes beyond a few adjacent notes (e.g., the principal theme of the *Chorphantasie* and the *Ode an die Freude*, which is derived from it, the Andante in the third movement of the *Ninth Symphony*, and the second theme in the finale of the *G major Piano Concerto*). Sometimes these two types appear together with remarkable effect, either in the same melody or else in close conjunction, as in the Benedictus of the *Missa solemnis*, or the beginning of the late *String Quartet in E flat major* (op. 127). Mozart and Beethoven were both given to constant re-working of their themes. The thematic material of Mozart's famous fugue in the finale of the *Jupiter Symphony*—so emphatic, yet curiously Gregorian—was re-worked no less than ten times in various works from his youth upwards. Beethoven too finds it extremely important to make frequent returns to the same theme, thereby achieving an even clearer and more pungent statement of his thought. The process is familiar enough in the case of the Leonora themes, the thematic material of the *Fifth Symphony*, and the *Ode an die Freude*, but less familiar elsewhere. In some of his later works, a particularly important role is played by the melody-type with a restricted compass:

98

Beethoven: a) Cello Sonata, Op. 102, No. 1 (Andante)

b) String Quartet, Op. 135, 3rd movt.   c) Piano Sonata, Op. 10, No. 3
(Lento assai)   '(Largo e mesto)

The fact that these melodies occur so frequently may help to explain why some of his older themes come to look the same in his later works. It explains for instance how and why the lilting, idyllic theme of the *Sixth Symphony* is able to merge into the mysterious message of the *Ninth :*

99

Beethoven:
a) Sixth Symphony, 2nd movt.   b) Ninth Symphony, 3rd movt.
(teneramente, dolce cantabile)   (cantante e tranquillo)

For Beethoven's thematic types originate in many places and like Mozart's before him, gather up the results of the 18th century. Their sphere of action is perhaps more limited, yet for that very reason the themes interact with all the more consistent and tenacious intensity.

The most striking melody-type to be found in his early works is the ardent 'bayonet motive', a resolute, rebellious and even aggressive call to action. This is heroic and bellicose marching-music, loudly proclaiming the vigour of the Empire; obvious examples are the opening of the *C minor Trio*, op. 1, the *E flat major String Trio,* op. 3, and even more important, the second subject, last theme, of the first movement of the *Second Symphony,* and the *Kreutzer Sonata* :

100

Beethoven: a) Second Symphony

b) Kreutzer Sonata

etc.

Just as characteristic is the festal 'Processional Motive', which occurs in his later works, from the *First Rasumovsky Quartet* to the great *B flat major Trio* :

101

Beethoven: a) String Quartet, Op. 59 No. 1

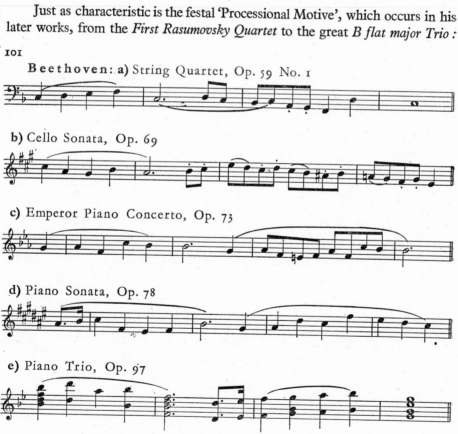

b) Cello Sonata, Op. 69

c) Emperor Piano Concerto, Op. 73

d) Piano Sonata, Op. 78

e) Piano Trio, Op. 97

But the new 'sentimental' approach also finds its most complete expression in his 'humanity' melodies—in *Fidelio*, for example:

102

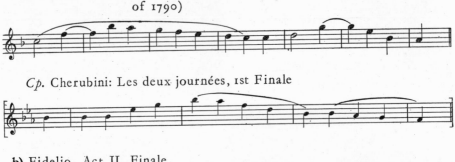

B e e t h o v e n: **a)** Fidelio, Act II, Finale (occurs in an earlier cantata of 1790)

Cp. Cherubini: Les deux journées, 1st Finale

b) Fidelio, Act II, Finale

Es   sucht   der Bru - der   sei - ne   Brü -   der

His melodies on common chords are related either to Haydn or to Cherubini. His famous *parlando* motives (in fantasias and scherzos), on the other hand, are connected with C. P. E. Bach and Clementi:[7]

103

a) C. P. E. B a c h: Adagio assai from the "Probesonate" No. 5 (1753)

b) *Idem:* Andante from "Preussische Sonate" in F major (1742)

144

c) Clementi: Allegro from the sonata "Didone abbandonata," Op. 50, No. 3

diliberando e meditando

During the period of the *C sharp minor Sonata*, these themes lie somewhere between C.P.E. Bach and Chopin. His 'shooting' and 'whirling' themes, on the other hand, are indebted to Hassler, Rust and the Mannheim School, while some of his slow themes are reminiscent of Mozart (as in his early *E flat major Piano Trio*, or the broad 'humanity' themes of *Fidelio*, which are related to Sarastro's scenes in *Zauberflöte*). But the explosive way in which Beethoven sweeps away all melodic tradition in the *Eroica* assumes symbolical significance, and endows an ancient pastoral formula and a common-chord melody with entirely new meaning. From then onwards, with ever more insistence, Beethoven forsook 18th-century melodic idiom, and with it the classicism prevailing at the turn of century. But like Mozart in his later works, Beethoven still had to make one more encounter with history. Towards the end of their careers, both composens entered the realm of J.S. Bach, and this encounter changed the nature of their melodies.

Beethoven's dance-themes also play a distinctive part. With its alternation of tensed and relaxed rhythms, Beethoven's melody stands mid-way between the folk-style of Haydn and Schubert. After Beethoven—and indeed after Mozart as well—Schubert seems to make a sudden and deliberate return to the countrified, provincial quality of Haydn. For Schubert was simpler and more 'sentimental' than either Beethoven or Mozart, although he was influenced by Mozart's tender and mysterious side (for instance, in the *E flat major Piano Trio*), and learnt much from Beethoven about the expression of loneliness and nostalgia, though little of tense, combative effort. His milder temperament, and his reluctance to brood and analyse, distinguished him from Haydn too; melody was always his salvation, that happy yet melancholy cast of folkish lyricism which runs through his entire output. In Schubert, the Viennese melody-style came back full-circle: setting out with the young Haydn, it returned with Schubert's premature death. What it had lost of Haydn's local colour it regained in Schubert's, and between them lay a whole universe.

For whether he realised it or not, Schubert never failed to pay homage to local colour, the sweet sadness of his native landscape, the 'golden melancholy' of Vienna. Hints of it had occurred here and there in Haydn's early works, but they had never been stressed. All of a sudden, marches and *ländlers* came to the fore—graceful march-rhythms finishing in an Austrian folk-cadence on the third, and *ländlers* with long-drawn-out codas and repeated snatches of melody.

(The key and tempo of the repetitive second-subjects in the first movements of both the *B minor* [*Unfinished*] *Symphony* and the *C major String Quintet* provide striking examples. The markings *noch einmal* and *immer wieder* seem to be characteristic of gentle, irresolute and lyrically gifted temperaments, and appear just as often in J. C. Bach's sonatas as they do in Schubert's.) Schubert's most natural idiom is a steady marching-pace, to be found in both his vocal and his instrumental music:

104
Schubert: a) "Winterreise," I

b) Impromptu, Op. 90, No. 1

c) Symphony in C major, 1st movt.

d) String Quintet in C major, 1st movt.

These themes show a natural fluctuation between major and minor; the 'Viennese third' is their natural ornament, and their normal contrast a tragic sound which is transformed into a plaintive game. Even the rhythm of the funeral march is soothed and uplifted by a soft, mysterious dance-rhythm which 'smiles through its tears':

105
Schubert: a) Piano Trio in E flat major, 2nd movt.

b) String Quintet in C major
c) String Quartet in A minor

146

d) String Quartet in G major

This is the highly distinctive swan-song of Viennese classicism. One step more, and it sinks into occasional music of restricted, local significance. In Schubert however there is still a connecting link which is strong and unbroken—or at any rate still taut. Schubert's melodies still have the power to evoke a lost wonder. The language of universals and a genuine art-form emerge from a single detail or the turn of a phrase. Yet these melodies also make it clear that the wonder is at an end; they already belong to Romanticism as well. In 1828, when Schubert died, the Romantic movement had half a century of masterpieces at which to gaze inbewildered amazement. These masterworks represented a completion and a self-sufficiency, and further development along the same lines was no longer possible.

*

To turn for a moment to see what has become of 18th-century melody. Seldom has any period had such clear notions about ideal music and musical thinking. Hence it is all the more surprising—though not contradictory—to find two sets of melodic theory coexisting—one French and one Italian, one 'intellectual' and the other 'emotional'. The famous theory of *affekt* claimed that melody should be capable of representing definite states of mind in a pictorial and formula-like way. It would have liked to tabulate the various kinds of mood and pace in terms of equations and dictionary definitions. The aesthetics of the period began to feel less sure when thinking in terms of type began to lose its hold, when belief in classified lists of mood and movement no longer gripped the imagination. Yet the eager search after the exact representation of accurately defined feelings went on. Melody took a long time to free itself of theory; every category was well entrenched—as well the rationalistic melody of Rococo as Rousseau's, and the folkish type of the 'back to nature' trend. Melody was also beset by other dangers, and the best composers were the worst offenders. Rameau announced that "harmony comes first, then melody", and even Gluck, busy searching for a universal language in music, declared that melody should be like colour in a drawing, that is, with a subsidiary function. Melody was not of course the strong point of either composer, yet they were representing the normal French standpoint in what they were saying.

This rational and theoretical outlook was directly opposed to the view of the Italian composers, who approached music through their senses. Metastasio considered that melody needed a clear, flowing line (memories of Mancini's *cantabile sia la cantilena!*), an idea which was also stressed by Galuppi and others. Later on Mozart too came out in support of the Italian outlook, with its insistence on clear, shapely line. He never made a definite statement about it, even in the most communicative of his early letters; O'Kelly was probably the sole ear-witness of his remark that "Melody is the essence of all music."[8] Yet even at this early stage there are many scattered comments in his letters which make his views clear (e.g., in a letter from Paris, he reproves the composer Anton Schweitzer for never learning to write properly for the voice). Later on he made what was virtually a declaration of principle, if for his word 'music' we read 'melody': the 'music' of one of Osmin's arias was running through his head, although not a line of the text had been written, and the text of Belmonte's A major aria "could scarcely have been better written for the music" (kaum besser für die Musik geschrieben werden können). This is what he means when he says in reference to the Italian operas that the text must obediently follow the 'music'. The 'music' should not only be beautiful, it should also predominate (meaning of course that it was the sort of melody that could assume dramatic significance). In this sense Mozart assumed his heritage, instantly raising it to the level which allowed for fusion with the artistic achievements of more northern parts of Europe.

This merging of styles only lasted during Mozart's lifetime, and even then did not survive the whole classical period. From South European music Mozart took over the idea of '*stofflichkeit*', by which is meant the close connection between melody and instrument, and clear associations of tone-quality, tone-colour and time-duration. The ideal sound of the 18th century was a luminous and uniform brilliance. It was the secret of the success of the *castrati* during the first half of the period, and, in the second half, of the 'sunny' melodies in high registers by Hasse, J. C. Bach, Piccinni and Mozart. It was here that 'substantialised' musical sound originated. For to discover its full stature, a melody depends on more than mere line; it needs colour too. It needs a cultural setting, in which the sound, the single note, and even the very timbre, with all its concrete associations, can become the object of detailed care and attention; in a word, it needs Rococo. Take, for instance, a melody which can only expand on a clarinet, in slow tempo, in A major, and round about top D; such a melody depends for its inspiration on a definite register, tempo, key, rhythm and instrument. Every melody needed its own key-colour, and every key its own type of melody. A Mozart melody in E flat major could never be mistaken for one in C major or D major. In this respect, Mozart's melodic style marks one long steady progress, and he seems to have had the same attitude from the outset: he generally takes over borrowed melodies in their original keys. The distinctive appearance of his themes is directly opposed to the fugal and elaborating styles, which depend for their working on ambiguity, transposition and minute dissection of the melody. Mozart did not feel at home in either type; for him they were long-winded and laborious methods of procedure.[9] An abrupt halt was called to the indifference of Northern Baroque for material problems of space, time and substance. Even Haydn was aware of the close relationship between gradations of pace and melodic texture—while for Mozart it was nothing less than axiomatic.

It is all the more surprising that the close connection was once again severed after Mozart's day. Beethoven's development sets melody free of the fabric of sound of which it was woven; his latest works almost reach the realm of disembodied sound. It is music which is close to J. S. Bach, the self-same point from which J. C. Bach and the Italian composers once set out towards Mozart.

Schubert's melodies then add a new element. They make instruments sound vocal, and blur the dividing-line. Their deepest magic lies in the fact that they constantly hover between embodied and disembodied sound, that they can fit voices as well as instruments, fit into a closed or an open form. In Mozart's later works, the symmetrical, enclosed melody of Rococo becomes progressively freer, until total liberation is reached in Beethoven's last string quartets; while Schubert's melody soars freely, and is only enclosed with difficulty.

Rhythm appears to follow the same course. Viennese classical music had almost parted company with Rococo dance-ideals, perhaps for the very fact that it originated with Germanic composers. Grétry's dance-rhythms had much less influence than the symphonic conceptions of Stamitz. Even Haydn, with his strong predilection for dance-movement, and Schubert, the most Viennese of all, gave dance a symphonic character which was most un-dancelike, and which tended to develop and stylise the melody, wrapping it in broad folds. Gluck, Mozart and Beethoven were probably all indebted to the colourful, pulsating rhythms of both the courtly and 'sentimental' types of French comic opera,

106

a) **Rousseau**: Le devin du village (1752)

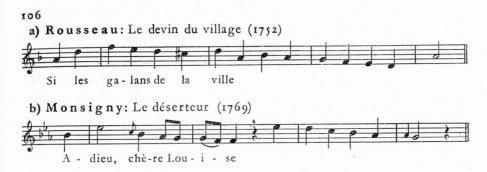

Si les ga - lans de la ville

b) **Monsigny**: Le déserteur (1769)

A - dieu, chè-re Lou - i - se

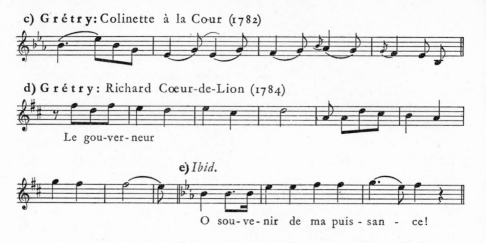

c) Grétry: Colinette à la Cour (1782)

d) Grétry: Richard Cœur-de-Lion (1784)

Le gou-ver-neur

e) *Ibid.*

O sou-ve-nir de ma puis - san - ce!

yet the luminousness of the original rhythms has vanished in all three. For Gluck, dance formed part of the drama, for Mozart it was a spontaneous expression of life, while in Beethoven it was used to celebrate the Dionysian liberation of man. It was made into drama, raised to the height of poetry, or transformed into a vision. Rococo dance had nothing in common with all this. It only wanted to be itself, a rhythmical physical movement in a fixed beat or pattern—nothing else. What followed was quite inevitable: Classicism caught up with dance, took what it had to offer, then cast it aside. Once abandoned, Classicism never returned to it. The marches in *Zauberflöte*, in Beethoven's last works and Schubert's sonatas were already trying to restrict rhythms which knew no limitations. Asymmetry made a return to symmetrical patterns quite inevitable.

The feeling for a general sense of proportion grew stronger in other composers too, particularly towards the end of the classical period. Haydn and Mozart absorbed into their music the cult of fantasias and minor keys—the melancholy, fervour and pre-romantic restlessness characteristic of Vanhal and C.P.E. Bach. The fact that Haydn and Mozart reached a vital turning-point in their relationship to Romanticism at the same time (1772—1773) served to show how far both had gone in adopting minor and chromatic keys. Later, they both redressed the balance: Haydn's *Symphony in E minor* and *Sonata in C minor* are as little related to his later music as the early *Symphony in G minor* (K.V. 183) and the small *String Quartet in D minor* (K.V. 173) can be said to represent Mozart. Their melodies came to fruition under the sign of diatonicism, and were always more faithful to the major than the minor. Yet minor and particularly chromatic music were pointers to the ever-present crises of Romanticism lurking in the background of Mozart's music, showing themselves even in the last change of style which led to the great revolutionary masterpieces of 1788—1789. Even here, diatonicism was victorious, succeeding in re-establishing balance and harmony—but how many chromatic currents of doubt and despair lurked in the shadowy depths! Even the lofty, sunlit grandeur of his last melodies are suddenly overshadowed by looming, menacing darkness. Mozart's *Organ Fantasy in F minor*, a work which comes very close to Beethoven—and late Beethoven at that—is the best indication of the period's change of feeling. It is a case of the swing of the evolutionary pendulum. First a melody with an individual, personal quality emerges from a melody-type. This is then refined to the point of becoming impersonal, and so reverts to type, or rather gives rise to a higher type. So it is that typical structural devices appear by a parallel process in both Mozart and Beethoven, apparently stimulated by similar processes of thought. These include building by means of a single theme (monothematic construction) and development by variation. J. S. Bach lies at the back of them both, yet 1789 and 1825 are both so far away from Bach! Between Bach on the one hand and Mozart and Beethoven on the other there yawns the gulf of a whole period which had totally submerged Bach's modes of thought and expression. But the laws of evolutionary growth are stronger than the passage of time, and the three composers join hands over the centuries.

*

Here to conclude are some typical melody-patterns of the period. They are melodic commonplaces, or 'wandering-themes' which symbolise the great change in outlook—the trend towards a personal mode of expression, and its opposite. They represent in essence a whole half-century of classical development. Mozart's youthful works are full of these Rococo types, and scarcely anything else. Whenever he needs melodies to start or finish a work, or provide a connecting link, he turns like a good pupil to the general supply of vocal and instrumental *bel canto*:

107

a) J. C. Bach: Sonata in G major (1765)

b) *Idem*: Sonata in C minor (1779)

c) F. di Majo: Ifigenia (1762)

d) *Ibid.*

e) Paisiello: La bella molinara (1788)

f) Galuppi: Marchese villano (about 1770)

g) Gassmann: La casa di campagna (1773)

They take on quite another aspect in his later works, or at least appear with altered stress and compass. Beethoven's development may have been more independent, but it was slower. Mozart at eighteen had already reached the stage Beethoven reached at thirty or thirty-two, so far as invention and a personal melodic style were concerned. But Beethoven's development is probably the more significant from the standpoint of melodic history. At twenty-two he stepped out of the South-German atmosphere of his youth into the classicism of the century's close. There, in the 1790's, he was greeted by the later works of Haydn and Mozart, and parted company with them after two great shattering changes of style, in 1803 and 1816.

The social art-form of the period was *par excellence* the concerto. The concerto-melodies of both Mozart and Beethoven reveal their attitude to society, and also their relationship to the general supply of melodic patterns. Rococo tradition only prescribed, for example, the rhythmical outline of the *siciliano*, and this had held good from the time of Vivaldi and Porpora. Mozart's lovely *siciliano* in the *Piano Concerto in A major* (K.V. 488) already constituted a daring exception. Its restrained use of the broken chord and the plaintive sound of broken sixths produce not merely a diffused feeling of melancholy, but an effect of improvisation as well; particularly is this true when the almost unreal quality of the Neapolitan is unexpectedly evoked by the common chord. The *siciliano* theme in Beethoven's *5th Piano Concerto (Emperor)* contains so much concentrated contrast that it gives the impression of being an innovation. The broad opening is at once followed by a characteristic chromatic passage starting at the sixth—Beethoven's pet degree of the scale for change or camouflage. The expansion that follows is even broader:

108
  a) M o z a r t : Piano Concerto in A major (Andante)

  b) B e e t h o v e n : Piano Concerto in E flat major (Rondo)

One step further, and the fate of one of the period's melody-types, the dotted march-rhythm, can be observed. Mozart and Beethoven use it as closing themes in their piano concertos:

109
  a) M o z a r t : Piano Concerto in A major, 1st movt.

b) Beethoven: Piano Concerto in G major, 1st movt.

These melodies are so saturated with personal feeling that their subject-matter cannot be further individualised. But they appear at the height of the trend, and are immediately followed by an ever-growing cult of impersonal ideas. Those tapping, insistent *fugato* themes with repeated notes, which appear as second subjects in the slow movements of Mozart's *C major String Quartet* and the *E flat major Symphony* (K.V. 543), seem to herald a change of style. Yet for Mozart there is really nothing new. He has two basic themes, two 'timeless' melodies which accompany him the whole of his life. One is a Gregorian credo-type theme, with its symbolical tetrachord. As we have seen, Mozart re-worked this theme in ten works, symphonic, sacred and chamber in type.[10] Its fullest statement is in the finale of the great *C major Symphony* (the *Jupiter*), and it is at its most mysterious in the slow movement of the *G minor Symphony* where it looms up in a shadowy, ominous way, divided up amongst the strings of the orchestra (E flat, F, A flat, G). It is a theme with a long ancestry: amongst Mozart's stylistic predecessors it occurs in certain Flemish composers, and later in Alessandro Scarlatti, Josef and Michael Haydn, and even in Bach (*Wohltemp. Klav.* II, fugue in E major); after Mozart it appears in Schubert (*F major Mass*, 1814). Here Mozart enters Bach's magic circle, and there is no escape from it.[11] His other theme, which he also has in common with Bach, is the descending minor pentachord, which drops from the dominant to the tonic, or beyond it to the leading-note. He continually returns to this theme—and not only he, but Beethoven too. It is a figure which accompanies him from the early *D minor String Quartet* (K.V. 173) and the *A minor Piano Sonata* (K.V. 310) to the *adagio* introduction of the finale in the *G minor String Quintet* (K.V. 516) and Pamina's G minor aria, *Ach ich fühl's*. When Beethoven quotes it in the *Arioso dolente* of the late 'great' *A flat major Sonata* (1821)—and already in essence at the end of the *C sharp minor Sonata*—he seems to be looking back a whole century, beyond Mozart's re-evocation to Bach's *Es ist vollbracht* in the *St. John Passion*.

With these works we reach the great fugal themes of Mozart's and Beethoven's polyphonic works. They are themes of extreme austerity and concentration, and come to life in both composers as a result of strict polyphonic treatment. That well-known fugue with the leap of a seventh which is found in Handel's oratorios (*Israel in Egypt, Messiah,* and *Joseph*) and the *Wohltemperiertes Klavier,* may have found its way into the *Kyrie* of Mozart's *Requiem* with the help of Haydn (*String Quartet in F minor,* op. 20, No. 5), or Mozart may have taken it over directly, without an intermediary. Another fugal theme from the *Messiah* (with a double descending sixth) takes on a new lease of life at the end of the *Missa Solemnis (Dona nobis pacem)*, and Beethoven's *String Quartet in C sharp minor* (1826) opens with a fugue which is closely related to Bach in every respect. Yet it is recreated in Bach's spirit rather than copied, and appears to testify to its lineage in an episode which actually stems from Bach:

110

a) B e e t h o v e n : String Quartet in C sharp minor, Op. 131

b) B a c h : Organ Fugue in G minor

c) B a c h : B minor fugue from the Well-Tempered Clavier

Mozart had already revived this episode in his *G minor Piano Fugue* (1782) and Beethoven uses it again in the last movement of op. 135. (Recent research has shown that Beethoven's last string quartets are linked together by hidden melodic filaments of *maqam* type.)

These impersonal, floating themes constitute a starting-point for highly elaborated styles of composition requiring the use of variation, a central, unifying idea, and building out of a single theme. They seem to signify the last stage of the journey back to Bach, and both Mozart and Beethoven attempt it, albeit experimentally and full of doubt and hesitation. In the course of this arduous experiment, and at a distance of decades, the always experimenting Beethoven and the seldom-or-never experimenting Mozart meet each other as well as Bach. Mozart in some of his early works had already touched on mono-thematic construction, only to come back to the dualistic principle of sonata-form. But he took the plunge in some of his later works, and adopted the idea of the single main *motif*, summed up in the principle of *omnia ex uno*. (Examples are the two *D major String Quartets* of 1786 and 1789, and the overtures to *Così* and *Zauberflöte*, the first two with themes based on common chords, the second with generic melody-patterns, drawn from the central source of supply.) Even *Zauberflöte* itself illustrates this age-old device, since however much disguised, its themes are definitely recurrent. Haydn was drawn to this device in the

1790's, in some of his chamber-works and the last great *(London)* symphonies—
he generally liked to draw on the same thematic material for his first and second
themes; but as a rule he was drawn to two-theme and not single-theme structure. Beethoven waited until 1801 before re-evoking the central section of a sonata in its finale (op. 27, No. 1). The principle was even more marked in the
Fifth Symphony, and in 1815—1816 he twice attempted to combine extensive
sonata-form with the idea of the recurrent motive (in the *C major 'Cello Sonata*
and the *A major Piano Sonata*). He seems to have come nearer to solving the
problem in the last fervid series of variations and fugues. In the great *Sonata
in A flat major* (op. 110, 1821) and the *C sharp minor String Quartet* (op. 131,
1826) strict unity is achieved by fusing the thematic material of the opening and
closing sections, and all the last chamber works seem to be linked together by
tenuous thematic filaments. In the *Great Fugue* for string quartet, the last piano
sonata and the variations of the *Ninth Symphony* a new process emerges. The
thematic discourse threads its way through the entire work, so that any sort of
transformation is possible. It is a melody-style which seems to burst out of its
frame in just the same way that Beethoven burst through the framework of
classical music.

Yet further work along these lines was out of the question, for Viennese
classicism had exhausted the century's evolutionary potential. The new West
European style which showed signs of life about 1820 had a radiant new
quality of sound with which its elders were quite unfamiliar. It was as if some
long-lost magic needed to be re-evoked, and Romanticism was the one to rediscover the buried treasure.

NOTES

1. All contemporary travellers are agreed that Vienna was an international meeting-place.
"Here one can see people from every part of the globe," wrote Von Loen about 1720,
"Hungarians, Hussars, Haiduks, Poles, Moscovites, Persians, Turks, Moors, Spaniards,
Italians, Tyrolese, Swiss, from every nation in Europe, in short . . . Nowhere else in the
world can be seen such variety of national costume and manner of dress." Or as Montes-
quieu wrote in 1728: "There are so many foreigners here that to be a foreigner is to be ac-
counted a native of the place." Paris used to be described in this way (and so were ancient
Athens and Alexandria, according to Strabo and Philostratus).
2. Related melodies occur in J. C. Bach (Overture in B flat major to *Temistocle* and to *Lucio
Silla*, respectively, 1772, 2nd movt.).
3. E.g. the themes in the finales of Beethoven's *Pastoral Symphony* and *Violin Concerto*, or in
the Largo of Haydn's *Symphony in D major*, No. 93, 1791 (a). But Haydn nearly always gives
a quiet, homely gaiety to his folk-like themes built on the common chord, as in the closing
section of this Largo (b):

(M. Pincherle in *A. Vivaldi*. Paris, 1948, I, p. 131 maintains that the opening themes of more than twenty Haydn symphonies are based on broken common chords.) This clearly harmonic form of major melody gives rise to the use of double turns for melody-openings, much favoured by Boccherini, Haydn and Clementi between 1770 and 1790. They treat the keynote of the chord like a central pillar, and cling to it either from above or below:

Quite a different kind of energy is released when the arpeggio of the common chord is coloured by the change of harmony. There are many examples amongst Mozart's broadly lyrical themes, the most obvious being his slow themes in G and D major from the mid-1780's:

a) Piano Concerto in G major, K.V. 453, 2nd movt.
b) *Ibid.*
c) Sonata for Two Pianos in D major, K.V. 448, 2nd movt.
d) Terzetto 'Mi lagnerò tacendo,' K.V. 437

4. For 18th-century German melody, see amongst others L. Riedinger's excellent thematic type-index of Dittersdorf: *Studien zur Musikwissenschaft* (Supplement of the D. T. Ö.) II, 1914, pp. 330—335. For the classical type of Viennese *lied* as opposed to the 'motive-spinning' technique of Late Baroque, see particularly W. Fischer: *Zur Entwicklungsgeschichte des Wiener klass. Stils*, in the series quoted, III, 1915, as well as the same author's critical appendix to A. Schnerich's book on Haydn (2nd ed., 1926).

5. The important role played by the dominant in the 18th-century melody is well illustrated by the minuet in Boccherini's *D major String Quartet* (1769), op. 6, No. 1, where Ex. 30 (a) is given in its repeated form as (b). Another example is the Scherzo-Trio (c) of Cherubini's *D major Symphony* (1815):

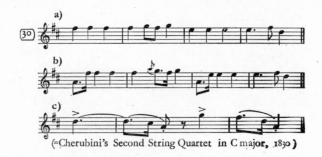

(=Cherubini's Second String Quartet in C major, 1830)

6. For Beethoven's handling of this double aspect (which even occurs within a single theme) see S. Jadassohn: *Das Wesen der Melodie in der Tonkunst*. Leipzig, 1899, p. 8. For another characteristic feature (climax occurring in the 6th bar of 8-bar melodies), see *ibid*. pp. 94—98. For similarities between the melodic structure of Mozart and Beethoven, see W. Danckert: *Ursymbole melodischer Gestaltung*. Kassel, 1932, pp. 122—158. For differences, see D. Bartha: *Beethoven*. 1938, pp. 95—124 (in Hungarian); A. Molnár: *Musical Aesthetics*. II (1942, Hung. mss.).

7. See study by G. de Saint-Foix in *Musical Quarterly*, 1931, entitled "Clementi, a Precursor of Beethoven." For the *parlando* style of C.P.E. Bach and others, see Bartha's cited work, pp. 76—77; A. Schering: "C.P.E. Bach und das redende Prinzip in der Musik." *Peters-Jahrbuch*. 45, 1938.

8. Haydn held the same view, if we are to believe Carpani (*Le Haydine*. 1812) and Stendhal (*Lettres écrites de Vienne*. 1814). ("Melody is the soul and the magic of music ... discover a beautiful melody, and your music will be beautiful ...", etc.)

9. It is however worth mentioning that Mozart's own contemporaries held quite another view of his melodies. The adherents of the Italian school considered them to be over-orchestrated, whereas most Germans thought of him as the 'audacious creator of unusual melodies' (e.g., the musicologist Ernst Ludwig Gerber, even as late as 1813). The theorists of the Age of Reason considered most of his music to be 'irregular and shapeless', 'an outrage to the ear' and 'crude'. They even accused him of being a musical *sansculotte* (e.g., Zelter, Sarti, Naumann, etc.). For the general aspects of his melody-style, see W. Siegmund-Schultze: *Mozarts Melodik und Stil*. Leipzig, 1957.

10. Mozart's works referred to here: *Symphony in E flat major* (K.V. 16, 1764), *Tantum ergo in D major* (K.V. 197, 1772), *F major Mass* (K.V. 192, 1774), *C major Mass* (K.V. 257, 1776), *B flat major Symphony* (K.V. 319, 1779), *E flat major Violin Sonata* (K.V. 481, 1785), *B flat major Divertimento for 2 clarinets and bassoon* (K.V 439 b, and Wyzewa-Saint-Foix, No. 535, *4th Divertimento*, 1st movt., 1783), *C major Symphony* (K.V. 551, 1788), also *G minor Symphony* (K.V. 550, 1788, 2nd movt., disguised), *D major Fugue for Orchestra*, fragment (K.V. 291—variant), and *G major String Quartet* (K.V. 387, 1782, last movt., variant). *Cp.* Abert: *Mozart*. I, p. 374, II. p. 585 and Wyzewa-Saint-Foix: *Mozart*. 1936, I, p. 464, II, p. 154. Also C. Schneider: "F. H. von Biber als Opernkomponist." *Archiv. f. Musikwiss*. VIII (1926), p. 337. The principal theme of the *Recordare* in the *Requiem* should perhaps be included as a hidden variant. One of the most important re-workings of the four-note Gregorian hymn is A. Scarlatti's *C major Mass*, dedicated to Pope Clement XI.

11. Handel's influence went even deeper. See Walther Siegmund-Schultze: "W. A. Mozart unter dem Einfluss G. F. Händels." *Händel-Jahrbuch*, 1956, pp. 21—56.

THE ROMANTIC MELODY

"In music, there are two ways of arriving at pleasure, by
way of Haydn's style or by way of Cimarosa's: by sublime harmony or delightful melody. Cimarosa's style is
right for southern peoples . . . Melody reached its zenith
about 1780; after this date, music changed its nature,
harmony won the upper hand, and the singing line de-
clined." (Stendhal: *Rome, Naples et Florence.* 1817)

"You must invent daring new melodies." (Schumann)

Classical melody at the height of its development, between 1780 and 1800, was
the most plastic, poised yet flexible of phenomena. One has only to think of
Mozart's masterpieces, which gathered into themselves the essence of a whole
cultural epoch, so that they shine out for a space like a beacon-light of human
achievement:

III

Mozart: Andante from Sonata in C major for Piano Duet (1787)
(K.V. 521)

There is no doubt that this represents a type: a familiar variant of the melody appears in the late *String Quartet in B flat major* (K.V. 589), where it is the chief theme of the Larghetto. The closing theme of the first movement of the *Jupiter* is a more prosaic dance-type variant which stems from the same source. However different the individual shape, definite signs of kindred and affinity are still apparent in similar modes of expression, a similar pitch of emotional tension, the same kind of tone-colour and rhythm. As a type it is as closed and self-contained as a lyric poem, a single act in a play, or a whole symphony movement; witness its almost song-like four-line structure, its matching line-endings, and the clear, balanced symmetry of its melody-lines. A historian is also aware that it is a 'sentimental romance melody' of the type which flourished in French opera during the 1780's, and won popularity in German classical music by being adopted by Mozart in his maturity. (The Andante quoted above is clearly constructed as a 'romance' movement, like its counterpart, the slow movement of the *D minor Piano Concerto*.)

How, and in what ways, is it possible for a balanced entity of this sort—expressive, polished, and vitally articulated in its minutest part—to be 'broken up' and reshaped? The ways are numerous. Certain elements, e.g. rhythm, can be emphasised and exaggerated, others can be omitted, the climax can be displaced, and most important of all, a new factor—that of tone-colour—can be introduced. If the melody is imagined in a different tempo with different rhythm, in another register, and in a minor instead of a major key, it at once changes its character, and becomes one of the favourite melody-types of Romanticism. The chief difference is that the sunny tranquillity has disappeared.

Why did composers who grew up amongst peaceful, balanced melodies, show such a longing for movement, passion and colour? What was the cause of their uneasiness?

The static solution of melody implied a regular, fixed framework which in all probability no longer satisfied them. Their more restless nervous systems expected colour and movement, and slowly the entire melody was reshaped from this point of view. Melody conceived in terms of colour; of this Vivaldi, forerunner of all impressionists, had already provided examples, and Mozart gave it prime importance in his style by linking melody with a particular instrumental texture and quality of colour. Yet Mozart's melody, though drenched in colour, is fundamentally a linear art, and lives and moves in clear outlines. But by the turn of the century, aesthetic values were changing their meaning to such an extent that melody's 'atmospheric' elements were all being used exclusively to provide tone-colour. Mozart has relatively few examples (the *Siciliano* in the *A major Piano Concerto*, and the Statue's utterance in *Don Giovanni*). The use of tone-colour as a structural device did in fact give rise to a significant new trend, which seems to have made its first appearance in Lesueur,

Méhul, and Weber. It is interesting that both Méhul and Weber made it their business to stress colour-values throughout their output. They wrote entire operas in which they assiduously avoided bright tone-colour (e.g. *Peter Schmoll*, 1803, *Uthal*, 1806). Many of Chopin's melodies are conceived entirely in terms of colour, and Schumann's request to composers to invent 'daring new melodies' was primarily a request for melodies in colour, that is, completely new and romantic. There was also another factor which was constantly gaining ground in this renewal of the spirit and content of melody—the element of movement, the dynamic upthrust contained in a melodic phrase. The opening theme of the Mozart melody quoted proceeds from its lower fifth to the tonic, and then rises to the third, from which point it returns to its starting-point. In this respect it is related to Beethoven's early type of Andante, found in the slow movements of the *First*, *Second* and *Fifth Symphonies*. Mozart, Haydn and Beethoven were all familiar with its minor form, too, as in the minuet of *Mozart's G minor Symphony* and the 'tragic' Minuet of the *Haffner Serenade*. In Haydn's *Symphony* No. 95 *in C minor* (1791) it becomes the kernel of the minuet, and in 1798 Beethoven made it a leading motif of the finale of the *Pathétique*. (The Minuet—or rather Scherzo—in G minor in Schubert's *5th Symphony* [1815] is also derived from it.) The minor form seems to have shown a strong dynamic impulse from the very outset, and it was natural enough that the 19th century should have turned it into a type. It is found as an evocative melody-symbol in the orchestral works of Mendelssohn and Wagner (e.g. *Scottish Symphony* and the 2nd Act of *Walküre*); in Donizetti (closing scene of *Lucia*) and even more strongly in Verdi (*Macbeth*, Act IV, *Forza del Destino*, Act IV, and the *Lacrymosa* in the *Requiem*), it becomes a typical opera-lament. In addition, it is worth noting that consciously or not, it is a re-evocation of an old chorale (*Wer nur den lieben Gott lässt walten*) :

112

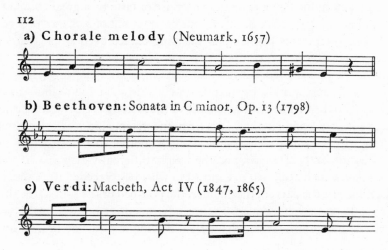

a) **C h o r a l e m e l o d y** (Neumark, 1657)

b) **B e e t h o v e n**: Sonata in C minor, Op. 13 (1798)

c) **V e r d i**: Macbeth, Act IV (1847, 1865)

d) Verdi: La Forza del Destino, Act IV (1862)

e) Verdi: Requiem, Lacrymosa (1874)

A similar transformation can be observed in any classical melody that was taken over by Romanticism. Beyond a certain point composers could no longer be satisfied with the stress, outline, substance and construction of the older melody and its rhythmical impulse. So they were all displaced, and their meaning and purpose changed. The melody was constantly being broken up and reshaped in relation to the new demands. These demands may well have been barely conscious, but they brought with them a new, changed conception of tempo and dynamic pulse, a different grading of emotional intensity. Melody is a more conscious and civilised element of music than sheer rhythm, and as such obviously comes later in time, yet still belongs to the world of spontaneous feelings and passions . . . For this reason it is always quick—and even first in the field—to reveal the changed emotional outlook of a new generation, to mirror its tendencies, sense of period, and state of mind, as well as its attitude to the past and the immediate future. When it comes to the choice of rhythmical patterns, a trend may be determined just as surely by the preferences of a whole generation as by individual taste. The pace may even be set by purely social considerations. But where the essential substance of a melody is concerned, that is, the density of its texture, its symmetry and its articulation, the choice seems to be determined by a deliberate exercise of taste by a great composer, in relation to his own particular needs. A rule emerges out of a chance occurrence, and the composer seems to make an unerring choice even when there are a multitude of possibilities. A composer such as Mozart, for example, will choose from the stock of his predecessors and contemporaries the most humanised melody-types—i.e. the most expressive, intelligible and close to life—and then use and develop them. The entire meaning of the melody-style is transformed by this change in stress and rhythm. It is then understandable why other intervals are chosen, why the whole melody-line assumes another shape, why the melody-rhymes are differently arranged, and the weight differently disposed. It may be the *style galant* which is chosen in contrast to what has preceded it, or the 'sentimental'; it may be the curved, the angular, the polished or the rough; the rhythm may be vague or sharply defined, the melody repetitive or continually varied, decorative or functional. It may have rich, flowing lines, or be broken up into sections; it may be conceived for voices or instruments, embedded in its own harmony, or given a tonal—and even an atonal— framework. What matters is that the new melodic form always comes into existence as a living expression of a new ferment and sense of period, that it is a direct, forceful and often unveiled statement of new awareness, with all its desires, fears, joys and sorrows.

In this sense it is possible to assert that Romantic melody came into existence as a result of the French Revolution, or rather, that it owed its liberation to the French Revolution, for it had been waiting in the wings of European music since the 1770's, forced to make a temporary retreat before the powerful onrush of Classicism. About 1770, everything in European music was ready for Romanticism, but the musical *Sturm und Drang* embodied in C.P.E. Bach, Franz Beck, Schobert, Vanhal and Hassler was prevented from leading directly into High Romanticism as a result of the unexpected purification and clarification of style achieved by Gluck, Haydn and Mozart. Literary Pre-Romanticism was held up in just the same way by Goethe's Italian journey and his sudden turning to the authors of Greece and Rome. From the standpoint of today, it is of course easy to see that this pre-romantic music has a lack of sound and substance when compared with the many-voiced tornado of later High Romanticism (*c.* 1800); it is possible to unearth all the evidence which showed that both the period and society in general were unprepared to have great inner and outer crises expressed in artistic terms. Yet because such clear dividing-lines exist, it would be easy to overlook the potency of individual intervention—the influence, in other words, which can be exerted by a great artist or statesman. He may appear to put forward individual claims, or claims that are in opposition to the feeling of the entire period; but he is in fact only bowing to the deeper evolutionary laws of his period, and in so doing obeying his own. Beethoven's emergence is a most convincing proof of this, for his art liberated Romanticism as much as it held it up; he checked its progress as much as he sent it on its way. Gluck, Haydn and Mozart gradually suppressed Romanticism by polishing their own art to ever greater perfection; they took the wind out of its sails. Beethoven, on the other hand, slowly reintroduced it, and encouraged its development. From the *Eroica* onwards, and in particular in the song-cycle *An die ferne Geliebte,* he even outdid the Romantics in renewing 'without Romanticism' the musical language of his time. The Romanticism which was suppressed in 1770 was naturally very different from the Romanticism allowed back in 1810. Forty years of spiritual exile on the outer perimeter, and relegation to minor composers, had deepened and widened its basic self-awareness.

The chief characteristics of the new style—colour, excitement and expansiveness—first appeared in their new significance on the heels of the French Revolution. They showed in two critical decades, between 1795 and 1815, and were at their most powerful in the operas of Méhul. These operas were the direct predecessors of the great scenes in *Freischütz, Euryanthe,* and *Oberon,* and abound in recurrent situations of crisis and catastrophe, of escapes from dire and dreadful deaths. They show a new feeling for Nature and tend towards descriptions of their environment; they wax ecstatic about sunrises, volcanic eruptions, Alpine storms and sea-storms, deep forest magic and midnight spells. The operas of Méhul and some of his contemporaries bridge the gap between Gluck's classical French ardour and the typically 'northern' transport of Romanticism. So it is that the typically 'Latin' features of a German composer (Gluck) gradually change into the 'German' inspiration of a French one (Méhul!). It is no mere coincidence that it is Méhul who comes closest to Weber in the use of the *leitmotif ;* that his melody-style anticipates Beethoven's revolutionary ardour (in his marching themes and 'bayonet' motives), Weber and even Spontini. The impassioned and inspired 'dramatic motive ' and the purely descriptive 'nature theme' are constantly appearing in Méhul's operas *Mélidore et Phrosine* (1794), *Ariodant* (1798) and *Uthal* (1806):

113

Méhul: a) Mélidore, Act II (1794)

b) Ariodant, Act III (1798)

c) Uthal, Prelude (Forest-music) (1806)

Here, in embryo, is everything which will later develop into the turgid, dramatic melodies of late Romanticism. The basic mood of these melodies is almost always one of heroism, battle and excitement. They share the same tense upward flights, sudden springing leaps and occasional moments of exhaustion: the rolling, surging movement of an ocean breaker. The melody bursts out of its frame and becomes a line of movement, able to shoot up to the heights of ecstasy and make itself heard far beyond its natural limits. Weber's *Oberon* has some typical examples; one important type, presumably derived from Beethoven *(E flat major Concerto)*, appears in Wagner's operas, where it blazes up white-hot at the moment of rapture:

114
   a) **Weber**: Ocean aria from "Oberon" (1826)

   b) **Beethoven**: Piano Concerto in E flat major (1809)

   c) **Wagner**: Walküre, Act III (1856)

   d) **Wagner**: Tristan and Isolde, Act III (1859)

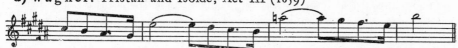

Wagner's great *Ring* motives almost all derive from this early romantic crucible of ever-restless, ever-extending melody, to which they owe their dramatic impetus. Other examples are the vehement principal theme of Brahms' *D minor Piano Concerto*, the various great melodic climaxes of Verdi and, even more obviously, of Liszt, who often depends on a broad, dramatic 'gesture theme' to open and develop his melody, and generally give it vitality:

115
   a) **Verdi**: Requiem, Offertorio (1874)

   b) **Verdi**: Othello, Act IV (1887)

165

c) Verdi: La Forza del Destino, Act II (1869)

d) Liszt: Faust Symphony, 2nd movt. (1854)

e) Liszt: Sursum Corda (1877)

This heroic rhetoric is clearly the century's deepest and most typical form of expression. It involves more of a hint and a symbol than concrete reality, more rapture than genuine involvement; it is more a paean of praise to feeling and destiny, than feeling and destiny in themselves. Yet it is more than just rhetorical speech; it rises to the intensity of real drama, it actually battles with destiny, but being theatrical and theatrically minded, it requires magnificently coloured backcloths! Liszt's *Sursum Corda* (1877) is a single dramatic gesture, that points upward with the harrowing poignancy of a 7th; nor is it mere chance that makes the basic pentatonic theme of *Les Préludes* (1850) echo on unchanged in César Franck's *D minor Symphony* (1889). The urgent pace and power of the single basic figure, underlining a whole composition, stimulate the creative imagination of the romantic composer, and goad him on to the end.

Even the softer and more lyrical style of melody, best described as *romantic bel canto*, are full of these dramatic gesturings. The dramatic gesture-melodies of the Romantics may in fact be regarded as the descendants of those of Baroque: the *belcanto-parlando* of Romanticism is a new form of *stile rappresentativo*. This is particularly true of Schumann's melodies, behind which can always be heard the pulse-beat of speech, diction and declamation (e.g. *Fantasy in C major*, the *A minor Piano Concerto*, the *E flat major Piano Quintet*, *Abendlied*, etc.):

116

Schumann: a) Piano Concerto, 1st movt. **b)** Piano Quintet,
(1841)　　　　　　　　　　　　　　1st movt. (1842)

c) "Abendlied" (for piano duet) (1849)

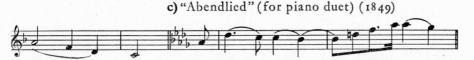

Berlioz and Liszt, too, often 'declaim' in this way. Liszt, for example, discovers a purely instrumental way of 'declaiming' Petrarch, whereas his settings of words are quite different from Schumann's 'dotted' type of declamation. In addition to the declamatory rhythm, which has its origin in the words, a yearning, open-form *lied* style characterises this particular kind of *bel canto*. Again, it is a form which owes its inspiration to the human voice, and one which allows ornamental figures (which are normally turns, etc.) to develop within an instrumental framework. The lyrical styles of Chopin, Berlioz, Liszt and Wagner are equally rich in relevant examples:

117
a) Chopin: Nocturne in F major (1834)

Cp. Field: Nocturne No. 1

b) Berlioz: Romeo and Juliet, Part III, Garden scene (1839)

c) Liszt: Sonata in B minor (1853)

Cp. Chopin: Nocturne in B major, Op. 9, No. 3

d) Wagner: Meistersinger, Act III (1867)

167

e) Chopin: Sonata in B minor, Op. 58, 3rd movt. (1845) (the belcanto line has been split up into ornaments)

Out of this 'breaking-up' of *bel canto* into instrumental ornaments springs one of the period's most typical and recurrent melodies, the one which in its descent describes a broken 6/4 line:

118

It has a 'home' quality about it, and threads its way through the entire 19th century like an almost continuous *maqam*, from Beethoven to Brahms and Verdi. Mozart uses it in the minuet of his *'Hunt' Quartet*, Beethoven in the slow movement of the *F major Violin Sonata;* Schubert uses it to express the demonic lure of the *Erlkönig* (at *Du liebes Kind*) but also the peaceful, evening atmosphere of the family home (in the *Schöne Müllerin*, in the song *Am Feierabend*, at the phrase *Euer Werk hat mir gefallen*); in Weber it expresses the naive joy of a child *(Der kleine Fritz an seine jungen Freunde);* Mendelssohn sets it at the head of his *Rondo Capriccioso;* in Brahms (*Sonatas in C major* and *F minor*, and *Waldeinsamkeit*) it describes the melancholy, intimate charm of Nature, quiet homecoming and rest. Wagner weaves it into Hans Sachs's *Abendmonolog (Dem Vogel, der heut sang . . .)* as an invocation to night, spring ecstasy and melancholy resignation. It would seem a typical German melody, but for its appearance in Chopin's *A flat major Ballade* and in the middle of the *Fantasy-Impromptu*, and we learn from Kleczynski that in the *Polonaise-Fantasy* (1846) Chopin used it to describe Poland's blissful patriarchal past. It is applied with equal authority by Cimarosa, Donizetti, Verdi and Puccini (2nd finale of the *Matrimonio Segreto*, *Don Pasquale*, tenor aria of Act II, the quartet in *Rigoletto*, the duet between Philip and Posa in *Don Carlos*, Act I, and the Manon-motive in the 1st Act of *Manon Lescaut*).[1] The melody-type does in fact span a whole century and encompasses the whole range of romantic lyrical emotion relating to happiness and homeland. (It also inspires the great baritone melodies of romantic opera, and stands for Kurwenal, Sachs, Posa and Simone Boccanegra.)

During the Romantic period, *maqams* of this type also recur in the evolution of individual composers. Schumann's development was accompanied by

C. D. Friedrich : The Moon is Rising (about 1820) — a typical landscape of German Romanticism.

the recurrent idea of the descending major sixth, which he took over from Beethoven's song-cycle *An die ferne Geliebte*. It appears in the *C major Fantasy*, the closing movement of the *F major String Quartet*, the last movement of the *C major Symphony*, the *Ländliches Lied* of the *Album für die Jugend* (1836—1848) and one of the *Frauenliebe und Leben* (*Süsser Freund*). The melody leaves the tonic with an upward leap of a third or fourth, then dips down to the lower sixth with a vigorous stress on the fourth. It manages to maintain its Beethovian character in spite of being tinged throughout with Schumann's personal idiom:

119

Schumann:a) Symphony in C major   **b)** Phantasy in C major
     (1846)   (1836)

c) String Quartet in F major   **d)** "Süsser Freund" (1840) from the song-
     (1842)   cycle "Frauenliebe und Leben"

e) "Wanderlied" (from "Liederreihe," 1840) *Cp*. **Mendelssohn:** Second
                                     Symphony (Hymn of Praise), 1840

Brahms' recurrent melody-idiom is even easier to trace. It is the 'home-melody' of Romanticism, described above, which on closer examination proves to be akin to Schumann's *maqam*, if the sixth is imagined a third higher; in other words, if it is taken as a 6/4 chord written out into the melody. Significantly enough, Brahms considered this melody to be a quotation: he sent it to Clara Schumann in a letter dated 12 September, 1868, as an alphorn melody (*also blus das Alphorn heut*)[2] and used it in his *First Symphony* to introduce the Allegro of the finale:

120

Hoch auf'm Berg, tief im Tal, grüss' ich dich   viel   tau-sendmal!

It occurs in many other of his works, and is a familiar theme of the *Violin Sonatas in A major* and *G major*, the slow movement of the *Violin Concerto*, and in *Lieder*, such as *Sapphische Ode* or *Waldeinsamkeit*. Its horn-like sound plays a part in all Brahms' melody-style, suggesting the horn's broken

169

chord, its register, and even its solemnity; witness the opening themes of the *G major String Sextet* and the *B flat major Piano Concerto*. In late-Romantic music it is presumably intended to evoke a real or imaginary closeness with Nature, the longing for familiar woodlands. But in a wider sense, it is a symbol of the endless, deep nostalgia with which urban civilisation pines for the freedom of Nature. Even decadent Western Romanticism was affected by it—Mahler's trumpet motives are a case in point. Yet Wagner's feeling for Nature shows no such attachment to music symbols, and his horn colouring—used from the time of Weber to evoke the magic of German forests—has quite a different quality from that of Brahms. It is associated with rising, not falling, melodic lines, and is only linked with the melancholy fall of Brahms' melodies in two very significant instances from *Meistersinger*. One of these is *Dem Vogel, der heut sang* from the end of Sachs' Monologue (mentioned above), and the other is *Huldreichster Tag*, at the end of the Prize Song, two melodies which appear in similar guise in Brahms. Brahms' *A major Sonata* may reasonably be described as the *Meistersinger* Sonata, and the Andante of the *F minor Piano Sonata* anticipates Hans Sachs' *Vogel* motif.

The exceptional attachment evinced by Romantic composers for repeated motives and *maqam* methods of thought seems to be bound up with the practice of variation, which during the 19th century had such a decisive role to play. The melody is responsible for shaping the whole form, and hence for renewing it as well. From the time of Beethoven's last works, the Romantics laid ever greater stress on the principle of construction by means of the single-theme, even applying it to the building of large forms. Beethoven's last sonatas and string quartets repeatedly exploit the idea of a common basic theme, a central unifying idiom; this method was continued by Schumann, in *Carneval* and the *Symphonic Studies*, and by Berlioz, in the *Fantastic Symphony* and *Harold in Italy*. Liszt arrived at the bold notion of a sonata, a symphonic poem, a piano concerto, compressed into a single monothematic movement. Wagner built the new music-drama by endless variation of a series of set motives. Although in other respects Brahms is at the opposite pole from Liszt and Wagner, he comes closest to them in his liking for monothematic construction and variation, and several of his works (e.g. the *Sonata in F sharp minor*) reflect very clearly the form at which they are all aiming. And what is more natural than that a unified melodic texture should imply a unified structural scheme, that a work built round a single theme should try to turn into a work in one movement, a single giant span? In this way, the whole construction tends to become a variation on the same basic theme—or themes—whether it is a work in many movements, a single act in a music-drama, an entire opera, or even an entire series of operas. Wagner's tetralogy is at the extreme limit of this expansion of form. It is startling and monumental evidence of the application of the monothematic principle.

Whatever Romanticism understood as form is represented here at its zenith, yet, irrevocably, it also marks the beginning of decline, since the component parts are only held together artificially, as the result of superhuman effort. After Liszt and Wagner, monothematic construction did not often regain such dangerous heights. It seemed on the point of petering out, when at the turn of the century Franck, Debussy and Strauss decided to return to the monothematic symphonic poem, string quartet, and symphonic variations: when Bartók, as Liszt's successor, built a string quartet, a violin concerto, out of a single theme, and revived Berlioz' *idée fixe*, creating from the same musical material a picture of the 'ideal' and the 'grotesque'.

In the meantime, another fermentation was in action, and was even having its effect on classical Viennese music. Western European music in major keys was subjected to a gradual change of colour and a process of expansion, later to be followed by crisis and disintegration. The Hungarian and Oriental motives of Haydn, Mozart, Beethoven, Schubert and Weber were isolated, exotic instances, which did not involve any basic change in the musical texture. Chopin was the first composer to create a new texture from the melodic style of an East European background. It may well have been Field and Bellini who were responsible for firing Chopin's youthful imagination so far as the written-out ornaments and ecstatic swing of his melodies were concerned. It seems, in fact, as if certain passages in late Beethoven directly anticipated Chopin's style (e.g. op. 106, 2nd movement, bar 31—35, and the same point in the reprise: op. 109, 3rd movement, beginning of the first variation, etc.). But all this was only the beginning of the general loosening-up of tonality which permeated Chopin's 'ornamental' style. The major itself, and not merely the fixed rhythms of classical music, began to disappear beneath the arabesque-like ornamentation and the free flow of these loosened streams of melody. Lydian and Dorian melodies, dance-melodies with augmented seconds would begin to appear (see the *Rondo à la mazur*, op. 5, and the so-called *Mazurka in C major*, op. 24, No. 2): a pentatonic *étude* with freely used passing notes, or a fantasy in an unusual key. A sonata-movement in 5/4 taken in connection with the general change in melody, would seem to herald a revolution in West European rhythm . . . There is an analogy in antiquity for this. At the end of the classical period, the stressing of Classical Latin was broken up in the first instance by men from the provinces, barbarians in origin, for whom Latin was not a natural mother-tongue. In the 19th century, classical music in major keys was similarly broken up by composers from East Europe—Chopin, Liszt and Mussorgsky—for whom it had ceased to be a natural language, though for a time they had adapted themselves to its formal requirements. The disintegrating process was hastened by the beleaguered fortress, as it were, itself offering a rope-ladder to the besiegers. German, French and English romantic composers 'betrayed' classical major melody by introducing elements of chromaticism. Spohr, Wagner (particularly in *Tristan*), Franck, and later Reger broke up the old nature of the classical scales, and overloaded and overstrained their harmonic functions. From Field onwards, the creeping chromatic melody became more and more common, progressing by altered degrees of the scale. This was particularly true after Wagner's *Tristan*, when melody became nothing more than the outside edge of piled-up, chromatic blocks of harmony. In this period, Italian operatic music alone remained true to pure major melody, as will be discussed in the next chapter.

121

a) **Field**: Nocturne No. 16

b) **Chopin**: Nocturne in C sharp minor, Op. 27, No. 1 (1836)

c) **Chopin**: 3 nouvelles études, No. 1 (1840)

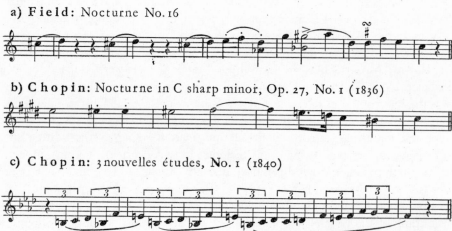

Melody had certainly never been so fluctuating and changeable as it was in these decades. In the middle years of the century, romantic, time-inspired melody began to show a fleeting quality, that endless longing for the 'evanescent world of Faery', which first appeared in Keats' poetry and Schumann's languorous arabesques. Even Schubert tended towards disguise and camouflage, so that his melodies were displaced in time, and 'present' melodies acquired a past meaning of 'long ago' by the use of suspended pedal points in the upper parts. Later on, the nostalgic quality of melody was to be even more intensified in Mendelssohn, Schumann, Chopin and Brahms. This 'eternal longing for remoteness' best sums up romantic *bel canto*, which has an innate capacity to convey something which earlier music had known but rarely, if at all. In Beethoven's *Lieder*-cycle *An die ferne Geliebte*, the glimpse into the distance only lasts a moment; the distant mountains suddenly flash up behind a typically Schubertian suspended pedal-point at *Wo die Berge so blau*; but in the melodies of Schumann, Chopin, Liszt and Brahms—and in the actual melodies themselves—the 'magic casement' is open all the time. The vista is a world of rapture and dream, the past, the far distance, regions beyond life and reality. (Schumann springs constantly to mind and in particular the quotation at the head of this chapter.)

a) S c h u m a n n : Arabeske, epilogue Op. 18 (1839)

b) C h o p i n : Third Scherzo, Op. 39 (1840)

c) L i s z t : Sposalizio (Années de pèlerinage II) (1839-1858)

d) B r a h m s : String Sextet in G major, Op. 36 (1865)

Yet the very ease with which this music could be transformed already marked it out for decay. An entire view of melody, a whole musical outlook, and hence a whole culture, was in decline. These were the last stages of European major music, for the dissolution of romantic melody also implied the eclipse of the major key. For a very long time, the various forms of melody seemed to be in crisis by virtue of their very quality as melody. In differing directions, Bruckner, Wolf and Mahler represented the break-up of romantic melody. They overstrained it, converted it into recitative or made it excessively chromatic. With them, and after them, as we have seen, melody became simply the outer edge of harmonic movement. Wagner began a trend in this direction which was patently followed by Wolf, Reger, and sometimes Debussy.

In this, as in so many other respects, Debussy's music was on the border-line. At a critical moment, he invoked the help of East Europe from his position on the edge of Western Europe. The fate of European melody at the point of its dissolution was to be met by the fresh, invigorating influence of Eastern Europe. Mussorgsky's revolutionary reform followed closely on Wagner's, yet Europe did not become fully aware of it for some twenty years, along with that of Debussy. The encounter soon took on the dimensions of a historical meeting-point. For the diatonic and pentatonic folk-melody of East Europe almost unconsciously recalled earlier, submerged levels of European music, and thus opened up for Western Europe new horizons for renewal and development during the last years of the century.

NOTES

1. Here are the first two examples:

2. See Clara Schumann—Joh. Brahms: *Briefe aus den Jahren 1853—1856*. Ed. B. Litzmann, 1927, vol. I, p. 597, No. 271.

THE MELODIES OF ROMANTIC OPERA:
LATE ROMANTICISM

In places where Western Europe was still able to renew itself through its own traditions, there was no need to turn to the East and the music of Eastern Europe. 19th-century Italian music was the chief and most obvious example of this, the music of the composers who had inherited *bel canto*.

19th-century Italian music was primarily operatic, and consisted in the majority of cases of late *bel canto*, which was still surviving, although it had sometimes passed its prime. This almost unprecedented flowering of Golden Age melody had spoilt Italy in three ways: *bel canto* expected too much of melody, that is, of *certain* types of melody; it demanded sublime achievements of the human voice, but always expected them to be realised in terms of technical bravura; it permitted a certain type of drama, or theatricality, yet refused to acknowledge another and less melodic kind, even obstructing its progress. It negated the darker, deeper and more tragic drama of Monteverdi with its more fluid structure, and took no note of Jommelli's and Traetta's experiments along the same lines. At best, it admitted Paisiello's melody-style as model and forerunner, yet at a stage of his development in the 1780's when his *opera buffa* style was saturated with 'sentimental' elements, and nearer grand opera in conception; when it had achieved almost as complete a fusion between *opera seria* and *opera buffa* as had taken place in the contemporary operas of Mozart. By 1800, the adventure-story type of grand opera, adopted by Sacchini and Salieri, was already flourishing, as well as the 'sentimental' *opera buffa*. At the hands of Mayr and Zingarelli, this latter was unobtrusively being mixed and watered down into the smooth declamation and strident crudity of the stage Romanticism of Mercadante and Pacini. All this was primarily the result of melody's need for 'enclosed' arias and effective finales: the art of Rossini, Bellini, Donizetti and, later, Verdi, sprang from this source. The melody-style which they took over and developed was, after all, concerned with *enclosed* melodies, a most important point which needs stressing, since it constitutes the essential difference between the musical and dramatic development of Germany and Italy. Mozart's melodies are also enclosed, but the 'enclosedness' of Italian operatic melodies is so much more sensuous, robust, vital and poignant! Verdi was the only one who managed to find a way back to the forgotten dramatic laws of Shakespeare and Monteverdi—sometimes instinctively, sometimes in full awareness—but even in his last and most mature works, he never repudiated the claims of enclosed melody.

What exactly is meant by enclosed melody? A glance at 19th-century Italian operatic sources is sufficient to give the answer. Rossini, Bellini and Donizetti, with Verdi in his early days following in their footsteps, use melodies of which the main strength—apart from a smooth, expressive vocal quality—consists in their symmetrical shape, and in the symmetrical way they are placed within the operatic framework. They do in fact govern the shape of the whole dramatic structure. In this sense, Italian romantic opera composers without exception all followed Paisiello, who as early as 1784 described the Italian approach to melody in very clear terms: "We Italians care only about the melody; we use modulation just to enhance the expressive value of the words." Paisiello held that Italian composers approached the beginning of their pieces more easily, whilst the Germans "end before they have begun." Further, German composers knew very little about melody, and were therefore forced to substitute contrived harmonies for the beauty of lovely sound. This rather mechanical and rigid distinction could easily be challenged by exceptions and contradictions; but all the same, 19th-century Italian composers considered it to be fundamentally true. The strongest support came perhaps from Verdi, whose letters contain numerous statements indicating that in this he felt almost exactly the same as Paisiello about the different musical attitudes of the two nations. In his view, Italian composers were above all inventors of vocal melodies, or *melodisti*, and in spite of a certain amount of overlap, they had always been distinct from German composers, even the classical German composers, whom he maintained to be primarily composers of chamber music, *quartetisti*, that is to say, composers of instrumental music, as he called them in a letter of 1878. In his opinion, these were tendencies and accepted facts which could not and should not be overridden. The North, with its instrumental conceptions and harmonic complexity, and the South, with its *cantabile* melody and simple harmonies, were always bound to be in opposition.[1] As mentioned earlier, Italians did not include all and every type of melody under this heading; subconsciously, enclosed symmetry was as important for them as the natural requirements of the human voice, and the ability to express drama or lyricism; they measured their melodic requirements by the tradition and ideal of a *bel canto* which was already in decline. Even Paisiello's strange comparison between the Italian talent for beginning and the German for ending could well stem from the same idea of *bel canto*, for it lay in the very nature of the flourishing Italian melody-style to initiate movement and development. It was less suited to 'stand still' than German music, which not being 'melodically minded' could end at any point, without having really begun or developed at all. That at any rate was the opinion of an Italian opera-composer who never had the opportunity of making closer contact with the Northern style of melody, which was so alien to him.

Enclosed symmetry in the melody was supported by the rhythm as well. 19th-century Italian opera music was full of the traces of dance. Never before, except perhaps in French music at the turn of the 17th and 18th centuries, had music been so permeated with dance rhythms; nor should it be forgotten that so far as Italian opera is concerned, the vivid song-, dance- and marching-rhythms represent the rhythms of the drama as well! In this respect, the music of the individual composers naturally showed sharp differences, and striking differences might also exist between different phases of development of the same composer. Of them all, Rossini was the most stimulated by rhythm, Bellini the most poetically lyrical, whilst from the fifties onwards, Verdi abandoned the dance-like concept of melody, and aimed instead at melody of greater dramatic impact. It is noticeable that, at various phases of their lives, all three were considerably influenced by French music. Rossini only came under French influence at the height of his Parisian activity; and his harmony—which was more under German influence—simultaneously became more refined and complex. Up to that point, his melodies had belonged to the specifically Italian world of late *opera buffa* and watered-down *opera seria*; they now began to be typical of grand opera, of that particular Italo-French blend of a rather exaggerated and rhetorical form of musical declamation which for the whole of Europe had come to spell pathos. (In Eastern Europe, Glinka, Moniuszko, Erkel and Smetana all came under its influence; Chopin himself, when in Paris, learnt most from Bellini's style of melody; Liszt reflected its influence almost to the end of his life; Wagner was subject to it up to the time of *Lohengrin*, Verdi until *Aida;* and even Mussorgsky and Tchaikovsky found it the best Western style *par excellence* whenever they wished to refer to Europe in their works.) The inner workings of all melodies in this style can be laid bare by the analysis of a single example. The famous *Preghiera* in Rossini's *Mosè*, for instance, a work which gained world-popularity in the Paris Opéra version of 1827, and gave rise, amongst other works, to Paganini's famous *Moses-Fantasy*, is typical of grand opera melody at the peak-point of its development. It embodies a set of formulae which became axiomatic for decades of European opera composers, extending, as has been seen, not only from Spontini to Meyerbeer, but from the last works of Paisiello and Zingarelli up to the last works of Verdi. (Verdi, for instance, emphasised that the *Preghiera* was a genuine melody, although he dismissed Rossini's cavatinas as mere *solfeggi*.) The opening is sharply rhythmical and declamatory, with some tragic, pathetic or religious turns of phrase; it normally works up quickly, has a clear, symmetrical shape (often a sequential question-and-answer); there is a gradual climax and an effective finish, generally with recourse to some familiar cadenza. This is the normal shape of slow melodies by Rossini, Bellini and Donizetti, whether they be solemn, lyrical or 'relating'. Verdi would later on shape from them his much more individualised dramatic melodies, which are none the less still filled with general formulae. Such formulae can be seen in action in the famous Sextet in Donizetti's *Lucia*, the lyrical numbers of *Don Pasquale*, and the ensembles of Bellini's *Norma* and *Sonnambula*. They should be compared with Verdi's treatment of cadential formulae in operas between *Traviata* and *Falstaff*:

123

Verdi: **a)** Traviata (Aria from Act I)

b) Don Carlos   **c)** Don Carlos   **d)** Forza del Destino

e) Trovatore   **f)** Aida

g) Requiem   **h)** Boccanegra, Aida, etc.

i) Otello, etc.   **j)** Falstaff

k) Falstaff   **l)** Aida   **m)** Don Carlos

n) Don Carlos (Romanza from Act I)

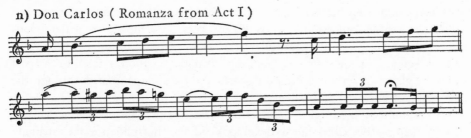

In the Quartet of *Rigoletto* it is already possible to see how he throws off the fetters of set conventions and formulae, applying or adapting them in an ever freer, less rigid, and more dramatic way. In miniature this sums up the whole of Verdi's artistic development, from his robust folk-opera (or 'suburban' opera!) to the masterpieces of his latter years. These last works also form the climax of the whole *corpus* of Italian opera; in them the voice of the 'folk' is heard again, but with an altered meaning, both newer and deeper.

Three of Verdi's melody-types, taken at random, merit closer study. One consists of ornaments which have been written out into the melody—the so-called *doppelschlag*, or turn,[2] for instance, which in 18th-century music, and even in Beethoven, is abbreviated to a simple graphic sign (a horizontal letter S). This ornament played an important role in classical melody—in the Adagio of Mozart's 'great' *F major Sonata* (K.V. 332) for instance, and in numerous themes in Beethoven's *String Quartet* op. 18. But in romantic melody, it is noticeable that the turn nearly always expands into a broad melody, as for instance in Schubert's *Ave Maria* and the *Hostias* in Verdi's *Requiem*. (It is worth commenting here on the more or less concealed threads which link Schubert's and Verdi's melodies. Examples of this written-out ornamentation also occur in the declamatory-style melodies of Schumann, Chopin, Berlioz and Wagner.)

Two other melody-types might be described as 'melodies of public life'. One is the marching-hymn of the Italian *Risorgimento* (ranging from Bellini's oath-taking scene in *Puritani* to *Aida* and *Otello*); the second uses a different rhythmical device—the dotted figure associated with the world of soldier, knight and courtier. The earliest example probably occurs in *I Lombardi*, and other well-known examples include the soldiers' chorus in *Trovatore*, the court ensemble in *Rigoletto*, and the Letter-Trio in Act I of *Don Carlos* (Elisabeth—Eboli—Posa). Renato's first aria in *Ballo in Maschera* ought also to be included because of its emphasis on the courtly and chivalrous. (The device probably traces its ancestry from a court-scene in Meyerbeer's *Les Huguenots*, 1836, and Donizetti's court-chorus in Act III of *La Favorita*, 1840.) Very few examples of these melody-types occur in *Otello* and *Falstaff*, and if they do—as in the *Otello* 'Brindisi' and some of the ensembles—they appear as isolated instances in the midst of a different and highly personal language. For the melodic line of *Otello*, and even more particularly of *Falstaff*, with its built-in, condensed style and written-out ornaments, is already very far removed from the joyous vocal abandon of Verdi's youthful works, and has entirely outgrown conventional forms; it springs directly from the dramatic situation, related to the past only by virtue of certain *bel canto* features and natural symmetry, through the principle of enclosed and balanced phrases.

It should be mentioned that French influence probably played a decisive role in helping these formulae to develop. Verdi felt this influence most strongly between the time of *Ballo* and *Aida* (1859 and 1871), presumably because of his close connection with the Paris Opéra. Verdi's version of the *leitmotif*, already clearly evident in *Don Carlos* (1867)[3] also matured during the same period—though not in a Wagnerian sense.

There are two reasons why the melodies of Italian romantic opera-composers are historically important. One is that from the outset they were rooted in the people, which not only explained their exceptional influence in Italy, and gave them a national stamp, but also greatly facilitated their propagation abroad. A traveller from a Northern European country would constantly hear the great melodies of *Rigoletto* in Italian street-songs and in the folk-songs of Tuscany or Calabria: it would convince him of the elementary force of this music, of its popular origin and mission. The other decisive factor was that they represented the last group-appearance in Europe of major-minor music. This form of melody had appeared in the West some six hundred years earlier, to dominate operatic music for two hundred years, from Pergolesi to Puccini, and indeed the whole of European music during the Viennese classical period. This uniquely Western type of melody had its last showing in the operas of Italian Romanticism; after them, and even in the last of them, the melodic and harmonic world of major and minor began to show signs of upheaval and decay. This was not confined to Italy: almost at the same time, signs of crisis appeared in the works of German and French composers, and in their own way, almost all were stimulated by the 'fermentation' received from Eastern Europe. And all this took place during the period of Late Romanticism.

It *was* another world, for sure. French and German late-romantics were generally far removed from folk-song. Wagner was never much interested in folk-music, and even his most folkish work, *Meistersinger*, conjures up the sound of an imaginary community rather than a reconstructed one. Brahms was enthusiastic about folk-songs, but his characteristic style suffers no basic change when he turns to folk-music arrangements, or evokes the sound of folk-song in sonatas and choral works. Berlioz and Franck, for their part, excelled at quite other things than imitating or reconstructing folk-songs. Late Romanticism in Central and Western Europe did not favour folk-elements; musicology regarded all such endeavours as naive and out-of-date, particularly where the language and formal equipment of art music had developed a stifling tradition (as for instance in Germany). Even if such an effort were made, during this period it was bound to begin in Wagner's shadow, as was the case with Cornelius, Götz, Humperdinck, Siegfried Wagner and Kienzl. Closely related to this trend was the process of making melody completely chromatic, for German academicism is as close to German chromaticism as Italian folk-style to Italian diatonicism. The need for symmetrical shape relaxed its hold at the same time as the need for fixed tonal relationship. It was an inevitable consequence of chromaticism that melody should lose its natural centre of gravity (a stage soon reached by Reger and Schönberg), leaving no trace except a vague striving in certain directions. If Verdi's carefully balanced diatonic melodies, interlaced with folk-elements (triplets, ornaments and typical folk-cadences) are compared with those of Wagner, it is clear that Wagner's tend towards a certain blurring of form and outline, in spite of their rich emotional content and their strong claim to create atmosphere. Wagner in fact proudly claimed this 'art of transition' as his own invention—the merging of darkness and shadow, of flashes of light and colour in a continuous, undulating stream, without sharp edges or clearly defined outline:

124

W a g n e r : a) Meistersinger, Act II

b) Tristan und Isolde, Act II

While some critics welcomed in Wagner's new achievements the deep and studied reflection of the soul-life, a worthy realisation in music of modern man's psychic make-up, there were others who from the beginning criticised the new style for "knowing nothing about drawing": the reproach that Burckhardt was contemporaneously levelling at Rembrandt—and through him at 19th-century painters. The accusation is largely true: Wagner's prime concern was with painting, or rather, with composing in large dynamic colour-surfaces.

'Drawing'—that is, melody—was pushed into the background. German and French music at the close of the century fulfilled Paisiello's prophecy of a hundred years before: the Northern composer was trying to substitute "studied harmonies for the lost magic of *bel canto*"—melody's natural and deeply musical function—and making up at the same time for the lost magic of general intelligibility. The melody-style which emerged from the 'cultivated' melody of the end of the century was artificially constructed—stifled, stunted and decadent.

It was at this point that East European music gave promise not only of a new type of music, but pointed the way to what was to come. The influence of the Russian realistic revival only made itself felt in the West in a general way some decades later, and Mussorgsky's message was still scarcely understood at a time when the more comprehensible and popular music of Tchaikovsky and Rimsky-Korsakov, with their more familiar methods and subject-matter, was rapidly gaining ground in European concert-halls and salons. Mussorgsky's message was always destined to reach at the right time those who needed it: first it reached Debussy, then Ravel and Delius, finally returning through their agency to Eastern Europe, to the workshop of Bartók and Kodály.

The importance of Mussorgsky's music for melodic history is that it brought a radical return to folk-diatonicism and even pentatonicism. This implies a backward movement as well, since great revolutions are also great regressions; but it also represents the first break-through of folk-music into art-music, so that its revolutionary significance is much greater than its significance as regression. In spite of the narrow range of its operations—Russian historical music-drama and the genre art-song— its influence on the whole of Europe was as effective as it was symptomatic. It is easy to detect the other sources of Mussorgsky's melody—the echoes of Schubert, Schumann, Liszt and French grand opera. What is much more important is that the music of the Russian 'folk' is to be found at the very heart of his melody, sometimes in the form of direct quotations (as in many scenes of *Boris Godunov* and *Khovanshchina*) but even more in the form of expressive idioms originating from it and directly linked with it. As is evident from his letters, Mussorgsky was in sympathy with the literary and political outlook of the great Russian and Hungarian poets of the time; as Petőfi put it: "The people had taken over poetry and were almost taking over political power as well." Mussorgsky felt himself to be a forerunner, the preparer of a new world, and was very aware what forces he had conjured up from the womb of time. He studied Great Russian, Ukrainian and Tartar melodies, listened enthusiastically to *maqam* melodies in the Crimean Peninsula (the source of the Persian Dances in *Khovanshchina*), and from childhood believed in the omniscient, all-expressive power of peasantry and peasant-song. In this way the principal source of his melodies were East European peasant-song and Russian *parlando*, or the natural melody of speech.

In both fields he had predecessors, but neither Glinka's fresh and vigorous folk-feeling, nor Dargomijsky's experiments in declamation ever reached the same degree of artistic intensity which Mussorgsky's music, and particularly his operas, had shown from their earliest, tentative beginnings. Even after Chopin and Liszt, it was still unprecedentedly new to hear pentatonic melodies of the kind heard in the chorus of welcome to the Khovansky Princes, and in *Promenade*, from *Pictures of an Exhibition*. Even if they were not actual folk-melodies, they were couched in a personal idiom inspired by folk-song:

125

Mussorgsky: a) Pictures of an Exhibition (1874)

b) Khovanshchina, Act I (1875)

It was new to hear the people uttering such authentic melodies in the great dramatic choruses, as if they were using their own folk-idiom. Seldom, if ever, did even Italian folk-Romanticism (represented by Verdi) and French veristic opera (represented by Bizet) succeed in doing anything like this. Broad, soaring melodies in re-discovered folk-modes, diatonic and pentatonic: in this setting chromaticism acted as a stimulating novelty, as if it were some rare foreign guest. "Music should give back not only the agitation of the soul, but also that of words," Mussorgsky declared, and by allowing the word to flow freely he did in fact free the metre and rhythm of melody. At times Haydn and Mozart had also enjoyed experimenting with such irregular devices, but the asymmetrical bar did not appear until Chopin and Glinka (Chopin's *Ist Sonata*, about 1828, *Ivan Sussanin*, 1836) and in some of Mussorgsky's songs; the 5/4 bar had ceased to be unusual by the time of Tchaikovsky's *Pathetic Symphony*, and had become a natural form of expression.[4] Other new factors appeared, which were partly a reflection of the harmonic experiments; for instance, the whole-tone scale, which probably appeared for the first time in Glinka's *Russlan* (1842), and shortly afterwards in Dargomijsky's *The Stone Guest* (1868), Mussorgsky's *Fair of Sorochintsy*, and in Rimsky-Korsakov as well. Simultaneously it also appeared in yet a fifth East European composer, Franz Liszt, from whom Scriabin and Debussy would inherit it at the end of the century. The course of development was indicative of upheaval and rebirth, and for the time being its path lay directly towards the West, until such time as East European music was ready to make its second appearance in the scheme of things.

1. But this was a generalisation expressed in a letter of 1871 (the year of *Aida*), in which Verdi explains that since music is more than just melody or just harmony, the greatest composers, Beethoven and Palestrina, were "no melodists," that is to say, no mere melody-makers.

2. "This ornament consists in the alternation of a main note with two subsidiaries a step above and below . . ." "There could be no more impressive instance of the characteristic transformation of what began as improvised embellishment into the raw material of composition proper." (Robert Donington in *Grove's Dictionary.* 5th edition, 1954, VI, pp. 418 and 423.)

3. Some striking examples from *Don Carlos* :

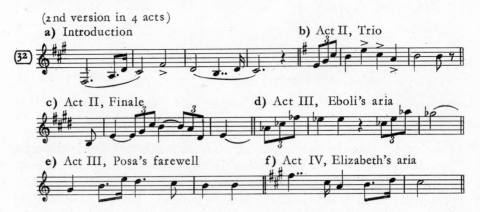

4. There are naturally earlier examples as well, e.g. Belli's melody quoted on p. 84 of this book (1616); such bars also occur in Saracini's canzonettas, around 1620; Handel uses the 5/8 bar in *Orlando* (1733), B. Marcello the 5/4 bar in a cantata for soprano solo, and Clementi, in the Adagio-Introduction of his *Capriccio in C major* (1821).

Van Gogh : Landscape (1889). Music of the Impressionist period shows the same capacity to charm nature into movement as have Van Gogh's drawings and paintings.

THE MODERN MELODY

At the beginning of the 20th century, the pioneers stood face to face with followers-up, and even with laggards; but naturally the pioneers were also followers-up themselves (as often only emerged later on). To make things even more complicated, they often appeared masked as such, just as the followers-up would disguise themselves as pioneers. Slowly it became apparent that Strauss and Mahler were the descendants of Wagner, Liszt and Brahms, that Debussy was working in the tradition of Machaut and Couperin, rather than that of Massenet and Fauré, that Bartók was Liszt's heir in quite another sense from what seemed to be the case in his youth, and that Kodály was a successor of Palestrina, rather than Debussy.

National traditions, individual characteristics and the set notions of different generations often cut across each other's path and contradict each other; sometimes they reinforce each other, but they hardly ever appear in a way which is plain, simple and easily worked-out. All at once the entire past assumed importance, in that the 20th-century composer took up his inheritance of past centuries in a more conscious and decided way than any of his predecessors, yet perhaps under greater compulsion at the same time. His education was in great part historical, his orientation a conscious choice between various traditions. This is what generally happens in late and self-conscious periods, when new eras are beginning or ending, and at great historical crossroads. Bach, Haydn and Mozart were chiefly concerned with their own contemporaries, only encountering their predecessors at turning-points in their lives, the result of a chance flash of insight. But Beethoven already showed a much more conscious interest in the music of Bach and Handel. Schumann, Liszt and Brahms had an unusually rich cultural background of literature and musical history; Weber and Wagner criticised their predecessors, and held opinions about them. Verdi, source of the remark that "Progress consists in returning to the old," made out an exhaustive list in his old age (1887) of earlier composers whom he considered to have been important . . . But a definite historical bias of this sort was never the compelling ideological necessity it is for the 20th-century composer. In Debussy's repudiation of Gluck and Wagner and his approval of Rameau, in

Ravel's irritation with Beethoven, Stravinsky's passing enthusiasm for Pergolesi or Tchaikovsky, and Bartók's aversion to Hungarian amateur Romanticism, there is always the implication that the composer has taken up a very definite and conscious stand, which affects his own leanings and aspirations. Yet it seems to be a characteristic of composers of this period that without exception, all pay homage to Bach and Mozart—whether their leanings are atonal, 'objective', or straightforwardly 'collectivist'.

Every whit as important and indicative as the composer's relationship to the past is his attitude to folk-music. The profound social and political crises of the 20th century were bound to affect composers and musical life generally. The composer of the 18th and 19th centuries was a bourgeois, even when he appeared to be outside society, a romantic genius at the head of the masses. At the beginning of the 20th century—up to the time of the Russian Revolution, and in the West even later—the composer was living, spiritually speaking, in an unstable and undefined environment, even though he was a better and more dutiful member of society than his romantic forbears. It was obvious that the essential ties of bourgeois society were becoming looser, more contradictory, more burdensome, and more brittle. So at a certain moment he was inevitably bound to turn traitor to his social environment. He took to championing the art or melody of an unknown or unrecognised people, class, country or continent; a spokesman and supporter, say, of East European peasant peoples, or the lost regions of Iberia. To do this, he naturally needed to be scholar, researcher, folklorist and possibly historian as well!—for these were the great years of folk-music research and of European comparative musicology. The characteristics of different national cultures and the different levels they have reached are seen here at their most fascinating. From the beginning of the 20th century, the musicians who turned most successfully to folk-music stemmed from the outer periphery of Europe: they were Russians, Hungarians, Rumanians, Bulgarians, Greeks, Poles, Englishmen and Spaniards. The territories which had given rise to European musical history—Italy, Germany and France—could no longer be stimulated by folk-music. (Honegger made a significant comment à propos of this in 1927, to the effect that France has no real folk-music; at the same time, Schönberg and his school were showing an equal lack of interest in German folk-music.) Searching for exotic folk-colour, Debussy travelled to Spain and Java, while Puccini fantasticated about Japan, China and the Wild West—how vast, yet how small, the 20th-century worlds had become!—yet Stravinsky and Prokofiev in Russia, later joined by Shostakovich and Khachaturian, Bartók, Kodály and Enescu in Hungary and Rumania, Vaughan Williams, Bax and Britten in England and De Falla in Spain, were still discovering living folk-melody and rhythm. Using Mussorgsky to some extent as their model, they were able to let an individual musical idiom come alive in their music, a 'freely used mother-tongue' as Bartók put it, such as can only exist in the creative artist by the 'intensive experiencing' of folk-music.

Hence the Europe of living folk-music was to be sharply distinguished from the Europe of 'extinct', no longer functioning, or at best resuscitated folk-music; and from these two entirely different relationships of the composers to the 'folk' there arose two intrinsically different ways of handling melody, and in two different cultural environments. For Central Europe 'without folk-music' had its own strong melodic traditions too; indeed, if 20th-century composers in this area are studied from this point of view, it is clear that they needed no folk-traditions because their forbears had already absorbed them; they took them over second-hand, in a ripe and often far too ripe state, quite exhausted. This decadent and often already defunct major-minor style of melody still lived on in some 20th-century German and Italian composers. It is as easy to recognise the German and Russo-Polish romantic ancestry of melodies by Strauss and Mahler, as to make out the Italian Ottocento in the operas of Puccini and Mascagni:

126

a) R. Strauss: Don Juan (1889)

b) Mahler: Das Lied von der Erde (1911)

Herbst-ne - bel wal - len

(*Cp.* Mahler's *Herbstnebel* with Liszt's *Vallée d'Obermann* and with Lenski's famous farewell aria in Tchaikovsky's *Onegin*.) In the most folkish of these melodies, generally conceded by universal taste to be 'great melodies':

127

a) Puccini: Madame Butterfly (1904)

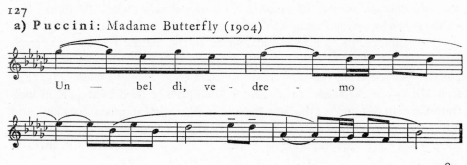

Un — bel dì, ve - dre - mo

187

b) Tchaikovsky: Fifth Symphony (1888)

there are numerous sensuously expansive and gently undulating features, typical of the music of *fin de siècle* society: as in Tchaikovsky's colourful, yearning and passionate melodies (e.g. the themes of the *Violin Concerto*, or the famous 5/4 movement in the *Pathetic Symphony*). Instead of organic development and clear linear treatment, there is often sequential repetition, a rhapsodical, almost accidental outpouring of melody, or—as in Puccini—a structural organisation effected through dramatic gestures rather than through formal devices. All the same it is obvious that, up to now, this is the last operatic music to be genuinely capable of stirring the masses and satisfying the longing of a broad public for drama, music and splendid spectacle. Every other composer is still trying to find the way to this audience, this lost universal society.

A new stylistic trend was beginning to emerge in Northern Europe alongside this late and overblown manifestation of 'major-minor' music. It was indeed a reaction, though quite unrelated to *this* type of Romanticism: with passionate enthusiasm it preferred to pursue another form of it. This was the double trend of over-rich chromaticism and speech-melody, sometimes separating, and then again reuniting, rooted in Wagner's *Tristan* and in Mussorgsky's and Dargomijsky's experiments in *parlando*. Up to the middle years of the 20th century, this movement found its most consistent leadership in Arnold Schönberg. It is curious that chromaticism and inflectional melody momentarily engrossed the attention of the most significant composers of the period—and sometimes both at the same time—to be later abandoned with a greater or lesser sense of dissatisfaction. Only Schönberg and his small circle remained true. There was a very considerable output of speech-melody in this period, for it attracted the 'new' music-cultures, based on folk-music, which would now and then attempt to build their larger forms from the *parlando* and the folk-form. The stimulating influence of Debussy's *Pelléas* (1902) had far-reaching effects, and was followed by Janáček's *Jenufa* (1904), Bartók's *Bluebeard* (1911), and even Stravinsky's *Les Noces* (1922), all of which attempted from different standpoints to give musical shape to the natural melody of speech. But Schönberg was the only one who followed up the new road with dogged persistence, requiring the same basic solution from *Pierrot Lunaire* (1912) as from the *Ode to Napoléon* (1942). At the same time he tried to liberate melody from the grip of tonality; this was the aim of his theory of atonal harmony and his system based on twelve equal degrees of the scale—'twelve note music' or, since 1923—24, 'dodecaphony'— which is a new version of the *maqam*:

188

a) S c h ö n b e r g: Second·String Quartet (1908)

Gön - ne die ru - he schwan - ken-den schrit - ten,

hung - ri-gem gau - me bröck - le dein brot!

b) A. B e r g: Wozzeck, Act I (1922)

Es wird mir ganz angst um die Welt, wenn ich an die E -

wig - keit denk?

Composers such as Berg or Bartók who came into contact with this very specu-lative system recognised its threatening blind-alley much quicker than did Schönberg himself, and left it much earlier (yet Schönberg in 1934 was again writing a *Tonal Suite for String Orchestra,* and some of his later works show tonal influence). Bartók came back under the influence of folk-music; after a longer or shorter journey away from it, Hindemith and Prokofiev returned to tonality via the acceptance of classical models. Some, like Kodály and Malipiero, were never influenced by the possibilities of atonal experiment. Yet for all this, it is inconceivable that twelve-note music, and the particular form of chromaticism associated with it, vanish from present-day European music. The art of 'com-bining' it appears perhaps at its most interesting in Bartók, at points where he is experimenting with a form of chromaticism which is seemingly irrational, most gloomy and close-set[1]; in the *Music for Strings and Percussion* (1936) for instance, where a secret and sinuous melody, half-way between speaking and wailing, runs motto-like through the four movements (it is built round Bartók's most charac-teristic interval, the tritone, once called the *diabolus in musica* by mediaeval theo-rists because it was so unvocal). This oppressive 'natural' chromaticism per-vades the whole work, only resolving into a diatonic variant in the 4th movement:

129

B a r t ó k: Music for Strings, Percussion, and Celesta (1936)

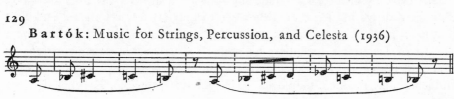

The new chromaticism, with its typical fragments of melody, actually reached its point of culmination about 1920, in the course of the so-called Expressionist movement; in most cases it yielded to Neo-Classicism about 1925. Particularly in countries without a folk-tradition, or under the influence of Stravinsky, Neo-Classicism revived the great 'self-propelling' melodies of the Baroque; it assumed instead a folk-like flow of melody in lands with a living folk-tradition, such as the Soviet Union (particularly in Khachaturian and Kabalevsky) and Hungary, largely under Kodály's influence. Today the lands of living folk-traditions in East Europe are also countries of socialism and new mass-culture. It is no chance that one of their chief art-types, the 'mass song', stemming from the Soviet Union, should for years have borne witness to the renewed power of popular and folk-inspired melody. During the course of the thirties and forties, Neo-Classicism and melodising in a folk-idiom joined forces as frequently as had atonality, chromaticism and *parlando* in the previous decade. It is worth noticing that this trend of the thirties and forties, whether it occurs in Ravel or Honegger, Bartók or Kodály, De Falla or Britten (to whom might be added Prokofiev and Shostakovich, at certain phases of their development), is made in terms of a return to strict tonality, consolidation and retreat from 'revolution'. Equally typical of this trend is the ostentatious dependence on folk-diatonicism, counterbalancing the fragmentation of the earlier decades, in the form of twelve-note music, serial music or quarter-note music— counterbalancing also the decadent major-minor style of the older generation, the stragglers from Romanticism. The archaic or folk-type melody obviously found itself in as new a harmonic setting as the more modern chromatic melodies, yet there is little doubt that its influence on the shape of the composition as a whole was more and more marked. From this point of view, West European music of the thirties and forties should not look for its pioneer and precursor in Schönberg, but rather in Claude Debussy, of whom little mention has so far been made, but who in fact became the pioneer of 20th-century art by carrying out the last and most effective experiment in Romanticism.

During the two decades that it flourished (1892—1912), Debussy's melody-style was a unique phenomenon in European music, not to be explained merely in terms of its environment without reference to Mussorgsky's prior example. Yet it does in fact have many roots and antecedents. From French music it has refined Fauré's song-style, and from German that of Wagner (his influence occurs not only in the early Baudelaire songs, but in *Pelléas et Mélisande* too). But the decisive influence on Debussy's melody-style was Oriental and East European melody, first revealed to him by Mussorgsky. Even if nothing were known of Debussy's melodies, his remark that musical ornamentation, or arabesque, lies at the heart of all music would lead one to suspect some Oriental influence. His practice, moreover, bears out this principle. His melody does in fact consist mainly of arabesque, a playfully abstract, fleeting outline, but never abstract in the sense that Bach's melodies are abstract. He remains true to Mozart and his French forbears, in that he always respects the claims of musical texture, and makes it his starting-point. The predominance of church and folk-diatonicism in Western music about 1900 was clearly not entirely due to Debussy; signs of it were already appearing about 1880 in the works of Fauré, and in Debussy's time it was familiar through the work of Delius and some other English composers. All the same, it was through Debussy, and the acceptance of Mussorgsky's influence that took place through him, that it became an organic, historical phenomenon. Even Italy, which had long been averse to the trend, finally came to terms (though not till 1922) in Respighi's *Concerto Gregoriano* and in works by Casella and Pizzetti . . . In his early works, Stravinsky characteristically adopts East European folk-modes not only as a national inheritance from Mussorgsky and Rimsky-Korsakov, but also as an echo of Debussy. A biographer of Debussy would have to concern himself with Franck and d'Indy as well as Fauré; yet it was through Debussy that Ravel and Stravinsky formed this 'neo-archaic' style into a natural musical language, and it is familiar that from 1907 he inspired the work of the new Hungarian school. The rediscovery of pentatonicism, that living patrimony of Mussorgsky, forms part of the 'regressive renaissance' through which Western music renewed itself from ancient forms of diatonicism. (In France this was carried out with far less prehistoric material: at best it meant drawing on Celtic sources.) It occurs in the *Nocturnes, La Mer, La Fille aux cheveux de lin,* in the folk-song imitations in *Pelléas,* and in the *Invocation* from the *Six épigraphes antiques*; sometimes it is pure, and sometimes mixed:[2]

130

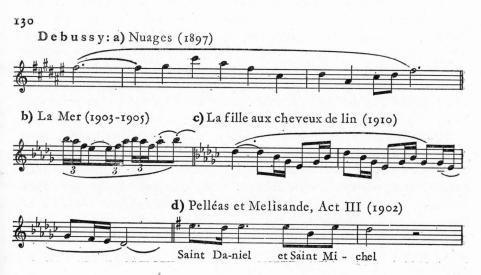

D e b u s s y: a) Nuages (1897)

b) La Mer (1903-1905)   c) La fille aux cheveux de lin (1910)

d) Pelléas et Melisande, Act III (1902)

Saint Da-niel   et Saint Mi - chel

e) Six épigraphes antiques (1915)

f) Reflets dans l'eau (1905)

But it is not the Celtic or the Oriental heritage which matters here; the 'return to modes' of Western music means more than mere exotic local colour or deliberate archaism; the infiltration of jazz melodies in pentatonic and Dorian folk-modes, imported from America, began in Debussy's time . . . Naturally it was an art of local colour and atmosphere, rather than a living use of a musical idiom; yet on occasions Wagner was already using pentatonic and diatonic melody of this kind in his nature-descriptions—in quotation marks, as it were. Yet what a living language it inspires, in Debussy: in the *Après-midi d'un faune,* the *String Quartet,* and the themes of *Pelléas!* In these works there are as many innovations as there are types. There is a new technique of *parlando* melody, which from *L'Enfant Prodigue* evolves through *Pelléas* and the *Chansons de Bilitis* to the *Ballades de Villon;* a new 'Greek' dance rhythm which Debussy uses to conjure up the 'divine serenity' of the ancient world and its pagan customs (as in *Fêtes*). He also has a related melody-type which could be described as 'reflex', 'reflection' or 'glimmer' melody, because it is nearly always connected with a visual allusion, picture or vision. A brief flash of impressionistic notes reaches down into the subconscious depths where thought-associations and emotional relationships are formed, as in the famous *Reflets dans l'eau.* This melodic figure is almost entirely the result of the harmonic play; it is no longer real melody, but only a reflection, mirrored in the water . . . Without realising it, Debussy has here turned ally of that over-harmonised, melody-less 'new German' music, against which he struggled so implacably in his conscious mind. In both directions he brought about the great turning-point of his period; by dint of breaking up and opening up, he also set free. He released Europe from the domination of German Romanticism, in part by breaking up the German tradition more radically than had German music itself.

It has been rightly stated that the 19th century came to an end with the First World War. 1917—1918 was the year of revolutions, and a turning-point in the history of music—Debussy's death in 1918 symbolised the end of the period of Western Romanticism and, with it, of radical individualism. The new was breaking out of the old—yet for a long time, the old lived on in the new. The period between the two world wars stiffened the spine of European melody, or rather, it expressed the same hardening process that had also taken place in European melody. The melody-style of Stravinsky and Khachaturian, Bartók and Kodály, all born out of East European folk-music, as well as the more abstract and calculated thematic style of Hindemith and Honegger, lived in this colder and harsher new world, as though they had been made for it. It was primarily East European music that emerged first from Impressionism, then from expressionistic experiment, and finally from the style-play of Neo-Classicism. In their own way, all three trends represented a flight from reality, a taking refuge in one corner of the world; yet they all brought lasting results, already apparent in the new world language that was forming. Expressionism preferred melodies which were dramatic, ejaculatory or fragmentary; Neo-Classical objectivity needed the play of 'self-propelling' Baroque-type melodies; but at the hands of East European composers both trends characteristically join forces with some form of folk-melody. In Stravinsky they turn into equalised, litany-like fragments of melody (*Sacre du Printemps* and *Les Noces*); in Bartók's concerto-texture (particularly the *1st* and *2nd Piano Concertos*) the clattering rhythms of Bach's *Brandenburgs* meet up with typical devices of the Balkans and the Near East—the asymmetrical forms of Rumanian, Bulgarian, Arabic or Turcoman music. In the broad melodies of Khachaturian's concertos they are absorbed into the folk-rhythms of Russian and Armenian dances:

131

Khachaturian: Violin Concerto (1940)

Whether or not this was the intention, this is a world of East and West, a new synthesis. It affects rhythm and melody alike, its diatonic and chromatic style throws a bridge across continents. 'East' no longer means only East Europe, the 'West' not only West Europe. Asia, Africa and America are emerging in the background, the whole Old and New World. Apparently it is natural for this typically European renaissance of our day to have as its slogan "Music belongs to everybody."

Earlier on it has been described how Bartók permitted the use of the strictest chromatic devices alongside pentatonic scales and certain folk-modes.[3] Kodály was drawn from the outset to a broader diatonic and pentatonic style, and followed a more or less planned route from the descriptive Romanticism of *Summer Evening*, with its evocation of the Hungarian landscape, to the Eurasian range of colour in the *Peacock Variations* and the Palestrinian handling of melody in the *Organ Mass*. His heroic and declamatory song-style had meantime come to characterise the Hungarian movement; it evoked the Hungarian past as effectively in works for solo instruments as in choral writing or the solo-song; witness the *Cello Sonata*, the *Psalmus Hungaricus* and the settings of old poets. Kodály formed an entirely new style of national *parlando* out of material taken from folk or historical sources. It was no accident that the melodies used as early on as those of the *Cello Sonata* should have found an echo twenty-two years later, in Bartók's *Violin Concerto*; nor is there any doubt that from the very beginning this style looked to find plasticity in the purest Greek and Latin models, succeeding with their assistance in ranging from peasant song to Gregorian chant:

132
a) Kodály: Sonata for unaccompanied cello (1915)

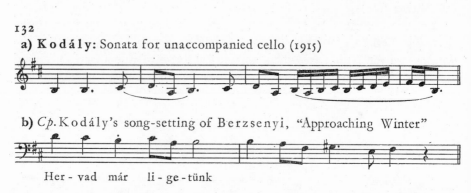

b) *Cp.* Kodály's song-setting of Berzsenyi, "Approaching Winter"

Her - vad már li - ge - tünk

It aspires to a vocal beauty of sound, its masters were poets of 'timeless song', and its aim is to unite humanity more and more through singing.

*

If from this point in the mid-20th century, we cast a backward glance at the course of development outlined in the foregoing chapters, we need to recognise and stress the existence of two basic laws. One is that in its periods of calm and unrest, its culminations and renewals, its periods of decadence and its new beginnings, European melody mirrors the cultural life of Europe. During the great stabilising, summarising periods of 'rest', it culminates in the form of classical periods, in more restless and crowded periods of crisis it is released in Romantic forms, and renewed all over again. Classicism is melody's crown, forcing it to stand still, while Romantic periods set it in motion, and stir it into action. Together they represent the ever-changing Janus-head of European life, the mirror of its soul; they are the beginning, the culmination, the starting-again; the morning, noon and afternoon.

The other basic law is that these phases are present in the development of the single artist. It can almost be said that the career of each composer is the history of a Romanticism or a Classicism (and sometimes of several such, as with Mozart). Each one within given limits accomplishes the same thing; each one introduces, develops, consolidates, and fulfils. These phases are as true of Bach's life as they are of Mozart's, Beethoven's, and Verdi's; and their lives come to be mirrored in melody, sometimes through progressive disintegration, and sometimes through consolidation and unification; to be followed once again by break-up, fresh stimulus and new achievement. Melody mirrors these phases because it comes from a superabundance of perception and emotion, so that it always presents an intensified and concentrated picture of human existence. It is not only life as reflected in the composer himself, but the life that surges around him! Even the immense tradition of melody, the embodiment of 'eternal melodies', takes on a different meaning in the midst of this endlessly surging sea which is the life of the composer. It creates his individual work of art in exactly the same way as the life of the 'folk' gives rise to a collective one.

The law of the greater process holds good in the smaller too; for the great stream of historical evolution carries life in the same way that the incident of a short life makes history. It is the law of the water-drop and the sea:—a law of history, which unites the moment of a human life with the breath of super-human aeons in a single, collective and continuous rhythm.

1. Already foreshadowed in the *Prestissimo* of the *4th Quartet* (1928) and then in Nos. 132, 135, 142 and 144 of *Mikrokosmos ;* of these the first is the most closely related to the *maqam* quoted from the *Music for Strings and Percussion.*

2. See the article by C. Brailoiu: "Pentatonismes chez Debussy" in the volume *Studia Memoriae B. Bartók Sacra.* Budapest, 1956.

3. This is Bartók's typical Lydian-Mixolydian scale-mixtures, the 'acoustic' or 'natural' scale which occurs earlier in Debussy—as in the principal theme of *La Mer* and in *L'Ile joyeuse.* Traces of it are also found in Liszt and Scriabin. It is particularly common in Rumanian folk-music: see the relevant material from Bartók's collection, or the *Ciobănaşul* of Paul Constantinescu (1951), etc. It is very likely that it reached Bartók not by way of art-music but through Rumanian folk-tunes. See also the comments of Ernő Lendvai, in *Béla Bartók, Weg und Werk.* Budapest, 1957, pp. 127—128 [in German and French].

APPENDIX

SPEECH AND MELODY

"The emotions which accompany speech, the subtleties of thought which need to be communicated but cannot be expressed in writing, are conveyed by variations in pitch." That is how the Hungarian linguist József Balassa puts it in his book, *The Hungarian Language*. And it seems as though Zoltán Kodály is following exactly the same line of thought when he writes: "Every language has its own innate tone-colour, tempo, rhythm, melody, in a word, its music. If the bell-like sound of our language is allowed to sound like a cracked plate, we must not be surprised if nobody takes any notice of us, and we vanish in a sea of peoples."

In the hands of an artist such as Kodály, who has deliberately set out to build up a cultural policy for his people, this idea has become a weapon of national defence. But it pervades the whole of human existence so thoroughly that anthropologists and musicologists are constantly bound to encounter it at different epochs, in different societies, and at every historical turning-point. The English phonetician, Henry Sweet, is not far from the truth when he asserts that "Intonation . . . . seems to survive longest"; intonation, the first speech-melody, is one of the most ancient and enduring phenomena in human culture.*
Intonation originated at the same point as music. At one time they probably both belonged together, and the oldest form of melody was little different from that of speech. The history of music began when man used his voice to imitate the sounds of Nature, and tried to communicate with the world; it began where natural speech-music—intonation—also began to exist.

For a long time, primitive man, like the Oriental, could hear no difference between speech and music. When the voice is raised, it slides unobtrusively into singing, and solemn declamation, or the formal reading of texts, turns into singing of its own accord. The word for 'word' (*davar*) and 'melody' (*shir*) are not clearly distinguished even in the Bible, and come together in the common concept of recitative (e.g. the Hebrew rubric of the 18th Psalm bears the instruction "to speak the words of the song" (*dibber et-divré hashirá*): the singing is

---

* For the distinction between intonation and inflection, see p. 12, footnote. (Translators' note.)

spoken, as the word is sung. Cantillation,[1] or the reciting of the sacred text, was practised in all Oriental cultures: in Jewish ritual, the Latin verb *legere*, to read—in Middle High German, *leinen*—always inferred the sung performance when used in connection with the Scriptures. The ancient Eastern practice of reciting aloud, so convincingly demonstrated by József Balogh in the twenties (*Magyar Nyelv*, 1926), is known to have lasted deep into the European Middle Ages and up to modern times. It is natural that Plato in his *Republic* should have judged ideal 'harmony' by the extent to which it could "imitate the tones and accents of a valorous man" (μιμήσατο φθόγγους τε καὶ προςῳδίας). In all classical cultures, the life of speech was inseparably bound up with that of melody. At the beginning of the Middle Ages, the term *tropus* was applied to the ornamented *text* as well as to the ornamented *melody*, and the *tropator*, or *trovator*, would be as much at home inventing one as the other. The words *mot* and *motto* still lie unremarked at the heart of a motet; the starting-point for the most prolific musical genre of the Middle Ages was a verse-text. In the 14th century, the main accusation against the motet was that it distorted the text, and broke it up until it became incomprehensible. This was because of a new humanistic attitude, as well as a purely clerical concern. In spite of the rich poetic diction and melodic invention of the Middle Ages, the text was constantly overlooked. To respect its demands was considered in some way inferior, materialistic and vulgar.[2] Not until the 16th century, and then with eager enthusiasm, was the new discovery made: musicians began to taste and caress the words, never tiring of listening to their sound. The chief function of the newly revived madrigal was "to pour life into the words" (*fondar spirito nelle parole*), or, as Palestrina put it, *dare spirito vivo alle parole secondo il significato* (bring the words to life in accordance with their meaning). Now that they had recovered from a distant past the declamation of classical tragedy, they wanted to shape European sung speech, or recitative, in the form and spirit of the antique model. From then onwards, on countless occasions in the course of its development, European music would turn to speech inflection, prose melody and free declamation to help stimulate a solution to its problems.

The writer and poet Vincenzo Galilei, father of the great astronomer, and one of the leading spirits in the reformist group of Florentine musicians, was probably the first to pose the problem systematically. As he wrote in 1581: "A musician should pay heed to the way a Prince talks to his subjects, or an angry and impatient man, an old woman, a young girl, or a simple boy; he should hearken to the speech of a querulous, quarrelsome, timid or joyous personage, or a lover as he converses with his beloved . . . even an animal has its own kind of voice which it uses to tell us whether it is well or in pain!" New composers of the Late Renaissance and Baroque followed Galilei's advice quite literally, and in its spirit discovered the *nuove musiche*, or dramatic style of declamation. Peri, the first composer of operas, searched for a "middle way between speech and song," basing himself on Greek models. In 1607 the claim was put very forcefully by Monteverdi, the first great composer of tragic opera: "Speech should be the master and not the servant of the music!" (*L'orazione sia padrone dell'armonia e non serva*). Forty years later, the German composer Christoph Bernhard had the same idea in mind when he distinguished the *stylus gravis*, or *antiquus*, from the stylus *luxurians*, or *modernus*, and the *stylus theatralis*; in the first, harmony dominated speech (*harmonia orationis domina*), in the second, the two elements were of equal importance, whilst in the third (*stylus theatralis*), speech totally dominated the harmony (*oratio harmoniae domina absolutissima*)—in other words, sung declamation or recitative was ideally suited to opera.

Yet the final results of the 'modern system' matured not in Italy, as might have been expected, but in France. The evolution of sung recitative in heroic French operas was closely connected with the dramatic conventions of French tragedy. Lully, the great French composer of his day, painstakingly set to music the classical stresses of French tragedy. Actors and actresses of Racine, Mlle Champmeslé for instance, learnt their tragic roles from musical notation, and Voltaire nostalgically recalled this melody-permeated stage tradition in his *Dictionnaire philosophique*. For him, classical tragedy was sung—*se chantait*; even as late as 1710, great representatives such as Mme Beauval were still able to recite an entire role by Corneille as melody. By contrast with today, continued Voltaire, when everything is played "drily" for "ours is a century of dryness." Rousseau was no longer concerned with such classical reminiscences; he delved further back into the past in search of the traces of primitive melody, primitive speech and primitive feeling. He wrote an *Essai sur l'origine des langues, où il est parlé de la Mélodie et de l'Imitation musicale* (1753), in which he explained that in the beginning everything was singing and poetry, and that melody itself was a most emphatic form of speech: *la mélodie parle, et son langage inarticulé mais vif, ardent, passionné a cent fois plus d'énergie que la parole même*. Lacombe (1758) followed Rousseau's lead, and so advised the composer "to preserve the natural accentuation of the language" and "always to study its intonation, because it is the instrument of feeling and passion"; "our most moving and significant melodies are based on natural declamation." At the end of the century (1789) the operatic composer Grétry took the same line: "the word is a sound which contains melody as well," "good vocal music copies the accentuation of the words," and "operatic music is made not *after* the words, but *with* the words." The 18th-century operatic reformer, Gluck, was perhaps a little less fanatical and less dogmatic, yet he too looked for abundant expression, for "noble, stirring and natural melody, a declamation suited to the prosody of every language, and the character of every people" (1773). Nationalism and internationalism were here closely related; the national style could only assert itself on the 18th-century world-stage if it was couched in super-national terms. But even though national feeling had not quite come to the surface, it was already on the alert and aware of its rights. The particular had to be respected as well as the universal, a special national tone-colour, as well as the collective voice of humanity. At the beginning this was only intended as a nuance, and as a means to an end, but later on it became an aim and object. When he arrived in Paris, the Italian composer Piccinni, Gluck's rival, took lessons in French prosody from Marmontel. However international the claims made for linguistic awareness, the French public would not allow their feeling for it to be outraged, even by distinguished foreigners! Another Italian opera-composer, Paisiello, showed himself even more sensitive to the problem of vocal declamation. "Let people sing as they speak," he wrote to his French colleague, Lesueur, in 1804, "according to the natural inflections of speech. I believe this to be the true art. This is the task which confronts music. Let us imitate Nature!" They did indeed try; all composers who grappled with recitative round about 1800 believed that they were imitating Nature. During this period, the problem was scientifically investigated: as early as 1776 and 1787, Steele and Walker analysed the laws which governed "the melody of speaking," and within a few decades—by the mid-19th century—it had become a key-question in musical life. Wagner's name was soon linked with the new style; in his *Oper und Drama* he set out in detail the laws governing speech-melody, for "we should wrest from the prose of our ordinary speech that intensified expression which alone is capable of commending the poetic intonation to our emotions." But Wagner was not the only one: in Russia, Dargomijsky and Mussorgsky were declaring that "melody should translate the word," and "music should express the agitation of speech, as well as that of the soul." New trends were emerging from this ferment, trends which were both folkish and non-folkish: romantic movements, aristocratic or demotic in stamp, which were to influence specialist research and scholarship more strongly. Köhler and Merkel treated the phenomenon of intonation most comprehensively, whilst a few decades later Jespersen was already trying to establish the major and minor tonality of speech, and others were measuring the slightest oscillation of a note with the help of graphs and electrical apparatus . . . Modern music itself has scarcely been able to keep pace with it all, although since Debussy, Schönberg and Janáček, the extent of its debt to living speech inflection and pure declamation is an accepted fact.[3]

But what is the real nature of the debt? It is difficult to give a definite answer, since speech itself is much less straightforward than used to be believed, let alone the nature of its relationship to music. Not so long ago, H. Christian Wolff pointed out that early operatic recitative, which was once held to be uniform, showed basic differences according to its nationality (Die Sprachmelodie im alten Opernrezitativ. *Archiv für Sprach- und Stimmphysiologie* IV, 1940). Yet another musicologist has pointed out that even the apparent naturalness of *Sprechgesang* is really a stylised simplification of speech-melody, in itself the most complex and shifting form of melody imaginable. (I. Szelényi: "The meaning, aims and means of parlando." *Magyar Zenei Szemle* [Hung. Musical Review], 1942, in Hungarian.)

What is the perennial fascination of speech-inflection? Why does it have such an electrifying effect on the music of every period? The answer is not difficult to find. Whether it is melody of a restricted or a wide compass, relying on few or many notes, it brings free-floating, pulsating rhythm which over and over again in the history of music has the impact of novelty, opening the door to every kind of innovation. It appears with liberating, revolutionary force, particularly when styles reach their zenith, at the point at which they become liltingly melodious, with smooth and supple lines, compact harmony and lively rhythms. That was the way it asserted itself between 1600 and 1770, and again between 1850 and 1900; how it will always be able to function in European art-music so long as the great European melody-styles endure. For rich musical styles quickly grow decadent and are constantly in need of rejuvenation—the release afforded by spontaneous declamation, with its colour and raciness. It bestows a magical moment of anarchy, a break-away from established traditions. It provides access to the instinctive melodiousness of the human larynx, to the basic common language or "elemental melody," as Wagner puts it, "from which the language of speech was once born."

NOTES

1. In the reading of the Koran, *al-lahn*. See, amongst others, the article by P. Kahle, *Ignace Goldziher Memorial Volume* I, Budapest, 1948, p. 173.
2. Early Christianity did its utmost to subordinate the emotional effect of the melody to the exigencies of the sacred text. (As S. Augustine wrote, *moveor non cantu, sed rebus quae cantantur*—I am not moved by the melody, but by the things that are sung.) The ideal melody was one which was adapted to the needs of the text. Hucbald in the 9th century was still dividing melody and phrase according to the same principles (*eodem modo distinguitur cantilena, quo et sententia*—the cantilena takes its character from the meaning), but with the growth of polyphony, it was thrust into the background. By about 1340, Pierre de Baume (Petrus de Palma) was angrily reproaching composers: in the old motets, he said, every part of the text could be understood, but in the new ones "*tot sunt fractiones, quod solum percipitur melodia, quae mulcet aures et nullam aliam facit utilitatem*"—"there are so many sections that only the melody is understood, which caresses the ears, and does nothing else useful." This

is the age-old dispute between text and melody, even though melody obviously springs to some extent from intonation, and poetry from melody. "Don't merely read! Always sing!" declared Goethe (in *An Lina*, 1799) and in 1828 a French poet wrote that "Poems are the offspring of the lyre: they should be sung, not read"(F. Baldensperger: *Sensibilité musicale et Romantisme*. Paris, 1925, p. 126).

3. From extant folk-music, American negro blues and the East European Yiddish songs of *shailo-utshuvo*, etc., still mirror the inflections of living speech.

THE MAQAM PRINCIPLE IN FOLK
AND ART-MUSIC: THE TYPE AND ITS VARIANTS

In this chapter an attempt will be made to clarify a subject which has long been familiar to folklorist and musicologist both as a basic fact of musical existence and an established form of expression. By this is meant the formation of variants, a phenomenon which has been interesting musicology more and more during the last few decades, the result of many independent researches carried out from various points of view. Countless small details have been thrown up in the course of these studies, which, so far as the researcher is concerned, shape themselves in perspective into two distinct standpoints. One view is that variant formation represents the essential difference which separates folk-music from art-music. The other finds this to be an exaggeration, and holds that there is no sharp dividing-line between folk-creation and the work of the creative artist. Both views will be illustrated with examples during the course of this chapter, and some sort of synthesis attempted. The term 'maqam' has been adopted because it is the term provisionally used by present-day musicology for the conscious or unconscious formation of variants by primitive communities as by highly developed ones.

What then is a 'maqam'? According to the Orientalist Idelsohn, it originally meant the dais on which an Arab singer used to stand when he performed at the court of the Caliphs. Another meaning is simply 'rule' or 'law', which, like the Greek *nomos*, applies just as well to music; yet a third is 'sound', and in a broader musical sense it means the melodic form, model, formula or typical form. The origin of the word is not what matters here, so much as the way in which it is used. Idelsohn and Lachmann trace the 'maqam' to the pre-Islamic era, when centralised urban communities of Arabs would keep track of the various local melodies of the tribes, even in later periods, by the use of special identification labels. Persian, Bedouin town and village tunes were absorbed into current Arab art-music, together with a permanent record of their place of origin. The geographical and ethnical origin of the chief Arab melody-types and derived types are immediately apparent. They are called Hejaz-maqam, Iraq-maqam, Ispahan-maqam, Adsham-maqam, Nahavand-maqam etc., all indicating some particular region where these melodies may once have originated.

(Adsham is the popular Arab name for Persia, the others are well-known place-names.) It is familiar that for centuries the Greeks used regional names to describe certain melody-types as well as scales — Dorian, Phrygian, Lydian, Aeolian, etc. But a more detailed explanation is needed to show how this practice developed in old high-cultures—particularly as even today it is the prevalent practice in all Oriental music. Obligatory traditions prescribe which *maqam* the Arab musician will perform on any given occasion, which *raga* the Indian, which *patet* the Javanese. And under this head one could also add the Greek *nomos* and the Byzantine *epichema*. What sort of melodic regulation is involved, and by what is it determined? What is laid down is normally the general outline of the melody; sometimes only the outer notes, so that the melody can move as freely as it likes within this framework, sometimes only the first and last notes. This may well sound easy-going and chancy, yet the Oriental player unerringly distinguishes the good performance which respects tradition, from the faulty one which disregards it. But this faultiness, this disregard of tradition, has nothing to do with the freedom of the individual performance, but rather the contrary; within certain limits, the performer is not only entitled to improvise his melody, but expected to do so, so long as he keeps to the model, the pre-established outline of the *maqam*. Hence 'maqam' clearly denotes a collective tradition, rule, or style, which sets limits for the performer's art. The improvisation, the melodic shape assumed, represents the expression of his personality within the stylistic bounds laid down by the community. That is why a melody can never sound the same twice. The essence of this art is the balance achieved between constraint and freedom, between the established model and the improvised performance, between collectivity and individuality, permanent tradition and the creation of the moment.

It will be seen straight away that folk-music (*every* kind of folk-music) is in essence no more than a consistent application of the 'maqam' principle. As he sings or plays his instrument, a folk-singer or instrumentalist becomes aware of certain melodic patterns he would like to realise. But this realisation depends on his personal inclinations, his skill as a performer, his cultural background, his physical condition, his frame of mind, his likes and dislikes; these change as much as the human face alters under the influence of different impressions, to quote László Lajtha's ingenious analogy. It has been said above that the folk-musician is *aware* of the melody-types he wishes to perform; and this requires some explanation. Recent research in this respect has produced some surprising results. Marius Schneider, for example, points out that the Egyptian, Negro and Indian folk-singer is still searching for his melody at the moment of beginning a performance: the melody gradually takes shape as he proceeds. (The folklorists Markov, Maslov and Bogoslavski have described how the singers of Russian rhyming chronicles, from whom they collected in 1901 in the Arkhangelsk province, "first recall the subject-matter of the saga," then "choose from the possible melodies." The final version of the melody "does not appear until the second or third verse," after which "it is always repeated with slight alterations.") Because of this, Schneider tends to the opinion that there are two kinds of variant-formation: the general or unconscious *maqam* (stemming from indecision, forgetting of words, or using existing formulae in a different way) and the conscious *maqam*, which invents structural variants as a way of clarifying an idea. Hungarian collectors in the last few years seem to have reached the same conclusion. Both Lajos Vargyas at Áj and Pál Járdányi at Kide found that a village community would accept certain variants as its own form of expression, and entirely exclude others; and although variant-formation is nowhere the result of conscious intellectual effort, the village singers were well aware, as one of the women at Kide said to Járdányi: "there are many versions of these village songs," or more briefly, as a gipsy in Gyergyóalfalu told the author: "It can also go like this."

"It can also go like this"—yet this awareness of the 'identity' of a song has its limits. Oddly enough, village singers often do not recognise their own melodies if they hear them with different texts. So far, it is not known how far they are able to 'identify' melodies. What then happens to melodies with "many versions" and what is the importance of this phenomenon? Let us take a look at an Arab or Turkish *maqam* and compare it with the melodic variants of one of the Hungarian folk-ballads (e.g. *Mason Kelemen*, of which Kodály has recorded more than thirty different strophic variants[1], see Ex. 133—134).

These melodies obviously exist in many versions; a single one is quite inconceivable. The folk musician is not trying to discover the one perfect form, clear and authentic; for him, such an idea would be quite absurd. So far as he is concerned, as for his audience and his whole cultural community, the melody exists in various guises; were there only one, it would be unable to survive, and would gradually become extinct. *Maqam* in folk-song is in a constant state of flux; it moves towards something, then moves away again without any precise intention. A singer of unusual sensibility may well be aware which is the better form, and even try to establish it; but it is beyond his power *completely* to accomplish this, because he is never in the same state of alertness and receptivity. It is worth referring at this point to Aladár Rácz, the great Hungarian cimbalon-player, who changed the prevailing notions about that instrument. He preserved this folk instinct to an astonishing degree; he would often declare that he could not possibly perform a piece of music twice in the same way. This links him with the tradition of the great creative performers of European music, who would improvise their arias and sonatas differently every evening.

This brings us to the essence of folk-music. The constant renewal of melody means its regeneration: the *maqam* principle affects not only the whole nature of folk-performance but of folk-creation too. The great discoverers of Hungarian folk-music, Bartók and Kodály, have never suggested that the peasantry were the creative "inventors" of folk-song. Where folk-melody is concerned, inventing and creating implies the use of *maqam,* that is, of variant-formation; performance is improvised within the limits of traditional forms. Even so, the possibilities are extensive, and the gradations of difference infinite. If a whole set of variations are examined, they will be found to range from the identical to the slightly resembling, the closely resembling to the infinitely distant.

It is worth taking a closer look at this age-old process, and trying to watch it in action. There are two closely related groups of problems which are of perennial interest to the Hungarian ethnologist and musicologist. One is concerned with how the living word is related to the written tradition, and the other with how melody-forms are transformed when they are taken over from art-music into folk-music. Neither problem is soluble without taking into account the age-old conventions of *maqam.* Zoltán Kodály's researches have shown the comparison of surviving folk-forms with old written records to be one of the most fascinating chapters in Hungarian musical history. Oral survival cannot be shown to bear a uniform relationship to written records, nor are general principles applicable, for so many different grades of transformation are encountered. In some melodies, the extant forms may confirm the authenticity of an earlier written record, whilst in others the rhythm or the melodic line may differ radically from the earlier written versions, and are most likely variants of more recent origin. Where most of the collated versions are concerned, it is characteristic that the extant version of oral tradition is older and more authentic than the inadequately recorded written version. This is particularly true of the richly ornamented melodies of the 17th and 18th centuries, the written or printed versions of which are almost always clumsy, hastily jotted down, and often full of mistakes. Here is one of the finest examples of Kodály's collated variants, the 17th-century lament known as 'István Dobai's Lament', given in its two most typical versions. One of these was recorded by 18th-century students, the other discovered extant by 20th-century folk-song collectors:

135

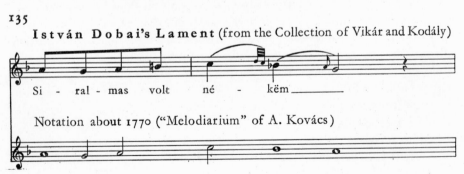

István Dobai's Lament (from the Collection of Vikár and Kodály)

Si - ral - mas volt né - këm _____

Notation about 1770 ("Melodiarium" of A. Kovács)

ti - zën - - - har-ma-dik   Ke-le-mën kő-mi- e - - ssə.

ők fë - - lə fo-ga-ggyák   ma - gos Dé-va vá - rát.

ők fë - - l fo-ga-ggyák,   hogy ők fë-lé₋ pít-sé - - kə. etc.

etc.

Noted about 1860

Original key

Azt   hal-lot-tam ró- sám   hogy el   a - karsz vál - ni?

Ballad of Mason Kelemen, after Z. Kodály (opening lines)

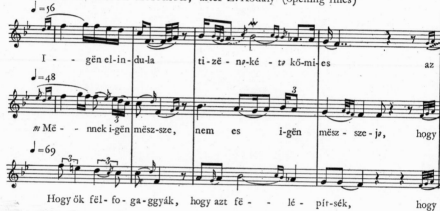

♩=56

I - - gën el-in- du-la   ti - zë - na-ké - ta kő-mi- es   az

♩=48

m Më - - nnek i-gën mësz-sze,   nem es   i-gën   mësz - sze- ja,   hogy

♩=69

Hogy ők fël - fo - ga-ggyák,   hogy azt fë - - lé - pít-sék,   hogy

Turkish Maqam after R. Lachmann

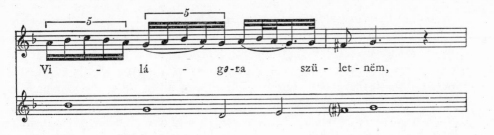

Here the 'eternal' principle of *maqam* can be seen in action, just as it has been practised in every epoch by the Oriental musician. General outline and basic features are all that is laid down; the rest is left to performance, which infuses the melody with meaning and vitality. Setting down the main outlines is the function of an impersonal and timeless tradition; the artist's task is realisation in an individual and immediate way. The whole existence of folk-tradition depends on the twin impulses of permanence and change, roots and foliage, everlastingly at odds, yet constantly in agreement. The picture may be completed with some examples showing the changes which have occurred in elements taken over from art-music. (One of the most felicitous examples was provided by folklorist Péter Balla, who in the thirties, in Moldavia, witnessed the transformation of a Budapest operetta waltz into a village folk-song through a process of four or five variants.) Here too the material at disposal is overwhelmingly vast, particularly if the bounds of enquiry are extended to include the whole of European folk-song as well as Hungarian folk-music. Only one set of problems can be singled out—one which also affects Hungarian folk-music—the extent to which ancient verse-forms can survive. It is common knowledge that towards the end of the classical epoch, a number of Greek and Latin verse-forms were transformed in Western Europe into popular and even folkish forms, and so continued to survive. Several of them reached Hungary, probably towards the end of the Middle Ages; among them was Sapphic metre, which produced a rich aftermath throughout Europe, and the so-called Alcaic metre, which in Western Europe, in the Middle Ages, turned into a typical hymn metre. It reached Hungary in this form, and found its way into Hungarian folk-melody in the 16th century through the songs of András Vásárhelyi, Sebestyén Tinódi and others. Several other Western forms also enjoyed the same sort of adventurous fate; Anacreontic verse, for example, took on new life in Italian folk-music towards the end of the Renaissance, thanks to Monteverdi and his contemporaries. A further example is the trochaic tetrameter, which can be traced from Sophocles to Beethoven; and West European vagrant poetry, which arrived in Hungary probably by the end of the Middle Ages, where it encountered the East European *kolomeika* form. The same principle that has been seen operating in melodic survival also applies to the way that these metrical forms have survived, chiefly because of their importance in folk-poetry. The original structure, outline and model are retained, but the details and the particular form required are built up in relation to the needs of the moment, and take any shape.

So far, we have been concerned almost exclusively with the continuity of folk-tradition. Is it the same when we turn to art-music, or does it present quite another problem? Are those scholars right who maintain that they are two separate worlds, cut off from each other by an unbridgeable gulf?

At first sight, folk-music and art-music, folk-tradition and artistic creation seem to represent totally different and opposing realms of the human spirit. Earlier on it has been described how the folk-musician—who is both executant and creator—retains more than one single, perfect version of poem or melody in his consciousness, and is constantly aware of the various ways in which it can be realised; that it has a Janus- or Hecate-like quality in that "It can also go like this," being a many-faced creation to which the idea of a single fixed version is utterly alien. The struggling development of an artist on the other hand appears to involve something diametrically opposed, since his aim is to embody his ideas in unique form, final and irrevocable. Beethoven would not have allowed anybody to perform the *Appassionata* in a "like this, also" way! A Mozart or Verdi opera cannot be performed in an improvised fashion, its final shape having once been laid down by its creator. Hence it seems as though in spirit and intention, artistic, self-conscious creation functions utterly differently from folk-creation.

But on second thoughts, one is tempted to ask whether this is really true, whether the spirit of *maqam* is really so different from conscious creation, so that there is no point of contact between the two types. The search for the mod-

el, which can then be realised in various ways; the necessity of change implying the destruction and renewal of the artistic shape as occasion demands; are
these so different from artistic creation? In this respect there are three relevant
factors to be considered if the principle implied by the fourth is clearly to be
understood.

Firstly, the flowering of great melodic cultures always and everywhere encourages the formation of *types*. In such prolific periods there are always *several*
specimens of *one* type, the harvest being bountiful. Because there are several
versions of each type, general taste tends to accept one specimen rather than
another. It is sufficient to mention the *bel canto* period, when a host of schools
taught the art of improvisation, and an artist worthy of the name would perform
his *pezzo di bravura* differently every evening—different, yet the same; it would
be in keeping with the generally accepted notions of taste and style, yet at the
same time free. Surely this is very like folk-creation, variation-building, *maqam*? We are familiar with the breath-taking variations of an aria, as performed by celebrated singers of the period, such as Farinelli and Marchesi;
surely their six, eight, ten, or fourteen richly ornamented variants of the same
melody show the same spirit as "it can also go like this." Even though Farinelli
and Marchesi had clearly never heard the singers of Kide and Gyergyóalfalu!

Secondly: the idea of variation has never been alien to the European composer. On the contrary, there were periods when his best energies were dominated by this idea, when it was the chief ambition of European composers to
construct new forms by varying certain set themes, thereby opening up new
possibilities. The psychological background of this phenomenon is thoroughly
familiar and straightforward. It evokes the primitive and almost childish delight
in concealment and discovery, hide-and-seek; the pleasure is the same whether
it is called out by the repetitive refrain of a nursery-rhyme or by the disguised
variation of the motives in Wagner's music-dramas. Centuries passed before the
medieval composer thought of doing anything other than elaborating and ornamenting the Gregorian chorale in various ways. Early instrumental music was
given a strong fillip by the strings of variations of dance-melodies, incorporated
in the so-called suite of variations. Protestant church-music reached its high-
water mark in the monumental structures which developed out of the variations
of the Lutheran chorale—the Chorale-Cantata, Chorale-Fantasy, Chorale-Pas-
sion. It speaks volumes that the greatest architects of European classicism, Bach
and Beethoven, were also supremely versatile in the use of variation. Some composers are at their best in constructing variations, in the various implications
of form, and elaborating of material, finding themselves more at home in this
than in the actual invention of melodies. Bach and Beethoven, as well as Liszt
and Bartók, all belong in this category. A love of variations inevitably leads on
to the idea of *omnia ex uno*, or monothematic construction. It is natural that

Liszt and Bartók have been primarily responsible in the 19th and 20th centuries for the monothematic symphonic poem, chamber music and concerto.

Thirdly: whether he realises it or not, even a self-aware European composer resorts willy-nilly to constant or ever recurring melody-patterns. All round him, the taste of the period, and its style and speech, are constantly affirming certain ideas and forms of expression, certain idioms, formulae and practical possibilities. If an artist were to disregard them, he would be denying his period, and renouncing the chance of communication. To neglect them would mean that he was no longer the product of his century, whether as collaborator or reformer. For whether reform manifests itself in a cautious or a revolutionary way, it still implies search and selection. By a gradual exchange of verbal idioms, models, *maqams*, it takes up what is best and liveliest, and discards what is feeble and outworn. That is why the 'wandering themes' of any given period acquire new impetus at the hands of some supreme personality; and nobody can possibly maintain that an artist of this stature has not made use of 'wandering themes' from the common supply. This applies as much to Shakespeare and Molière as to Handel and Mozart; they would be astonished if their individual inspiration were called in question on this account. In the past, public opinion expected composers to realise ideas in a fine and satisfying way; they did not expect originality. Palestrina and Lasso, Bach and Handel adopted countless themes which were not their own. Eighty per cent of Mozart's melodies turn up in works by his contemporaries, and many of his early works are scarcely distinguishable from those of J.C. Bach or Paisiello. There follows a selection of settings of the celebrated minuet from *Don Giovanni*, as treated by contemporary composers over a fifty-year period. (See also R. Haas: *W. A. Mozart*. Potsdam, 1950, pp. 7—9, for the earlier history of the melody-type in Austro-German folk-music, the role it played in Mozart's older Austrian contemporaries, and in Mozart's own works.)

136

a) **Rinaldo da Capua:** La zingara (about 1740)

b) **Piccinni:** La buona figliola (1760)

c) **F. de Majo:** Ifigenia in Tauride (1762)

d) J. C. Bach: Alessandro nell'Indie (1762)

e) Paisiello: Il re Teodoro (1784)

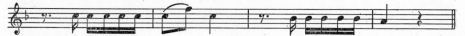

f) Paisiello: Gli Zingari in fiera (1789)

g) Guglielmi: Finti amori (1784)

h) Mozart: String Quartet (Divertimento) (K.V. 136) (1772)

i) Mozart: Don Giovanni (1787)

But even more exciting is to watch a great artist making a life-long occupation of re-modelling some self-chosen theme or melodic pattern. He approaches it from various angles, discovering in it ever new implications, merging it so completely with his thought that it is established as his own melodic idiom, the symbol of his entire creative achievement. A motive built out of a few notes, a sort of musical motto, accompanied Mozart, Beethoven and Bartók their whole lives long, acquiring greater significance at key moments, and so revealing a new and deeper meaning. (A good example is Mozart's four-note 'motto' which companioned him from beginning to end.) Such thematic unity can affect an artist's individual development just as much as it can influence the art of a period or a generation. The Hungarian ethnographer, Oszkár Dincsér, rightly quotes the Sienese school of painters as an example of this, and could just as well have quoted Raphael, Watteau or Cézanne as examples of individuals. The life and work of any really great artist are dominated in a deeper sense by a central *leitmotif*, which is continually receiving clarification. (Bergson said of philosophers that they keep on reshaping one single basic thought their whole lives long; the same could be said of artists.) "Every element of culture is essentially a range of variation," said Ralph Linton. (*The Tree of Culture.* New York, 1955, p. 34.)

In conclusion, it is clear that the links between folk-musician and composer are closer than at first appears, the one aware of the existence of many variants of equal value, the other in search of the one perfect embodiment of his ideas. For in essence, the artist's 'free' creation also implies a choice. Like the folk-singer, he has variants from which to choose; like the folk-singer, he is backed by a tradition of style and idiom, by what a period, generation or community allows or forbids him to do. He finds his raw material and a common vocabulary by operating within the restrictions of form acceptable to the community, and finds space within it for his own individual invention. Insofar as he is a conscious creator, he is free, yet all his efforts cannot entirely free him from his period and its conventions. They merely allow him a chance for self-discovery and development, for taking a conscious grip on himself. These two manifestations of creativity, seemingly so opposed, depend on the maintenance of a balance between permanence and change. These forces are related to each other in the same way as the immutable *maqam* is related to its transitory realisation, the basic theme to its variations. The number of basic ideas is comparatively small; variants alone are plentiful, being short-lived and transitory. It seems as though a basic fact of nature is reflected in this relationship: the roots are few, but there is plenty of foliage. The life of the root is permanent, even though it is mostly unseen, whilst the foliage, which all can admire, is constantly dyng and budding again.

NOTES

. A good example of the *maqam* style is the Greek song of Olympus, as sung by singers from Acharnania, Pelopponese, Livadia and Kardica. It was published by S. Baud-Bovy in the *Journal of the International Folk Music Council* I, Camb., 1949, p. 44.

(Aï - de) Dhen to 'lpi - za

vré(ŋ)O-lym - bé.

(mo-ré)to maï na syn -

ne - fia - ssis To Maï

To maï na - a - ri -

- xiss tiss vro - o - chess.

PENTATONICISM AND CULTURAL HISTORY

1. THE PROBLEM 2. DEFINITION OF THE FIELD OF RESEARCH
3. SURVEY OF THE MATERIAL 4. SUPPOSITIONS 5. CONCLUSIONS

1. *The Problem*

Family-histories abound in tales of old jewels and talismans, divided up from
remote epochs amongst the members of a family, by which late descendants
might recognise their kith and kin when scattered abroad. Human history, too,
is full of such relics, signs and symbols, a reminder of an earlier era when the
world's 'families' were united and equal. In the face of this phenomenon, even
the most credulous begin to doubt, and the sceptics to express astonishment, for
it represents something of which both alike have long declared themselves ig-
norant—something which has been forgotten by historical research for a very,
very long time, or never consciously known.

One such 'family heirloom' is the tradition of pentatonicism. The fact that
it turns up in different parts of the world, and amongst very different peoples,
has led researchers to assume that it is one of the oldest and most universal
of human relics. It has been repeatedly investigated by German, Russian, Fin-
nish, French and Turkish musicologists (Riemann, Hornbostel, Lach, Tolstoi,
Launis, d'Harcourt, Ragib). Since its discovery on Hungarian and Rumanian
soil, it has also been treated from the Hungarian standpoint in important works
by Bartók and Kodály. Kodály was also making a detailed study of the pentatonic nature of Cheremissian music* at the same time.

To begin with, it is essential to discuss the findings of German musicologists. In their view, pentatonicism** represents a universal stage of musical development, which they assume to have occurred everywhere at a certain period.

* The Mari, or Cheremiss, are a small people living in the Volga region. (Translators' note.)
** For use of term, see Translator's note on p. 11.

They explain the fact that today it is only met in specific places by saying that this is the remains of the ancient tradition, blocked and conserved in certain isolated areas, or 'areas of retreat'. Hence pentatonic remains presuppose a stage of evolution: a universal human tradition which survives in certain places, and harks back to the same 'musical Stone Age'—to what is known to students of cultural history as an *Elementargedanke*, or 'primary idea'. They consider that pentatonic systems probably existed wherever primitive music flourished, but that the remaining traces are not necessarily linked. The Neolithic cultures of Siberia and South Africa, for instance, are not necessarily connected. Yet on the other hand they find it impossible to believe that between one five-note system and another there is any difference of principle, style or historic development. In the absence of a common starting-point and a common standard of measurement, there is thus no relationship nor grade of difference between them. We are in fact confronted by a kind of musical uniformity, a *consensus gentium*, which at its most primitive level was probably once shared by the whole world.[1]

Does this represent the truth? Should we not rather assume that five-note organisation belongs with phenomena such as frieze motives, key patterns, swastikas, and similar ornamental devices? In scientific circles these are no longer regarded as simple manifestations of evolution, universal and parallel. They are no longer thought of as 'recurrent inventions', the result of chance coincidence, but are believed instead to conceal definite conscious links with specific ancient cultures. Surely pentatonic systems are more likely to be related to developed cultures? Is it not in fact inconsistent and unrealistic research which assumes that there are close links between Central Asia, Africa and South America, because the same standards of measurement can be applied to their instruments, while at the same time it denies the relationship which arises from the existence of pentatonic scales in these continents?

We shall discuss this a little later on. The author's conclusions are determined by his selected point of departure. Up to now, it is worth noticing, probably only Kodály, Danckerts, and M. Schneider (and, in passing, Schünemann and Lach) have linked pentatonic scales with melodic structure; most researchers are content to classify the phenomenon as a general principle. (Only in this way can it be understood why, for instance, several researchers have attempted to explain the origin of pentatonicism in terms of the technique of instruments and their historical development—a point of view which always assumes that the instruments enjoyed a parallel development in the various continents concerned. Of this more will be said later.) That is why for the most part the various problems connected with it have so far remained unsolved. It may of course be asked whether it is possible to study pentatonicism in the abstract as a general principle—independently of the melodic patterns in which it appears.

Is it not much more probable that in essence pentatonic style implies the *collective* and concrete manifestation of a five-note system *as well as* a special form of melody-construction?—that it is not a question of *one* pentatonic style but of several? An attempt will be made to answer this question by dint of examples, by examining a whole series of melodies. The various juxtaposed cultures are extremely diverse—they include 'historical' and 'non-historical', literate and illiterate cultures which are relatively original (that is, initiators) and those which are receptive and open to foreign influence. Of some (the Aztecs, for example) only the period of decline is known; of others (such as Central Asia), it is only possible to guess at their heyday and period of influence. Even the extent of time involved is variable and obscure; in Asia it may reach back to 3000 B.C., while in Southern and Central America it may be the 10th—15th century A.D. Yet they have in common the fact that they do not represent a primitive stage of culture, but a more developed one which has left behind it the unknown centuries, representing the oldest and most elementary processes of evolution. Musicology is particularly well qualified in our opinion to show significantly whether these ancient centres were interconnected, or whether they developed in isolation.

2. *Definition of the Field Research*

Contemporary Western musicology, as we have seen, considers pentatonicism to be a form of tonality which occurs universally at certain stages of evolution. Yet several music-cultures show no trace of it either in their present, surviving form, or in their pre-history, whilst others have flourishing five-note systems even today (see sketch-map on pp. 233-234). How can these contradictions be reconciled? Three explanations are possible:

1. The pentatonic systems surviving today are not identical with the forms assumed to have existed in the past (there is no proof of this).

2. The pentatonic system was everywhere prevalent at the same time, but was ousted in many places by factors of greater evolutionary strength. It survived in places where it did not encounter another type of tonal system which was richer or more adaptable; or because it was better equipped to meet the musical needs of some culture-zone which had remained 'frozen' at some stage of development. (To this it may be objected that pentatonicism is everywhere very tenacious; there is hardly an area, where it is known to have existed, which today shows no trace of it.)

3. A developing tonal system does not *necessarily* lead to a pentatonic one. This seems to be the most likely hypothesis; it does not involve the researcher in formulating a 'theory of disappearance', but tends instead to concentrate attention on such pentatonic systems as are still extant. It reminds him at the same time that there is nothing fortuitous about the survival of five-note scales in certain regions, that from the point of view of music and cultural history it is charged with significance. Wherein does this importance lie? We shall try and explain in the following pages.

★

Even in a rough preliminary classification, pentatonic material needs grouping into two categories. One type of pentatonic scale is characterised by its lack of semitone intervals *(without semitones = anhemitonic*)*; the other has two whole-tone intervals *(ditonic)* as well as semitone intervals *(hemitonic*)*. The difference may be set out as follows:

Anhemitonic five-note scale: *f-g-b flat-c-d-f.*

Ditonic or hemitonic five-note scale: *f-g flat-b flat-c-d flat-f.*[2]

Hornbostel points out that they have a 'permanent fourth' in common; he describes them as 'scaffolding fourths' *(Gerüstquarten)* :[3]

g-b flat-c-d-f,
g-a flat-c-d flat-f.

Every pentatonic melody-style shows examples of the first type, whilst the latter is typical of most late-Hellenistic and Japanese *(kumoi* scale) melodies, as well as of many melodies of New Guinea. Riemann has already pointed out[4] that the second type (which he calls 'imitated pentatonicism') is a later development than anhemitonic five-note scales. It comes into existence later on, through a process of modifying, mixing and archaising, and always in areas where pure anhemitonic types had once existed, areas where the old types had been eclipsed by a more recent melody-culture. So it was that in ancient Greece, the old 'enharmony'—or according to Riemann[5] the anhemitonic five-note scale of Terpander and Olympus—gave way to the late Hellenic 'new enharmony' or seven-note scale. In Japan, the earlier *ryosen* and *ritsusen* scales still survive alongside the *kumoi* and *hirayoshi ;* just as fragmentary remains of the original Chinese tonal system are still to be found in Java and Siam in the form of 'practice scales', alongside Indian and Malayan-Indonesian elements, alongside 'distance scales'; just as in India the *velavali* and *karnati* modes are probably the remains

---

* The author's terms have been adopted as there is no comparable English term. (Translators' note.)

of the original Chinese five-note scale. In any case the ditonic five-note scale is always a secondary formation by comparison with the original anhemitonic form, and for this reason will be disregarded in the course of this chapter. It is worth remarking that the *slendro*, the Javanese tempered scale, represents a third type of pentatonicism, one which divides the octave into five equal parts. The origin of this type is still obscure; J.P.N. Land thinks it was Chinese in origin, whilst J. Kunst believes it to be Indian. Others think that Javanese and Indian five-note formations result from the reduction of many-note scales.

The second group to be excluded—yet only so far as the narrow limits of this chapter are concerned—is the widespread group of pentatonic dialects which give the impression of having been borrowed, mixed and 'crossed'. Amongst these borrowed or mixed types, reflecting a later stage of development, should be included (*a*) all Japanese melody-forms. The Japanese tonal system (including ditonic scales) represents a relatively late historical stage, more likely to be traced to a basic Indonesian stratum, Mongolian-influenced, than to a purely Mongolian one[6]; (*b*) melodies of the Sunda and Polynesian Islands, in which the most primitive tune-types are curiously mixed with pentatonic scales and even with Western Asian Mohammedan influences (Arab-Persian); (*c*) Russian, Kirghiz and Rumanian five-note scales, which for the most part should be considered as an ancient Turkish folk-heritage; (*d*) the seemingly rudimentary or sporadic five-note scales of Bulgarian, German, Canadian, Patagonian and Chilean melodies; (*e*) the melodies of Lapps and Voguls, which, like some Scandinavian tunes, have preserved a fragmentary form of pentatonicism, possibly the defective form of the major scale. The Gregorian form of pentatonicism is not included in this list of exclusions because although it is not apparently 'original' or 'primary', it nevertheless reveals itself with far more classic simplicity in the pages of the Roman Gradual than in its sources in Oriental-Hebrew tune-types, as these are known today. In any case, it too is a form of pentatonicism which later creates its own mixed forms within its own sphere of influence, and these cannot be included in this summary. (*Christe qui lux es et dies* from the early hymn collections, and Hrabanus Maurus' *Veni Creator spiritus* from the later ones, are the best examples of pentatonic melody-structure at the stage of disintegration.)

Mention must be made of V. Belayev's view in connection with the mixing and breaking up of scales.[7] He assumes that pentatonic and diatonic scales have derived acoustically, and questions whether it is possible for these systems to be mixed. This view is refuted by the transitional tune-types which occur without exception wherever a pentatonic melody-culture meets a non-pentatonic one, in Hungary as in the Caucasus, or on the South-East fringe of China.

Thus the simplified selection which follows will limit itself to the most 'original' and 'predominant' melody-types—apparent 'source-types' of five-note structure. We have tried to represent each region by a developed and significant form so as to compare it with equally characteristic tune-types from other cultures. In order to simplify the survey—and because in the anhemitonic pentatonic scale the final often seems to be fortuitous*—each melody has been transposed into the same five-note series (*g-b flat-c-d-f*). The following thirteen melodies represent ten different pentatonic styles and ten pentatonic music-cultures:[8]

137
G r e g o r i a n p s a l m m e l o d y (from the Gradual)

138
A n n a m i t e m e l o d y (after Knosp)

139
T u r k e s t a n m e l o d y (after Nurullah Shevket)

* "The series is relative and the scale can begin with any of the five notes," C. Vega writes of Peruvian instruments. (*Acta Musicologica* IX, 1937, p. 43.) This is very often true of the final, particularly in areas of flourishing pentatonicism.

140
Nogai-Tartar melody (after Moshkov)

141
Kasan-Tartar melody (author's notation)

142
Hungarian melody (after Bartók)

143
West African Negro melody (after Tiersot)

222

North American Yuma Indian melody (after Herzog)

3 times

North American Chippewa Indian melody (after Densmore)

Indian melody from Peru (after d'Harcourt)

North American Negro melody (spiritual, after Burleigh)

148

Scottish melody (after Moffat)

Fine

D.C. al Fine

149

English melody (after Kidson)

3. *Survey of the Material*

What do these examples show? At first sight, as many different worlds and as many principles of melody construction as there are melodies. But a closer examination reveals that some types and style-groups are more closely related. To begin with, there is a connecting link between melodies Nos. 138—142. It is the Asian, or rather, the *Central Asian* group. Asia in the strict sense is represented in this table by three melodies, one of which comes from the South-Eastern coast of the continent (Annam, Vietnam), the second from Central Asia (Turkestan) and the third from Western Asia (region of the Astrakhan Tartars). To these the Kazan-Tartar and Hungarian examples are intrinsically related. The structural affinity and underlying identity of the five examples is immediately striking: they are all constructed from a melody-phrase which starts off 'high' (in the upper part of its compass) or is stated in its higher range, and then answered or repeated at a 'lower' level (in the lower part of its compass);

224

in this way the basic idea is transposed and to some extent changed, and a form built up. The Far-Eastern, Turkestan and Hungarian melodies show this principle almost faultlessly in all its purity, whilst the Nogai-Tartar melody—the most *parlando* of the five—shows certain modifications: here the third melody-line is entirely changed because it has been influenced by the first, whilst the fourth is more clearly reminiscent of the idea of the lowered phrase (corresponding second and fourth lines); this happens also in the Kirghiz, Chuvash, Mongolian, Chinese and Hungarian melodies.[9] The basic structure of the Kazan-Tartar melody is even more blurred: here the 'lowering' only appears in the second half of the third line and the first half of the fourth; the rest is modified under the influence of the first line, and through a plagal tendency. Both Tartar melodies show the same symmetrical structure as the Far-Eastern, Turkestan-Turkish and Hungarian melodies: opposing pairs of lines, with one pair answering the other. In this stylistically linked group it seems as though the *double-line* is essential to the musical structure, and transposition the chief principle of construction. (More seldom there is a repeated or slightly varied single line, as in the Hungarian, Turkestan and Far-Eastern examples, harking back to a still simpler, single-line structure: more often it is the double-line, with altered content.) These basic elements underlie even the more complex Chinese and Indonesian forms.[10] In this way a symmetrically organised four-line strophe emerges out of the basic structure—the single or double melody-line—as is still the case even today amongst the Buryat of Central Asia[11]; and this may be done either by changing the pentatonic system (Hungarian example) or by remaining within the same system (Far-Eastern, Turkestan, Tartar examples). The question of how this structural principle originated—manifestly the earliest universal form-building principle of Mongolian-Turkish folk-music in Asia and Eastern Europe[12]—has already been discussed elsewhere.[13] For the purpose of this survey it will be referred to as the 'Central Asian' transposing principle.

Gregorian melody (No. 137) provides a much more 'primitive' world of melody. Essential to it is a stepwise ascending three-note motif, the third and highest note of which 'echoes on' by dint of being stressed as a reciting-tone, thus indicating a three-note original. Its chief structural characteristic is its litany-like repetition,[14] its tendency to reiteration. It is entirely characteristic of the *pneuma* style of recitative psalmody. As already mentioned, its generic links are not European but probably Syrian-Hebrew, that is, it is *Western Asian* in origin. It is in fact the chief tune-type of Idelsohn's Arab-Jewish collection (particularly so far as the Yemen material is concerned, but also in connection with the melodies of old Jewish settlers in the Caucasus); the original three-note form (*b flat-c-d*)[15] does in fact occur here among their source-types, just as *g-b flat-c*—the three-note precursor of the Central Asian type—is found among the Buryat. Quite a number of the recitative formulae of Gregorian chant hark back to a basic three-note formula of this kind. Thus Western Asia possesses its own three-note form, expanded into a five-note form, and so has Central Asia. (It is quite possible that three-note formulae everywhere gave rise to pentatonicism.) Yet the pentatonic form of the first psalm-tone, that classic model of the Roman Gradual, seems to be particularly representative and significant in this culture-zone; in its Latinised form it may well represent a basic type (there is no trace of any such pentatonic type in the few extant remains of ancient Greek music). Because of its three-note opening motive, the psalmodic, pentatonic tune-type of Western Asia and the Mediterranean came in fact to influence other culture-zones as well. The similar openings of Transylvanian, Rumanian and Turkish folk-songs, for instance, may very likely reflect its influence in a direct or indirect way,[16] as may similar passages in Old German melodies. In any case, this so-called 'primitive' form of pentatonic melody characteristically presupposes at its rear an even more primitive level of culture, just as does the more developed type of Central Asia.

From the standpoint of European notions of form, the pentatonic structure of the *African* Negro melody (No. 143) appears only slightly more advanced than the litany-type. It is based on a short, rhythmical, note-repeating motive which develops into a chain of variations, here and there resembling a rondo. Here too, recitative is the predominant element, so that its basic form is a motive of few notes, and development proceeds by variation. Because of this, more developed variants such as ABCD and ABA sometimes make their chance appearance in African Negro music. The example quoted, taken from Dahomey, shows this kind of scheme. The 'return' of the main section is interestingly worked out through varying and displacing the rhythm.[17] It is an open question whether African Negro pentatonicism is related to the five-note style of Sudanese peoples, and in particular to the Dongola Barabras in the Nile Valley—and whether one may infer from it that in antiquity there existed an Ethiopian form of pentatonicism.

America's pentatonic style seems to be an organic, chain-like continuation of this line of development. Two traditions of pentatonic melody, the Indian and the Negro, encounter each other on this immense double-continent, and are joined by a third, the Irish Anglo-Saxon tradition of the early European settlers. These two, or rather three, traditions have many points of contact, so that they cut across each other and form mixed types. In connection with the remarkably developed South American (Inca) type and the widely ramifying Indian types of North America, it should be realised that of Indian and Negro melody, the indigenous Indian type was the more advanced, and the Negro the more primitive. Yet Negro melody-style was soon powerfully influenced by Indian models, and stimulated to form more advanced melodies. For this reason, very few stylistic links exist between the pentatonic Negro styles of America and Africa. The seemingly primeval pentatonic zone, which in North America extends from Florida across Dakota to Oregon and California, and in South America from Columbia to the Western sea-coast of Chile (and also to the South East by way of the Indian tribes of Brazil) suggests that a highly diversified Indian melody-culture once flourished here. However it is thought to have originated—whether in Northern, Central or Southern America; whatever it is called—Mayan, Toltec, Aztec or Inca—it is founded on a very ancient autochthonous American past, which simultaneously influenced Mexico, if it did not actually emanate from ancient Central America. The most primitive pentatonic style in the North appears to be that of California, and in the South, that of Tierra del Fuego; the most evolved is found amongst the Indians of Arizona and New Mexico (in the direct vicinity of California!)[18] and in South America amongst the Indians of Peru.[19] The style of the North-Eastern provinces (Appalachians) is clearly traceable to European sources. The music of certain East Siberian tribes (Chukch and Kamchadal) and of North American Eskimos[20] probably belongs in this evolutionary chain; from a geographical point of view this is probably yet another proof of the organic unity of the Mongol-Red Indian connection. From a purely musical standpoint, we are not yet able to say whether a connection once existed between the American and Asian pentatonic style-regions—in the same way that a connection existed between the Indian and Mongolian races, that American colonial history was bound up with Asia and Polynesia, and that various East Siberian and North American tune-types share certain features of performance. 'Central Asian' types, or forms which are reminiscent of Central Asia (i.e. built in a terraced way at different levels)[21] appear sporadically in America, but because pentatonic formations are so tenacious (sometimes thousands of years old) they would have to occur more often for the connection to be convincingly demonstrated. Sequences and the descending phrase occur on their own in the Peruvian style —amongst Bellakula, Chippewa and Dakota Indians, for instance—but the transposed double-line construction of the Asiatic type is relatively seldom found. It is almost certain that the ancient Indian tradition is fundamentally unconnected with the Negro style which was later attached to it. American Negro immigration—or rather, slave-settlement—is of more recent origin, and the principles prevailing today in American pentatonic structure are essentially different from those of Central Asia. What are these principles? The axis appears to be a double-line with a varied close (A_1A_2, or else AaAb). Hence a simple melody-line is the basic element, but the chief idea of construction has a strong bias towards three- or four-line song-form. The *quasi*-tripartite form is particularly interesting, as it is relatively the most evolved of Indian forms; the following schemes are encountered in the examples quoted: AAA/1BA/2 and

AABB₁A/2, where the second phrase is closely connected with some section of the first, and forms a more or less pronounced third section; or $ABCB_1A_1$, plus C_1C_2, as in No. 145, a miniature rondo.[22] The following forms are also found: ABCB, ABABA, AABB, ABA₁C (see the Negro example No. 147), ABB₁A, even ABBA (Appalachian), etc. The modern nature of this style is strongly emphasised by the new-style harmonic background to the melodies (e.g. the circling of the tonic major in No. 147), not to mention an almost entirely un-archaic rhythm which is particularly prevalent in the Negro melodies ('modern' dance-rhythms, dotting, syncopation in the spirituals, etc.). It should also be pointed out that such a markedly European character is shown in these melodies—and, in general, in most pentatonic melodies of North America— (e.g. the Appalachian style already mentioned) that the possibility of European influence (in the form of Irish settlers, etc.) cannot be entirely excluded. (During the last few decades, as a result of jazz, many of the typical features of spirituals have influenced Europe in just the same way.) Yet it is quite inconceivable that *all* American pentatonic melody should belong here. How could the more evolved Irish Celtic forms have influenced the more primitive forms of California, that 'enclosed reservoir' which formed a repository for older and more rudimentary streams of culture? How could it have affected Indian melodies in the South American Andes, which are equally primitive but quite differently constructed? What in any case is beyond dispute is that America provides the clearest evidence of the musical encounter of Whites, Negroes and Indians.

The series is brought to an end by the pentatonic music of *Western Europe*, which forms the natural last link, as it were, in this chain of development. In origin it is probably Celtic; its most remarkable examples were discovered in Scotland, Ireland and Wales (and occasionally in Brittany and Normandy as well). Its vaguer Iberian traces should probably be regarded as the heritage of Iberian Celts.[23] It is based on the modern period, rounded in a European sense, and the prevalent form of construction is tripartite song-form, with close-knit motivic unity (*cp.* Nos. 148 and 149). To complete this strict organisation, there is a dotted rhythm, or some other type of dance-rhythm, as though to stress the *harmonic* unity of the melodic concept (in addition to the examples quoted in the text, see also melody No. 49 in the Notes). Of all types it comes closest to the American, as though across the great distances of Celtic, Indian and Negro cultures, it reflected an old epoch of Western European and American history— a 'meeting of races'.

These few melodies are capable not only of provoking general questions of this sort, but of opening up ever wider-ranging problems of music and cultural history.

4. *Suppositions*

This investigation has brought to light two 'primitive' pentatonic dialects, and three 'developed' ones. Those of Western Asia and Africa may be called 'primitive', those of Central Asia, America and Western Europe are 'developed' (the Central Asian type may be termed Eurasian as it extends into Eastern Central Europe as the result of Hungarian influence). Relationship between these types can only be established by assuming that the Western Asian and African types, and the American and European types, are mutually linked. The Central Asian type stands on its own, and may at most be related to certain Central American types.

The most important formal schemes encountered in these culture-zones are the following:

AB_{AB} (Central Asia)

$AA_1A_2A_3$ (Western Asia)
$ABCB_1C_1$ (and its rondo-like variations) (Africa)
$ABCB$, $ABABA$, $AABB$, $ABAC$, ABB_1A and *quasi*-tripartite structure (America)
ABA (with strict motivic unity) (Western Europe)

The most important constructional principles are:

Transposition, and hence a balanced strophe divided into two sections (Central Asia)
Repetition (Western Asia)
Variation (Africa), and
Song-form (America, Europe).

The links suggested by this classification, and above all the gradual evolutionary progress (Western Asia—Africa—America—Western Europe) could well furnish a basis for the most ambitious and far-reaching assumptions. If it is true that musical styles always only migrate with the people who carry them (as Hornbostel and Lachmann maintain),[24] we have to imagine the ancient world as though in a state of perpetual migration. It would, for instance, be possible to maintain that American pentatonicism is the Mongolian heritage of the Indian natives; the five-note system came to Africa from Western Asia, although it might well be that the land of origin for both African and Western Asian types would have to be looked for on the North-Eastern coast of Africa (justifying those who believe in an 'Egyptian primacy'); it could also be maintained that at one time, and in some unknown way, the musical dialects of America and Europe were related; that there was a centre in North-West Europe which was related to Asia or America, etc. So far, all these relationships have received little or no confirmation from historical, archaeological or anthropological research.

But it is also equally hazardous to assume that five-note dialects originated from some single common territory in Asia.[25] One of E. von Hornbostel's most important observations deals with the migrations to East and West of the Central Asian, or Chinese, *paisiao* or pan-pipe, and its method of tuning. It spread through the Far East to Africa (as the xylophone) and across Melanesia to South America (as pipes and bundles of reeds).[26] The fact that the tuning method has travelled always suggests that the instruments have travelled too—that there was in fact a 'material' connecting link between the cultures. The three 'mother-continents' are thus seen as a unit with a common musical origin; the memory of pan-pipes, moreover, haunts almost every place where the earliest world-cultures flourished, leading us to assume that the five-reed pan-pipe and the five-note music-style spread in close conjunction through the ancient world. Yet even if the pan-pipe was the oldest bearer of the five-note system, this oldest form of pentatonicism could only have spread as a tonal system, independently of melodic shapes. We must assume this stage to have been followed by a second, more recent phase, in which the various forms of the primary five-note language accepted in their turn differently constituted forms, adapting themselves to particular 'regional' tendencies. The author considers the two phases to have been separated by the same time-gap as that which divides the primitive primary culture from the consciously developed high cultures. In consequence, he believes that the five-note system itself is the heritage of the oldest cultures, but that the series of pentatonic melody-shapes known today result from a much later cultural phase. The five-note system is the product of a general tendency, its melodic shapes spring from specific needs; the first is the basic phase, whilst the second follows it some hundred or thousand of years later.

If this theory is unacceptable, because music without a definite shape is inconceivable, but the need remains to establish a common land of origin for pentatonicism: then the differences between five-note styles can only be explained by new assumptions. Supposing we assume—on a strictly musical basis—that there was an emanation from some primitive key-region in Central Asia—similar to that established by Hornbostel in relation to the history of instruments. So far as the formative phase of melody-construction is concerned, it must then be assumed that this early emanation reached Western Asia and Africa at a relatively less developed, or earlier stage, or else stopped there at a more primitive stage; and that it reached America and Western Europe at a more developed, or later stage, or developed there to a higher one. As with the theory of five-note pan-pipes, this really involves abandoning the idea that pentatonicism is bound up with particular melody-shapes. We are in fact already assuming that the pentatonicism of one culture-zone is capable of influencing that of another, *independently of musical form*; that it causes one form to arise in one region, and another in another region. But perhaps this is the best way of approaching the heart of the problem—in the form of a third supposition.

Yet so far this is no more than pure hypothesis. We need to return to hard facts.

5. Conclusions

So far in this brief survey, it has been established that although *pentatonicism manifests itself in definite melodic shapes, yet these shapes develop and transform themselves*. Pentatonicism did not precede these forms, but it may well be older than the forms which are today associated with it.

For this there are various proofs. One proof, in the author's view, is that every pentatonic melody-type harks back to a less developed, earlier form; the Western Asian type to a three-note, primitive litany-form, the Central Asian and the American type to a one-line melody, the African to a rhythmical reciting-motive. Variation was preceded by repetition, regular tripartite form by a fluctuating, sometimes asymmetrical form in three sections. *Hence nowhere in the world today does pentatonicism appear in its primary form.* If it was ever dependent on certain instruments (which seems highly questionable), it lost this link a very long time ago.[27] In any case, the forms found over the global surface of the world today are much more recent manifestations than the 'original culture' of instruments with which they are supposedly connected. Hence on the one hand it follows that pentatonic melody forms, as known today, *never and nowhere represent the most primitive level of culture.* They already synthesise certain phases of development, and may even be described as 'high cultures'. On the other hand, the most primitive 'kernels' of form, and fundamental musical trends, are obviously not the same all over the world, in spite of elements they are likely to share. Rather do they tend to differ; sometimes they crystallise in repetitive, litany-like structures, sometimes in clearly articulated, balanced melody-lines; sometimes they give rise to basic rhythms, and sometimes to repeated phrases of melody.

Further evidence of the way that pentatonic shapes tend to transform themselves is provided by five-note melody-types which stem from the same source, but develop in divergent and even opposite directions. Chinese and Hungarian forms provide the best example of this, in that they probably once sprang from a common source (in Central Asia) but have developed in entirely different directions. Chinese melody leans towards more complex forms, but in its more recent strata it keeps to the traditional basis of its tonal system (although

231

theoretically it has been adopting other notes for more than three thousand years). Hungarian melody, on the other hand, nowadays shows the effect of European influence by progressively obliterating and extending the primary tonal system. All the same, it sometimes retains the old line-transposing method of construction, and adopts it independently of pentatonic scales; at other times, it preserves the five-note system, even in the strict and compact forms of more modern type, which have replaced the ancient Asiatic structure.[28] Related pentatonic traditions can thus develop in opposing directions; from a different point of view, each may appear to be conservative. There may well be other melody-types owning a common origin which today are even more separated and divergent than these.[29]

It is this capacity for development and transformation which the researcher must constantly bear in mind when dealing with basic common principles. The changes would obviously be determined by the particular type of formative influence encountered in each culture-zone by the basic idea of five-note organisation, that vagrant and adaptable storehouse of sound, which once, in a hidden past, emanated from the oldest centres of human culture—from Inner Asia, perhaps, but possibly at the same time from Asia, Africa, America and Northern Europe. They are changes which would take place as the result of particular regional trends and circumstances, local needs and potentialities. A tonal system did not yet imply a style; it had not yet become a world-language of music just by virtue of being shared. It was raw material which was held in common. The *differentiated,* basic style of each separate continent appears to have emerged gradually from the basic fabric of a *shared* and still older tonal system. Hence every type of five-note music known today recalls an unknown primeval era only in relation to its *tonal material*; its present-day *structure* reflects the life of ancient high-cultures.

There is a sketch-map at the end of this chapter illustrating the spread of pentatonic dialects. It was drawn up long before it was possible to compare it with N.I. Vavilov's map of the original locations of cultivated plants,[30] and so it is all the more astonishing that the two maps practically correspond. Musical history and natural science both appear to endorse the same cultural conditions: *that the oldest high-cultures of humanity flourished in certain focal centres, and radiated out from these.*

As yet, this is no more than a first glimmer of certainty, and yet it already sheds a little light. It is possible to describe the various pentatonic melody-styles as parallel, 'chance' phenomena only insofar as all mature and high-level manifestations of human culture are always parallel, 'chance' phenomena.

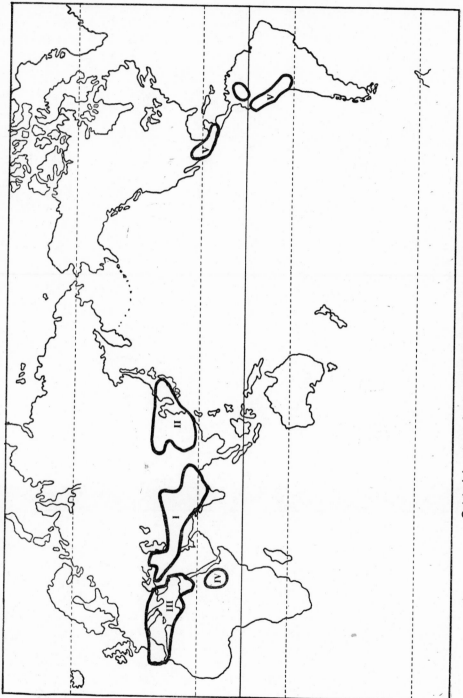

Original locations of cultivated plants (according to Vavilov's map)

The spread of pentatonic dialects

NOTES

1. E.g. Lach (Adler: *Handbuch der Musikgeschichte*. 1930, I, pp. 14—15): " . . . the question inevitably arises whether the appearance of anhemitonic pentatonicism ought not to be regarded as a manifestation of growth, that is, as the first stage in an evolutionary process which can be applied to the whole of human culture without distinction of races, peoples, lands, etc. Thus the five-note scale without semitones ought really to be regarded as the first and most ancient scale . . . " Idelsohn (*Hebräisch-orientalischer Melodienschatz*. II, 1922, p. 27): " . . . pentatonicism is a primitive characteristic occurring in all folk-song, a stage which represents the primitive state of song in primitive peoples." Lachmann (*Musik des Orients*. 1929, pp. 36—37): "Five-note music ought not to be claimed as a sort of distinctive characteristic of the music of some particular race or culture: Scottish, Berber, Creole folk-songs, and numerous other examples from folk-music and Eastern art-music, show it to extend throughout the world." Yet Lachmann is the only researcher who is concerned with five-note music as an individual manifestation of high cultures. (*Die Musik der aussereuropäischen Natur- und Kulturvölker*. 1929, pp. 19—20.) In his view, the pentatonic styles of civilised peoples differ from those of primitive peoples by reason of the "clarity of purpose which shapes and upholds these interval-relationships." *Cp*. also Mahmud Ragib Kösemihal: "Pentatonizmin evronselligi" (in the Supplement *Umumi Musiki Tarihi* of the Istanbul journal *Müzik ve Sanat Hareketleri*. Vol. 1935, Nos. 6—7, 9).
2. We disregard here the various methods of tuning which occur amongst the instruments of Eastern and Southern Asia. A. J. Ellis, the first to notice these differences, soon realised that their role in monophonic cultures was not a significant one. (On the musical scales of various nations, 1885; see *Sammelbände für vergleichende Musikwissenschaft* I, 1922, p. 64.)
3. *Zeitschrift f. Musikwissenschaft* XIV, 1932, p. 236. Lachmann (*Musik des Orients*. 1929, p. 41) traces anhemitonic five-note scales to the tuning of stringed instruments in pure fifths, while the semitonal forms are traced to the "blown fifths" of brass instruments. He also considers that the difference between the two main types of pentatonic scale lies in the characteristic way of splitting the fourth—one into a minor third and a whole tone (anhemitonic form), the other into a major third and semitone (ditonic-hemitonic form). See Lachmann: *Die Musik der aussereuropäischen Natur- und Kulturvölker*. 1929, pp. 20, 22.
4. *Folkloristische Tonalitätsstudien*. 1916.
5. A contrary view, which refutes Riemann's idea, is expressed by Abert and Sachs in the 2nd edition of Adler's *Handbuch der Musikgeschichte*. 1930, I, p. 54.
6. It should be mentioned that Japanese colonial history supports this observation (intermingling with Mongolian tribes in the North, and Malayan tribes in the South). Japanese musicology considers that the Chinese musical system was introduced in the 7th century. For the mixture of Siamese and Javanese elements in Melanesian melody, see Hornbostel's comments, *Sammelb. f. vergleichende Musikwiss*. I, p. 353. "Notiz über die Musik der Bewohner von Süd-Neumecklenburg." Both Siamese and Javanese elements influence pentatonic music by means of intervals which in a European sense are not tempered.
7. Acoustically speaking, pentatonic scales derive from *a)* a circle of fifths, or division according to stringed instruments (e.g. *b flat-f-c-g-d*); *b)* a tetrachord divided into *two*, i.e. a halved fourth (e.g. *c-d-f*, or, more exactly, 0—231—498 cent) which string and brass instruments transpose on to the fourth or fifth degree of the scale *(c-d-f-f-g-b flat or c-d-f-g-a-c)*. The diatonic scale derives from a tetrachord divided into *three*; that is, a third of the interval of a fourth (e.g. *c-d flat △ d-e flat-f*, or, more exactly, 0—152—316—498 cent); which will also be carried forward to the fourth and fifth degrees of the scale. It is a fact that the

phenomenon of the 'neutral halving note' nearly always occurs wherever pentatonic scales are acoustically derived e.g. in the case of scales consisting of 261 cent-distances: g . . $a \triangle b$ flat . . c . . $d \triangle e$ flat . . f (Old Chinese, Brazilian and Melanesian tuning)—where it may be assumed that a neutral note of this sort 'splits off', allowing for the formation of a threefold pentatonic system (g-b flat-c-d-f, g-a-c-d-f, g-b flat-c-e flat-f). These will only be held together by their shared 'scaffolding fourths', and should not be considered as being at all analogous to the 'affiliating' process that takes place in church modes. Yet such explanations only serve an indirect purpose: they proceed too much from theory and instrumental tuning. Even in the East, cosmological procedures involving the acoustics of instruments are of minor importance. Marius Schneider's theory of the origin of pentatonic music is very illuminating (Gesch. der Mehrstimmigkeit I, 1934, p. 18); in his view, f-b flat-c-f, followed by the scale f-g-b flat-c-f, and then by f-g-b flat-c-d-f, crystallised round the basic 'cell' of b flat-c, so that in its three forms (f-g-b flat-c-d-f, c-d-f-g-a-c, g-a-c-d-e-g) it became the basis of all tonal development That is why some of its modes are only of secondary importance. Some authenticated archaic Hebrew recitative melodies, also found in Europe, seem to centre round a double bichord fg-cd (b or b flat serves as a shifting middle-note between the two bichords). Other examples are built up from the double bichord fg-b flat-c. J. H. Lewis lays particular stress on the part played by the tone-distinctions of the Chinese language in Chinese musical history (Foundations of Chinese Musical Art. Peiping, 1936); it is very possible that these five tone-levels (Nanking dialect) have some connection with the pentatonic scales of Eastern Asia. On this subject there are some interesting data in A. Lübke's book (Der Himmel der Chinesen. Leipzig, 1931, p. 135); the kung scale, or old form of pentatonic scale, was already flourishing about 2250 B.C., at the time of Emperor Shun, when shao music was introduced (the five-stringed k'in); later, during the time of the Chu dynasty (1122—255 B.C.) the seven-note scale predominated in the North, whilst the five-note scale continued to flourish in the South (cp. the five tone-distinctions of the Nanking dialect).

8. Sources: for No. 137: Melody of Psalm-Verse and Doxology of the Advent Introit, *Liber Usualis Missae et Officii*. Paris—Tournai—Rome, 1931, p. 12; For Nos. 138, 143, 146: Lavignac: *Encycl. de la mus. Histoire de la mus.* V, 1922, pp. 3104, 3206, and 3355; for No. 139: Nurullah Sevket: "Dogu Türkistaninda Pentatonizm." *Müsik ve Sanat Hareketleri.* Istanbul, 1934, No. 3, p. 14 (in the original the note-values are halved). For No. 140: V. A. Moshkov: "Melodij Astrakanskich i Orenburgskich Nogajtzov i Kirgis." *Isvestiya Obshchestva Archeologij, Istorij i Etnogr.* Kazan, XVII, 1901, No. 1 (in this notation, the notes marked with an asterisk are shown as *acciaccaturas*, although the author presumably wished to indicate short quavers as there are words beneath them); No. 141: from the author's own recording of the song as sung by Tagan Galimdshan, 1936; No. 142: Béla Bartók: *Hungarian Folk Music*. 1924 (Eng. ed. 1931, O.U.P.), No. 71 (a); No. 144: *Journal of American Folklore* XLI, 1928, p. 212 (G. Herzog: "The Yuman Musical Style"); for No. 145: F. Densmore: *Chippewa Music* II, Washington, 1913, No. 110; for No. 147: Riemann—Einstein: *Musiklexikon*. 11th ed., 1929, II, p. 188; for No. 148: Moffat: *The Minstrelsy of Scotland*. 1896, p. 10; for No. 149: Kidson—Moffat: *English Peasant Songs*. 1929, p. 16.

9. In the Hungarian material see, for example, melodies Nos. 24 and 62 in Bartók's book, *Hungarian Folk-Music*. Eng. ed. 1931, O.U.P.

10. The particular way of 'lowering' a melody by combining transposition at the fifth and the octave may be seen in a Melanesian (New Mecklenburghian) melody published by Hornbostel (*Sammelb. f. vergl. Musikwiss.* I, pp. 356—357). Here is one of its verses:

The opening of a Javanese piece published by Lachmann (*Musik des Orients*, p. 111) shows a somewhat similar transposing structure (it interchanges intervals of fifths, fourths and octaves). Others, also Melanesian laments, combine the lowering process with a particular form of variation, e.g. (from publications by Neuhaus—Hornbostel and Thurnwald—Hornbostel):

A Madagascan flute-melody, on the other hand, shows an AA⁵AA⁵ . . . structure (recording of the Clérisse Mission, in the series of recordings of the Musée de l'Homme, Paris, D I. 46. 1. 4. B):

etc.

(noted by the author: the original is a fourth higher).

11. *Cp.* also Bashkuyev: *Sbornik burjat-mongolskikh pyesen*. Moscow, 1935, Nos. 3—6, 13—14, 19, 27—28, 30. A characteristic example, which shows how a four-line structure is built out of a one-line and even a half-line motive (Cheremissian melody from Vassilyev's collection, *Marij muro*, Kazan, 1919—20, No. 32):

12. Compare for example the following six melodies, which differ from each other little more than six variants of the same folk-song:

Sources: from Kodály's manuscript collection (see his book, *Folk Music of Hungary*. London 1960, p. 33); Vassilyev: *Marij muro*, Moscow, 1923, No. 96 (Var. Koukal—Tchet-karev—Rubzov: *Marij kalük muro*. Leningrad—Moscow, 1951, pp. 103, 228—229); Maximov: *Turi dovassen jurissen*. Shupashkar, 1932, No. 161; Rudnev: *Melod. mongolskikh ple-myon*. St. Petersburg, 1909, No. 58; Bashkuyev: *Sbornik buryat-mongolskikh pyesen*. Moscow, 1935, No. 31. (Variants, P. Berlinsky: *Mongolskij pyevez i musikant Uldsuj-Lubsan-Khurtshi*. Moscow, 1933, No. 41; H. Haslund-Christensen: *Zayagan*. Stuttgart—Berlin w. d., about 1940, p. 202, and H. Haslund-Cristensen—E. Emsheimer: *The Music of the Mon-gols*. I, Stockholm, 1943, Melodies Nos. 46, 84, 86); Tchao Feng: *Shi-King ti yin-yo ki k'i-t'o* (The Shi-King melodies and other songs). Singapore, 1948, p. 35.—A Korean melody (sung by the North Korean, Sen Van-ir, in Budapest in 1948, recorded by the author), combines transposition and variation within the framework of a double-verse:

It is worth noticing that some Turkish tunes have the same transpositional structure (but at the fourth, not the fifth); e.g. (M. Ragib Kösemihal: *Türk halk musikilerinin tonal husu-siyetleri meselesi*. Istanbul, 1936, p. 19; where the first bar is incorrectly given an octave lower):

Related idioms in Rumanian folk-music (see, e.g., Bartók: *Volksmus. der Rumänen von Maramureş*. No. 117, with transposition at the fifth) may reflect Hungarian or Turkish influence. Bartók's Anatolian collection (1936) shows that the descending pentatonic construction also occurs amongst the Yürüks.

13. "Eastern Relations of Early Hungarian Folk-Music." *Journal of the Royal Asiatic Society*, 1935.

14. Some Melanesian pentatonic pan-pipe melodies reflect an equally primitive form, though different in type; see for example those published by Hornbostel in the above work, consisting of varied repetitions of the motive:

15. See Idelsohn: *Parallelen zwischen gregorianischen und hebräisch-orientalischen Gesangsweisen*. 1922; Adler: *Hb. der Musikgesch*. 1930, I, p. 77 (P. Wagner: *Der gregorianische Gesang*). There are some significant comments by Jeppesen about the fundamental pentatonic element of Gregorian chant in *Kontrapunkt*, 1935, pp. 44—45. For the survival of five-note scales in this culture-zone see H. Loewenstein: "Eine pentatonische Bibelweise in der deutschen Synagoge." *Zeitschr. f. Musikwiss.* XII, 1930, p. 513 et seq. Also by the same author, "The Role of the Pentatonic Idiom in Jewish Music." *The Jewish Music Forum*, New York, 1946—1947; B. Szabolcsi: "About five-tone scales in the early Hebrew melodies," I. *Goldziher Memorial Vol*. Budapest, 1948.

16. Bartók—Kodály: *Transylvanian Folk-Songs*. Nos. 24, 31, 32, 44, 56, 63, 83, 88, 91, 100. Kodály shows that it also exists in other East European peoples (*Folk Music of Hungary*. 1960, p. 53). It also appears sporadically in Turkish songs, e.g. (Wahid Lütfi's collection):

(See Ragib's *op. cit.*, pp. 18—19.) Similar motives occurring in Rumanian folk-song (see Bartók: *Cântece pop. româneşti din com. Bihor*. Bucureşti, 1913, Nos. 225, 231, 233—234, 236—237, 240, 242) may also perhaps be traced back to Gregorian or Byzantine influence. It also appears in Armenian melodies, see L. Saminsky: *Sechs Lieder aus dem russischen Orient*. Wien, 1928, No. 2. Turkoman example, Gr. Lobatshev: *Turkmenskiye pyesni dlya golosa s fortepiano* (recorded by V. Uspenski). Moscow, 1937, No. 5. Italian example, E. Levi: *Per i vostri bambini. Poesie, figure, melodie*. Rome—Turin, 1906, p. 7 (Roman Lullaby).—As mentioned in Chapter II of the present volume, this rising 3-note form also appears in Hindu Veda-melodies, where it may well represent the oldest example of the type; in any case it seems to have a collective origin all over South and West Asia.

17. The 'Central Asian' principle, whereby the melody-phrase is heard again at a lower range, is very rare in the African sphere of influence. It appears in the following East African melody (from a recording by Bachmann) published by Marius Schneider in *Gesch. der Mehrstimmigkeit*, I, No. 185:

A. Chottin publishes some interesting examples of Berber pentatonic melodies in *Corpus de Musique Marocaine*. Paris, 1933—1935.

18. *Cp.* also G. Herzog: "Special Song Types in North American Indian Music." *Zeitschr. f. vergleichende Musikwissenschaft*, 1935.

19. The special character of Peruvian melody can be explained to some extent by the bold theory which considers that the Inca tribes migrated from Western Europe before 5000 B.C. (see E. Fuhrmann: *Reich der Inka*. Hagen, i. W., 1922, p. 31); but this idea has not been supported by more recent researches.

20. The most important authors in this connection are Leden (1911), Thuren (1911—1912), Thalbitzer (1923), Roberts and Jenness (1925), F. Boas (*Ethnol. Report* VI).

21. According to M. Schneider (*Gesch. d. Mehrstimmigkeit*. I, p. 25), the chief form of variation in Red Indian music is the transposition of motives; the present author was able to establish this only in a few cases. *Cp.* for example the following melody of the Bellakula Indians from British Columbia (after C. Stumpf: *Sammelbände f. vergl. Musikwiss*. I, p. 94):

According to G. Herzog, the 4-line, isometric, descending minor pentatonic melody-type plays a dominant role in a part of Canada which has close cultural links with East Siberia. The following Teton melody was quoted by him in the article "Plains Ghost Dance and Great Basin Music" (*American Anthropologist*, 1935, vol. 37, No. 3), after *The Indian's Book* (1923) of N. Curtis. It illustrates in many ways the difference between the Western Asian type and the 4-note, 'protopentatonic', *parlando* types of America:

M. d'Harcourt mentions the 'terraced', descending pentatonic melodies of the North American Red Indians in Lavignac, *Encycl. de la mus*. V, 1922, p. 3370.—Here is a Peruvian example (M. Béclard—d'Harcourt: *Mélodies populaires indiennes : Équateur, Pérou, Bolivie*, Milano, 1928, pp. 17—18):

Cp. also the present author's study "On the Spread of the Central Asian Melody-Type." *Ethnographia*, 1940, p. 242 (in Hungarian).

22. An interesting variant of No. 146 (in text) has been encountered in the Congo region (noted by Shebesta and published by M. Schneider in *op. cit.* No. 134):

23. It is a moot point whether the four- and five-note structure (generally major pentatonic) of old German folk-songs and nursery rhymes should be thought of as a relic of this 'Celtic style', or as the rather mutilated remains of the major hexachord, as found in Vogul, Swedish and Lapp five-note melodies—an age-old and universal tradition, European and Indo-Germanic. For old-German (or mediaeval German) pentatonicism, see Müller-Blattau: "Musikalische Studien zur altgermanischen Dichtung," *Vierteljahrsschrift für Literaturwiss. u. Geistesgeschichte* III, 1925, p. 548, also Lach's data in Adler's work quoted above (I, p. 14) and John Meier: *Deutsche Volkslieder mit ihren Melodien* I, *Balladen*. 1935, pp. 17, 142, 194, etc. Whereas these old tunes still show pentatonic passages and a pentatonic-type melody-line (the nursery rhymes have a litany-like structure), German folk-songs of more recent origin sometimes have a purely five-note structure (Meier's work quoted above, p. 79):

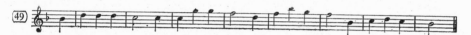

Some recently published East Prussian fairy-tale songs (Grudde and Müller-Blattau, 1931) appear to precede pentatonic formations with their three- and four-note range. For the sporadic Polish five-note system, which should possibly be treated as an extension of the same Baltic style-region, see H. Windakiewiczowa: "Pentatonika w Muzyce Polskej Ludowej." *Kvartalnik Muzyczny*. Warsaw, 1933; O. Kvitka: *Le système pentatonique anhémitonique chez les peuples slaves*. Lvov, 1927.

24. "Asiatische Parallelen zur Berbermusik." *Zeitschr. f. vergleichende Musikwissenschaft*, 1933, p. 60; "The Music of the Fuegians." *Ethnos*. Stockholm, 1948, p. 91.

25. The Turkish researcher Ahmed Adnan Saygun (*Türk halk musikisinde pentatonism*. Istanbul, 1936) supports this theory of diffusion. He considers that five-note music is of Central Asian origin, and extended from there via Eastern Europe to Scandinavia, via Central Europe to Scotland, via Hungary and the Balkans to Asia Minor and North Africa, via Arabia to Central Africa, via the Far East and Australia to South America, via China to Japan, and via Siberia to North America. There may be much truth in this theory, but it leaves unexplained why pentatonic melody cultures are encountered along the routes of development described, bound up with melody forms which are quite differently evolved and constructed. The study by M. Ragib Kösemihal: *Türk Halk Musikîlerinin Tonal Hususiyetleri Meselesi*, Istanbul, 1936 abounds in comparative material. C. Sachs in an article "Prolégomènes à une préhistoire musicale de l'Europe," *Revue de Musicologie*, 1936 formulates the theory of 'peripheral conservation' which is preserved in the North by Scottish and Lapp music, in the South by Hungarian, Gregorian, old Mediterranean and Spanish music; between these two archaic culture-zones is wedged the more recent culture-zone of major-minor music.—W. Danckert believes pentatonicism without semitones (anhemitonic) to be a "legacy of prehistoric

agrarian culture," "a song-style which is decidedly matriarchal in stamp" (see *Kodály Memorial Volume.* 1943, pp. 9—18, which also prints a list of Danckert's earlier studies on this subject).

26. See R. d'Harcourt's comments on pan-pipes in the Andes, and Hornbostel's on Melanesian, Brazilian and Peruvian pan-pipes (Lavignac: *Encycl.* V, 1922, and *La musique des Incas et ses survivances,* 1925, and *Sammelb. f. vergl. Musikwiss.* I, *Zeitschr. f. Ethnologie* 1911, *W. Schmidt Festschr.,* 1928). Also C. Sachs: *Geist und Werden der Musikinstrumente.* 1929, pp. 49—52, 79—80. The pan-pipe is the oldest instrument with notes of fixed pitch; the oldest Chinese data about it allegedly dates from 3000 B.C. See also I. Tregenna: *The Pipes of Pan.* London, 1926, and V. K. Steschenko—Kuftina: *Drevneishiye musikalniye osnovi grusinskoi narodnoi musiki, Fleita Pana.* Tiflis, 1936, resp. *Sovietskaya Etnografiya,* No. 4, 1937, pp. 193—198.—J. Kunst has pointed out the close relationship between the tuning of the Javanese gender and the African marimba ("Ein musikalischer Beweis für Kulturzusammenhänge zwischen Indonesien—vermutlich Java—und Zentralafrika." *Anthropos.* 1936, p. 131): both are based on the old Chinese tuning of blown fifths. Kunst thinks it unlikely that the same scale should come to exist in different parts of the earth at different times; if there is even the same ground-note, a separate and unrelated origin is quite out of the question. In addition, the ground-note of the scale of blown fifths is everywhere the same: 366 oscillations to the second (see Chap. I of present work).

27. It is significant that Mongolians, for instance, play pure pentatonic tunes on their diatonically tuned instruments. They consider the 'more developed' diatonic to be mere raw material, a tonal supply from which to choose. In general, the same is true of instruments of East and South-East Asia. See P. Berlinsky: *Mongolski pyevec i musikant Uldsui-Lubsan-Khurtshi.* Moscow, 1933, p. 42.—The same is true of Melanesian pan-pipes with 5—8 pipes, on which only five-note scales are played (see *Sammelbände f. vergl. Musikwiss.* I, 1922, p. 353). The same also applies to old Peruvian instruments, see C. Vega: "Tonleitern mit Halbtönen in der Musik der alten Peruaner." *Acta Musicologica,* 1937, IX, pp. 41—53, particularly p. 50.

28. See Kodály's entry in the *Zenei Lexikon* (Hungarian Music Lexicon), vol. II. 1930, p. 66, melody No. 4. Such schemes also occur in Chinese melodies, but as parts of larger forms, e.g. Melody Ex. No. 1 of J. H. Lewis, *op. cit.*

29. South Turkish peoples (Osmanli, Gagauz, Crimean Tartar, Turkoman, Khirgiz and Uzbegs) provide the best evidence of how a pentatonic tradition can become faded or blurred, even though this is not at all common. In this music, the Persian-Arab *maqam* system ousted the old pentatonicism, generally developing into a diatonic system. This also occurred amongst the Tarangis of Central Asia, under the influence of an Iranian or pentatonic basic layer. (Similar traits also appear in Bulgarian folk-music, where the advance of *maqam* style neutralised ancient Turkish and Byzantine elements.) Only of recent years has Anatolian research (Lütfi, Ragib, Bartók, Saygun) succeeded in revealing an indigenous pentatonic tradition, preserved in scattered traces within Osmanli culture, and seemingly once present in Oguz-Turkish culture as well (B. Bartók: "Folk-Song Collecting in Anatolia." *Selected Writings,* 1948, p. 33 [in Hungarian]; Ferruh Arsunar: *Anadolunun Pentatonik Melodileri Hakkinda Birkaç Not.* Istanbul, 1937, and *Kodály Memorial Volume.* 1943, pp. 322—327 [in Hungarian].) Present-day Kalmuk music shows an interesting mixture: it still shows striking pentatonic characteristics in spite of taking over a great deal from the Islamic style of the Southern Turks. Some idea of the strength of the pentatonic tradition underlying it can be gained by realising that the 'most recent' cultural layer to have overlaid it—the Islamic, Oguz style—probably dates from the spread of Islam into Europe, i. e. is a thousand years old. That stylistic diffusion did not inevitably follow on conquest is shown by Western

Central Asia, amongst other examples. Here in all probability the prevalent style was once pentatonic, but even the onslaught of Mongolians in the 13th century was unable to re-establish the hegemony of the ancient Mongolian-Turkish pentatonic style. For the South Turkish culture-zone, see publications by Pantusov (*Isvestiya Obshchestva Archeol. Ist. i Etnogr.*, Kazan, 1895), Uspenski (*Shash Makam*, 1924), Uspenski—Belayev (*Turkmenskaya Musika*, 1928), Mironov (*Obsor musikalnikh kultur usbekov*, 1931; *Pyesni Fergany, Bukhary i Khivy*, 1931), Fitrat (*Usbik klassik musikasi*, 1927), Zatayevitch, Olesnitzki-Gordlevski, Sherfedinov, Kontshevski, Efetov-Filonenko and others; for Kalmuk music, consult A. Rudnev: *Melodi mongolskich plemyon*, 1909, and M. Tritus: *Sbornik kalmickich pyesen*, 1934; also J. M. Hirshman: *Pentatonika i eyo razsvitije v tatarskoj musike*, Moscow, 1960.—The author has recently made some comparative studies of melodies which reveal that diatonic and even chromatic *maqams* are often based on pentatonic models. This implies that pentatonicism may lurk at the very heart of a *maqam*. Thus the pentatonicism of Central Asia and the *maqam* of Western Asia—these two 'opposing' principles which have played such an important role in the music of East European peoples, and particularly in that of Hungary, Turkey and Rumania too—may in the end lead back to the same sources. *Cp.* for example the melody-examples (5 variants of a *maqam*) published by Ferruh Arsunar in the work quoted above. It may not be a coincidence that in Arabic scales it is generally the *pien*, or accessory, notes which differ from the tempered tuning of the Eurasian basic scale; these and the chromatic notes have been added later on to the underlying pentatonic scheme.

30. Studies on the origin of cultivated plants. *Bull. Appl. Bot. Plant Breed* XVI, 2. Leningrad, 1926, and H. Hassinger: *Geogr. Grundlagen der Geschichte*. Freiburg i. Br., 1931, pp. 31—33.

EUROPEAN REGIONS OF ORNAMENTATION

The colourful, rich drapery and shimmering festoons of musical ornamentation are familiar to every practising musician, music-historian and folk-music collector, whether in 17th and 18th century keyboard music, old Hungarian folk-songs, Italian operatic arias, gipsy music or Hebrew chants. Yet for a long time—and to some extent even today—they were thought of as merely frivolous flourishes, pointlessly beautiful and usually superfluous finery which had nothing to do with the essence of music. Until the 20th century, for instance, most folk-song collectors were quite unaware of the importance of the adequate recording of folk-ornaments. Now that more recent researches—the work of E.D. Wagner, Germer, Dannreuther, Kuhlo, Harding, Kuhn, Goldschmidt, Beyschlag, Schenker, Lach, Écorcheville, Ficker, Orel, Brunold, Schmitz and others—have laid the foundations for a systematic study of ornamentation, musicologists in general have come to recognise that an important part of melody-construction, an organic part of the composition, is to be found in the ornamentation of ancient vocal and instrumental music. Its collection of formulae represent living melody in a 'petrified' and 'reduced' form, so that in a sense the ornament may be regarded as compact, concentrated melody. In past centuries, player and interpreter gave life to the composer's work—which in notation was just a framework, a bare sketch—by his talent for improvising embellishments, thus to some extent cooperating in the creation of the work; the composer of those days had in fact good reason to trust his often capricious interpreters, knowing that they would render the essence of his music, in spite of an addiction to exaggerated and affected flourishes. The practice fell into decay because of ornaments which had crystallised with the passage of time (Schering, for instance, emphasises that after 1500 fewer ornaments were fixed, whilst after 1650 they tended to be more and more written out). An art which up to that time had been a spontaneous culture, an organic part of life, stimulated by circumstances and the needs of the moment, had by then to be scientifically set down and taught.

But the technique of ornamentation had in fact been systematically expounded since the 15th century, and its practice had hardened into set mechanical conventions, beginning with the manuals of Paumann, Ganassi, Ortiz, Maffei, della Casa, Rognoni, Bovicelli, Diruta, Conforti, Zacconi, Bassano and Cerone, and continuing with those of Tosi, Agricola, Marpurg, Quantz, Hiller, Tartini, Mancini and Türk, up to the treatises of Gottlieb Muffat and C.P.E. Bach. To what extent the principles laid down in these manuals, and the formulae they describe, supply the key to the living practice of the art—or its reverse—is still not known; the extent, that is, to which they can be regarded as a reflection of what actually took place. But what is certain is that most of these formulae are to be found in the written-out notation of figurated works, and at a time, according to Schering, when ornamentation was normally extemporised.[1] A thousand years earlier, the melismatic melodies of Gregorian chant had undergone a similar process of crystallisation. Ancient Oriental folk-music, on the other hand, the parallel version of Gregorian chant, continued to preserve the immediacy of direct oral tradition, without any need of a written record. The noting down and fixing of ornaments in Western art-music was followed by a gradual process of decay (which Dannreuther and Lach regard as a process of 'absorption' into the melodic structure) and the last traces of living *fioriture* — already somewhat decadent—occur in 19th-century Italo-French grand opera. Yet it is worth noticing that during the 19th and 20th centuries—in the works of Chopin, Debussy, Stravinsky and recent Hungarian music—Europe's melody-style has generally drawn on East European if not Oriental sources. Even today, East European countries are certainly still able to bring to life some part of this ancient musical tradition; *mutatis mutandis*, the 17th-century tradition of improvisation and ornamentation in ensemble is still to be found amongst gipsy orchestras. In this way certain typical features of old Western musical practices can still be recovered.

This dying out of living ornamentation is in part the result of a more recent development, the ever greater dependence of European polyphony on harmony. The relationship between polyphony and ornamentation has been out of balance from the outset; not by chance did 16th-century lutenist composers, such as Vincenzo Galilei and others, turn repeatedly to polyphony as a reaction against excessive delight in embellishment. Freely flowering melody, complex chordal progressions and strict part-writing could not for long keep company on equal terms. German music during the 18th century is probably the best illustration of the seeming connection that exists between classical polyphony and built-in, structural ornaments (half ornament, half motive), and between homophony and decorative ornamentation (ornaments which are not motives). Yet there is no doubt that European post-Romanticism incurred the loss of the second of these traditions without ever having found its way back to the first.

Eastern Europe, as we have seen, is familiar with the idea of improvised ornaments, both from the traditions of its recently discovered folk-music as from those of its gipsy music; it is still possible to hear gipsy bands using the kind of ensemble improvisation which was being criticised in Western Europe by Praetorius some three hundred years earlier (in his *Syntagma*)! It is not improbable that by virtue of many characteristics of construction and performance, Eastern Europe can claim closer links with the older music of the West than has been preserved in Western music today.

*

Recent research into ornamentation has stressed that the ornament was not so much decorative as an organic part of the melody's construction: that it mirrors its form-building forces, 'sums up the whole of musical evolution'[2] —and thus even throws light on how melodies come into being. The conclusions reached in the brief description that follows need to be investigated in greater detail, but an attempt will be made to isolate a series of problems, on the basis of studies by Robert Lach and others, which hitherto have received but scant attention. The essential is that *ornamentation in European music is not always used in the same way, and so has different meanings.* Hence it refers to different kinds of melody-construction, and so indirectly affects musical thinking as a whole. It would appear that basic principles of ornamentation and melody-building *co-exist* in separate regions. (This idea is contrary to Lach's concept of trends of evolution, which fluctuate from period to period, but in the end form one homogeneous, 'geological' whole.) The idea of co-existing spheres seems to have been implied by Besseler in the distinction he makes between the 'textural ornament' of the Italo-Burgundian style, and the 'built-in ornament' of the English 15th-century style (divisions). (See *Zeitschrift für Musikwissenschaft*, 1928.)

A convenient starting-point is provided by the fact that two sharply differentiated epochs are recognisable in the history of European ornaments: two periods, comprising an older and a more recent outlook. (This has already been pointed out by Dannreuther, Beyschlag, and others.) The hundred years between 1650 and 1750 forms the dividing line; it is straddled by Bach, the most representative figure of this transitional period, who is on the border-line of both trends. In essence he is in complete *rapport* with the past, yet he also follows up and assimilates the imperative urgency of the 'new art' with all the powrerful and far-reaching vitality of an artist who is committed to his time. It is worth mentioning, moreover, that this transitional period witnessed a remarkable approximation between the vocal and instrumental styles of ornamentation, which about 1600 were still quite distinct. This was in marked contrast to the Southern European preference for 'substantialised sound'—to be discussed in more detail in a moment. Thus late Venetian and early Neapolitan composers (Cesti, Draghi, Scarlatti and so on) gave a new direction to instrumental and vocal *fioriture*; and during the 18th century instrumental and vocal ornaments generally came to be moulded out of similar material, particularly in the North, that is, in Central Europe. Only the most important composers of the period knew how to keep them separate, in practice as in aesthetic pronouncements.[3]

This dividing-line of 1700 presents a double aspect. After 1700, the ornament in Western music took on a more decorative function. The familiar 'petrified' forms—mordents (already foreshadowed in the 15th century), *pincés*, *coulés*, *chutes*, turns, etc. are all in their final shape the result of this more recent development. Before 1700 (i.e. the period leading to the full flowering of *bel canto* between 1650 and 1700), the ornament was still valued as an essential part of melodic flow, as 'melody within the melody'.[4]

For Lach, this dividing-line is marked by the spread of diminution; it is in fact very likely that diminution was directly responsible for the more recent, 'decorative' type of ornamentation. Both techniques overlay the native melodic flow with an international layer of readily available formulae; the only difference is that diminution appears to spring from Italian soil, and decorative ornamentation from Burgundian-French territory. These international formulae spring up alongside the instinctive need of voice or instrument (lute, viol, virginals, organ) to ornament for reasons of tone or technique. Once again it is a question of the association of sound and instrument—they are offshoots of Latin-Romance culture.

As a result of this dividing-line, the harmonic aspect of decoration became much more uniform after 1700, so that it is more difficult to distinguish the different ways in which it was applied.

Did such differentiated ways of handling ornamentation exist in earlier days too? Was melody differently embellished in different parts of Europe? To anyone making a detailed study of European melody before 1700 it is clear that this was so, in spite of frequent intertwinings and crossings, and plenty of borrowed practices. A comparison of the characteristic *fioriture* of old Italian, old French, old German and old Hungarian music will reveal striking differences in spite of obvious similarities, parallels and affinities. Even as early as the 11th century, Aribo Scholasticus found there to be a fundamental difference of principle between Southern and Northern forms of melody—i.e. between the Longobard and German forms. This has been confirmed more recently by the researches of P. Wagner (1925), who has been able to establish the existence of German and Latin-Romance liturgical dialects. Further evidence is provided by Johannes Diaconus, who inveighed against the French and German distortion of Gregorian melisma, etc.[5] The point can be illustrated by a wealth of historical data: Colluccio Salutati (1363) and Johannes Burchardus (1499) both regarded the Italian art of singing as a national characteristic; in the 17th and 18th centuries, Mersenne, Couperin, Telemann, C.P.E. Bach and particularly Quantz still recognised important differences between the French and Italian methods of ornamentation, etc. These deep, innate differences seem to have taken permanent root in the life of Western music cultures, to some extent splitting up European music history into the history of single regions. If an attempt is made to investigate the autochthonous language of ornamentation in each particular region—disregarding as the fashionable uniform of the period the internationally adopted, common vocabulary of diminution—then approximately the following regions emerge:

1. *Mediterranean region (Southern, Italo-Spanish)*

The ornaments are themselves extensions of the melodic line—they spring from what appears to be an overflow of melodic energy (even when their role is an illustrative one, as in the 16th-century madrigal). That is why they can hardly ever be stripped to plain interval relationships, as it has no effect on their own intrinsic melodic importance.[6] Even as late as the 16th century, it is quite astonishing what free and internationally valid offshoots of melody this Italo-Spanish collection of formulae can still produce; at a time, that is, when gradually 'petrifying' ornaments were already being taught from manuals. The following examples are taken from Ortiz (*Tratado de glosas*, 1553), Tomás de Sancta Maria (*Arte del tañer fantasia*, 1565), Conforti (*Breve e facile maniera d'esercitarsi a far passaggi*, 1593), Bovicelli (*Regole*, etc., 1594) and Rognoni Taegio (*Selva di varii passaggi*, 1620); every one of these examples is concerned with 'circling' a fourth, fifth, second or third, indicating that at the beginning no more was intended than the elaboration of a straightforward interval:[7]

150

Certain passages in this Southern region are clearly meant "not to be left unadorned," and manage to burst out into melody through diminution. In

248

the author's view these are highly characteristic. How frequently such traits appear in old Italian music, and how much they seem to be at home there! There can be no clearer indication of the extent to which this remarkable melodiousness, with its aversion to formulae, is deeply embedded in national tendencies. Here for example is a passage from Giovanni da Cascia's famous *Peacock Madrigal* (14th century), where an unadorned melodic phrase appears together with its ornamented form in what amounts to heterophony:

151
G i o v a n n i   d a   C a s c i a :   Madrigal

Here is another example, an ornamented cadence from Caccini's *Nuove Musiche* (1602), full of the same unrestrained melodic exuberance:

152
C a c c i n i :   Aria from the "Nuove Musiche" (1602)

The flood of ornamentation, free melodic flow and *fioriture* naturally lasted longer in this zone of Western Europe than in any other (in the shape of Neapolitan opera, Rossini); Zacconi (1555—1627) was already claiming that ornaments should be singable *(che cantino bene)*, and the melodic lines of these Southern *fioriture* seem to 'sing their hearts out' quite unrestrainedly. But at this point there is another problem. Undoubtedly this Southern world of melody is related to the Orient, though the single strands of the relationship have not as yet been fully unravelled. Gregorian chant, for instance, owns a double origin. Like the so-called church modes, it appears to be the collective result both of the Orient and of Southern Europe. The examples so far quoted have been embedded in polyphony, or interpolated into it, even when they were not the result of it. But the melody of Gregorian chant is the result of an unques-

tionably monodic culture which at the same time forms a bridge to the polyphony of Southern Europe. In part this is because the first attempts at polyphony in the Southern region crystallised round Gregorian chant, but also
because of a deeper kinship. Plainchant appears to have bestowed on Mediterranean melody the almost sensuous magic of unfettered melody. Take for example passages like these:

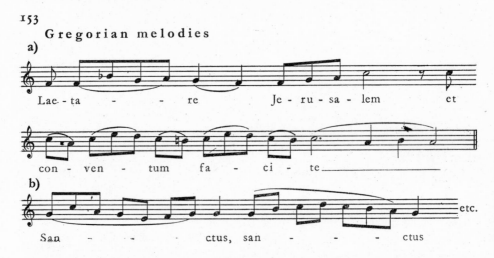

153

Gregorian melodies

a)

Lae- - ta - - re   Je - ru - sa - lem   et

con - ven - tum   fa - ci - te

b)

San - - - ctus, san - - - ctus   etc.

These can hardly be regarded as the ornamentation of a set melodic framework.
They really represent the spontaneous ebb and flow of 'melodic energy', yet
they also show clear affinity with Oriental melody-style, and are related to the
melodic embellishments of the Mediterranean (a mixture of Syrian, Hebrew,
Greek elements and Italian folk-tradition). Oriental and Mediterranean cultures
both developed under the sign of 'sung melody'; both developed their instrumental melodies in a radically different way from their vocal ones, ornamented
a slow melody quite differently from a fast one. Mediterranean culture naturally
fosters sound texture and tone-colour, whilst every melody performed in the
Oriental tradition, every performance of the same melody, is completely different. And this in spite of—or just because—the same 'unuttered' melody emerges
through its parts.[8] But in a time-sense it is possible to go even further. Even
in the 16th-century Italo-Spanish manuals of diminution, there are many
Oriental, or Orientalised, features. Where do they come from? From the living
streams of Gregorian melody, from Oriental sources continually available to
Southern Europe, from Byzantium, or from Arabic influences in Sicily and
Spain? Or from the Balkans, which for a thousand years was the melting-point
of Oriental, Western and South European cultures? So far there is no adequate
answer, although the link has long been established beyond dispute.[9] Summing

up the difference, this Southern melodiousness may perhaps be said to be more self-sufficient, more substantialised by comparison with that of the North, i.e. that its melodies are far more adapted to the needs of melodic 'matter' (e.g. colour and pace, the particular instrument used, tempo). So it comes to shape one style for voices and another for instruments, a fast style and a slow style. (So it is that Frescobaldi, for example, gives almost exact tempo-indications for the ornamentation in the Preface to his *Toccatas* [1614 – 16], whilst in Germany, the first composer to concern himself with such matters was C.P.E. Bach, more than a century later.[10])

2. *Atlantic region (Western European, comprising English, Flemish and French)*, perhaps with some general reminiscences of Celtic or Norman ornamentation.

Its chief features: the ornament becomes an element of movement, spurring on the motives which arise out of the harmonic structure, and helping them to flow along easily, with a good swing. This kind of ornament is a typically decorative formation, and inseparably connected with the homophonic and monodic mode of thought. Flemish polyphonists, considered 'masters of ornamentation', such as Okeghem, Agricola and the young Josquin, broke loose from the French tradition at the point at which it blurred the dividing-line between ornamentation and freer motives. The strikingly schematic ornaments of troubadour melodies should probably also be included here. The French in particular generally showed a marked preference for the fixed outline, stiffened into a formula; the three- or four-part *plica* in troubadour melodies is unmistakable evidence of this.[11] Hieronymus de Moravia commented in the 13th century on the unpopularity of certain forms of trill *(nota procellaris)* had become in France, thereby emphasising how closed and exclusive these formulae had become. Most striking of all are the 'vagrant formulae' which became international currency during the course of the 15th and 16th centuries—probably as a result of the 13th- and 14th-century practice of *déchant*. Palestrina, for instance, like almost all Western composers, took over these devices from Flemish composers, in addition to certain devices reminiscent of Gregorian chant. They include the diminution of simple groups of notes derived from *clausulae*, cadential formulae, *cambiata* figures, special kinds of turns. All these are devices of movement, and not extensions of the melody, like Italian ornaments. How easy it is to remove the ornamentation from these passages, and reduce them to their original structure! There follow some examples from the works of Josquin, Brumel, Agricola, and Palestrina in his Flemish manner. These are followed by excerpts from collections of *chansons* and *frottole*, and lastly—by way of transition to the third region—by some extracts from English virginal music, about 1600:

154

See also the English examples of this period quoted by Lach (*op. cit.* pp. 402–403). Where ornamentation is concerned, early English music presents a Janus-head with two, if not three, aspects. That it was open to Northern influence is clear from Giraldus Cambrensis' 11th-century description of the practice of pedal-points and parallel thirds in Northern England and Scandinavia. The Renaissance style of English melody, on the other hand, and 15th-century melody in particular, appears to be a Northern relative of Mediterranean melody. Its divisions form part of the melodic structure, and have an unrestricted flow.[12] Lastly, it will be seen to form a bridge between the *melopoeia* of Western and Central Europe. One of the chief characteristics of 'dynamic' ornaments is that the musical sensibility of the period grasps and adopts them as a set whole; not as living melody-structure, that is, but as stereotyped formulae. This explains their often unusual placement in the harmony, which Jeppesen has investigated in detail.[13]

(It is worth commenting at this point on the folk-like opening motives of Tinódi's *Egervár*, and on other, more recent Hungarian dance and song compositions in *verbunkos* style which should probably be included here as well. The motives they employ are familiar from 16th-century Italian lutenist literature, and are really no more than a circling of the tonic-dominant interval.)

Unquestionably, the far-reaching historical significance of the Western region lies in the fact that after 1650 or 1700 its methods of handling ornamentation were adopted by the greater part of Europe. (This was an explicit, conscious process in Germany, after the time of Froberger and the older Muffat.) The Western region was in fact responsible for forming the entire collection of modern European ornaments; the result of its pioneering (cp. French suite-composers!) was that the new type of ornamentation, effectively crystallised into formulae, was taken over by the whole of European music as an element of movement and decoration.

3. Baltic Region (Central European, German)

In this region ornamentation breaks up the musical idea into sections, and then elaborates and varies it; it does not generate melody or movement so much as supply energy for structural, form-building purposes. Ornamentation in this region does not bring new melodies into existence (as does the Mediterranean region) or new movement (as the Western). It is used instead to unfold the thematic texture, which it weaves into shape with strict attention both to thematic unity and the overall design (ornamentation composed of sequence-like chains or series, figurated melody). It is really a compressed form of motive-development. It seems that this represents the genuine older style of German ornamentation—including that of Bach himself. For him it does not consist, as Ehrlich, Beyschlag and even Hammerschlag maintain, in the trills, turns, mordents, etc. which were common international currency at the time. Also it would seem important that this architectonic form of ornamentation was closely connected with polyphony from the very outset. The German way of building up motives is closely allied with polyphony, which is probably why it appears to be less vocal than the Italian, less dependent on instrumentation and rhythmical shape; why, in a word, it is less concerned with material substance. The condensed melody in Bach's ornamentation (particularly in his slow movements, etc.) characteristically almost always appears as well in his larger, more developed and extended forms. Here is a parallel instance to illustrate this point: first the strictly ornamented Chorale-Prelude *Vater unser im Himmelreich*, followed by the opening chorus of the cantata *Brich dem Hungrigen dein Brot*:

155

Bach: a) Chorale prelude: "Vater unser im Himmelreich"   b) Cantata: "Brich dem Hungrigen dein Brot"

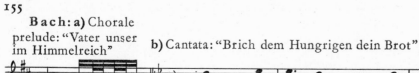

Cp. also Music Examples Nos. 69 (a) and (b); a figurated motive from the last movement of the *Third Brandenburg Concerto* is set alongside a familiar phrase from *Bist du bei mir*. Here figuration appears, always and in every respect, as the principal texture; as musical thought, it may be variously expressed and rhythmically ambiguous, but as texture it reigns supreme; whilst as a motive it forms the carefully thought-out basis for elaboration. This cannot usually be said of Hasse, Haydn, Mozart (sonatas, string quartets, e.g. the first two movements of K.V. 281, the slow movements of K.V. 173, 310, 332, 387, coloratura arias, etc.) or of 18th-century Italian composers. Here, and in the Southern region as a whole, the fundamental law of melodic progression and 'material substance' is in operation, so that smaller intervals are automatically linked up with faster tempi, and larger intervals with slower tempi. In this way—even in the 'singing Allegros'—a basic difference is established between the melodic and ornamental style of slow music and fast music, vocal and instrumental. The difference is immediately apparent by comparing any of Bach's Choral Variations with those of Mozart and his contemporaries: even as basic 'raw material', Bach's melody style depends less on tempo and instrument than does Mozart's. The decline of polyphony seems here to go hand in hand with the advance of the non-German, decorative type of ornamentation. In Bach the tendency is more Northern, less concerned with matter and substance, opposed to the Southern habit of bowing before pace and tonal texture. Variations in pace do not interest him, and in his melody-building he prefers concentration and 'motive-spinning' to the decoration or circling of intervals. Traces of this tendency already appear, of course, in the embellished transcriptions of 15th- and 16th-century German organ-composers (the 'colourists'). While the Gregorian-type adornment of *Meistersinger* still hovers between the 'Western' and German mode of ornamentation, this more 'Northern' method of melody-construction becomes quite typical of German choral adaptations in the 17th and early 18th centuries. The organ transcriptions by Adam de Fulda and Paumann, for instance (published by Schering in his *Studien zur Musikgeschichte der Frührenaissance.* 1914), already mirror the Central European outlook quite plainly in their built-in chains of ornaments, an integral part of the musical structure:[14]

156

a) **Adam de Fulda:** Organ Hymn

b) **Paumann:** Organ Hymn

The gap separating German tradition from the ideas prevailing in the West becomes still more obvious when some of Bach's typical figuration (conceived purely instrumentally) is compared with the typical embellishments of Couperin, Dandrieu or other French keyboard composers of the period:

157

Bach: a) Concerto in Italian Style

b) St. Matthew Passion

158

a) Couperin: 1er ordre, 1ère courante, double

b) Dandrieu: Le concert des oiseaux: Le ramage

c) Dandrieu: La lyre d'Orphée

The close-knit web of melody of the Bach examples appears in Couperin and Dandrieu as melody resulting from 'dynamic' ornamentation. The former is typically German, the latter typically French. This older German method of motive-building occurs much later too, in some of Beethoven's late works (e.g. the fourth variation in the second movement of op. 111). The style of ornamentation described here, which unquestionably penetrated deep into German composing technique, and in particular that of early German composers, seems superficially to have suffered eclipse when Western methods took over; but it survived in certain specific ways. One of the most interesting demonstrations of this is an *Adagio* by Vivaldi, transcribed in an ornamented version by Pisendel or one of his German contemporaries.[15] It is all the more interesting, in that the early German technique of weaving ornaments into the texture (using the ornament as a motive) came back in the last works of Haydn, Mozart and Beethoven; at a time, that is, when these composers had to some extent returned to polyphony (e.g. Mozart's *F minor Organ Fantasy*, K.V. 608, and Beethoven's last piano sonata, op. 111, where it appears—as mentioned above—in the fourth variation of the *Arietta*). In general terms, however, it is true to say that the three regions so far described appear to contract into two regions after 1700—1750 (into North and South, comprising German-French and Italian). After this time native German tradition appeared to go underground and conduct a hidden existence. The ornamentation of expression and feeling used by Mozart,[16] Haydn, Beethoven, Weber, Schumann and Wagner is plainly derived from the same set of formulae as that used by Méhul, Berlioz or Meyerbeer. These had been absorbed into the new cosmopolitan idiom, and were clearly schematic by comparison with the formulae available in earlier periods. German music of the 18th and 19th centuries was after all nourished from every side, but at the same time constituted a cosmopolitan world-language of music which emanated in all directions.

4. *East European region*
At present the concept is heterogeneous and artificial, adopted here merely to distinguish it from Central and West European music—particularly as it is made up of the folk-music of various peoples, collected for the most part in recent times. It includes the folk-ornamentation of Slavs, Hungarians and the Balkan peoples. Yet it is essential to realise that much Hungarian folk-music (and some Russian folk-music as well) lies outside any European system, since at bottom

both preserve numerous Asiatic elements and influences. (These are pentatonicism and ornamentation in ancient Hungarian folk-music, through which it seems to be the westernmost link of an ancient Asiatic chain; Tartar, Persian and Central Asian elements in Russian folk-music.) As yet it is not possible to analyse the whole vast East European territory from this point of view. Yet certain other East European and Oriental cultures appear to show traces similar to many of the features of ancient Hungarian ornamentation. To some extent —and this applies to every naturally monodic music—the Eastern ornament acts as an accompanying part and a substitute for polyphony. (In several Eastern cultures, ornamented performance has been shown to be a primitive form of polyphony—heterophony, in fact.) By filling out the framework and broadening its dimensions, ornamentation may be said here to substitute for the energy which in the folk-melody of other cultures is directed towards the development of polyphony (as P. Wagner has shown in the case of the *melisma* of Gregorian chant). Old-style Hungarian ornamentation springs as much from the physiological needs of singing as from the performer's artistry or some tradition of how the ornaments should be performed, yet it is remarkable for the range and variety of its ornamental designs, its arabesque-like elaboration of general formulae. It needs stressing that these are not loose and casually applied embellishments, but strictly executed, consistent configurations, drawing on a generally fixed, regular and permanent supply of notes. Their function is not only to 'sharpen the outline' as Hornbostel has remarked of East Asian ornaments,[17] but to give greater consistency to the melody. It is as if they were replacing some accompanying part, *ostinato*-like and uniform, and often imitative or illustrative in type. Like an extensive spider's web, this motive-like ornamentation surrounds ancient melody-patterns of which (like the *nomoi*, *maqam* and *raga*) only the main outlines are fixed. It shapes them into 'real' melodies, and gives them 'tangible' form. In simple peasant performance, too, a player will spin out long instrumental melodies from a vocal one, and still maintain the strictest motivic unity. As Kuhlo puts it, 'ornamenting' music is turned into 'ornamented' music, etc.[18] Most East European and Oriental peoples appear to share these characteristics, at least in part. In contrast to the West, all Oriental cultures appear to share the same motivic unity and clear tonal structure, which so far as ornamentation is concerned, produces a homogeneous *melos*. This is in spite of considerable structural differences (ranging from rows of Asiatic variations 'without start or finish' to the close-knit strophic design of Hungarian tunes), and of possible fluctuation in the characteristics of individual cultures.[19] (That certain groups of notes persist is partly due to the singer's physiological make-up and should to some extent be taken as a natural phenomenon, dependent on a physical organ. Yet it is clear from the way that a basic motive is rigidly maintained throughout a given piece that this springs from much deeper musical instincts and is not just the result of some physical habit or necessity. This is evident in countless examples of ornamented Rumanian folk-songs in Bartók's collection, in the ornamented interludes of North African Arab dance-tunes, etc.) To illustrate this unified style of ornamentation, by which the melody is moulded into a firm unity, there follow a Hungarian and a Russian folk-example. (The text and possibly the melody of the Hungarian folk-song is 17th century; see Bartók—Kodály: *Transylvanian Folk-Songs*, 1923, No. 76. The Russian folk-song comes from A. G. Novikov's *Russkiye Narodniye pyesni*, I, Moscow—Leningrad, 1936, p. 128.) In both songs the ornamentation of the second half of the melody is the diminution of one of the preceding lines, which gives the entire melody motivic unity and a uniform basic texture.

159

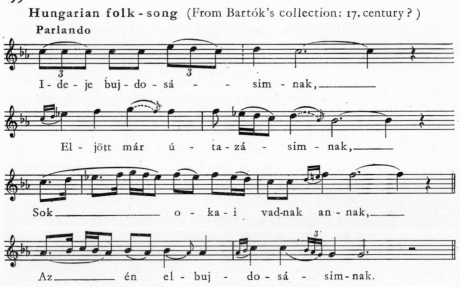

Hungarian folk-song (From Bartók's collection: 17. century?)

Parlando

I - de - je buj - do - sá - - sim - nak,____

El - jött már ú - ta - zá - sim - nak,____

Sok____ o - ka - i vad-nak an - nak,____

Az____ én el - buj - do - sá - sim - nak.

160

Russian folk-song (From Novikov's collection)

Лу - чи - на, мо - я лу - чи - - - нуш - ка,

бе - рё - зо - ва - я,____

что же ты, мо - я̲̅ лу - чи - - - нуш - ка,

не яр - ко го - - ришь? А - ли ты, мо - я лу -

чи - - - нуш - ка, в пе́ - чи не̲ бы -

ла, - - - зо - ва, не вы̲ - су - ше - на?

а - ли ты, мо - я̲̅ бе -

рё - - - зо - ва, не вы̲ - су - ше - на?

Older Hungarian *art*-music did not always adhere to this ancient Oriental tradition in the building up of ornaments and melodies; like old Hungarian culture generally, it was open to the most diverse European trends. The typical 'interlacing' ornaments of 17th- and 18th-century tradition, preserved orally or in manuscripts of the time, make it clear that a distinction should probably be made between the 'genteel' ornamented style of the Hungarian Baroque and the stricter, organic ornamentation of folk-tunes. This point is illustrated by several interesting 17th-century manuscripts of music for virginals, amongst them an instrumental piece in the *Kájoni Codex* known as *Chorea*, really no more than an ornamented transcription of an old hymn-tune. Its style of ornamentation is for the most part Italian, and so reflects the Western practice of diminution. Another interesting example of instrumental transformation is found in the *Chorea in A minor* from the *Lőcse Mss.* (about 1660), which probably paraphrases a well-known folk-melody. In contrast to this 17th-century trend in art-music, 18th-century student songs often incline to folk tradition, and here and there show traces in their ornamentation of melodies spun out of motives. The ornamentation of the recruiting *(verbunkos)* song and the *csárdás* is again closer to Western types. (*Cp.* also the excessively ornamented passages of *verbunkos* dances and folk-paraphrases, not to mention the *Rákóczi-March* itself, derived from a freely ornamented instrumental version of the Rákóczi-song.)

So far as the general idea of melody and melody-formation is concerned, Hungarian art and folk-music are thus seen to hover curiously between Orient and Occident. The Oriental method achieves structural unity by a melody-line which is organically constructed and concentrated; the Occidental method (and Baroque melody in particular) consists in building a series of motives out of minute sections of melody. It seems in fact as though the 'interlacing' ornaments of the 17th and 18th centuries counterbalanced the individual and minute articulation of Baroque melodies; they made it easier for Baroque melodies to seize hold of the closed and rounded structure, by means of which they were snatched up, and assimilated by the folk-tradition. Continual vacillation from period to period is quite unmistakable here, but it is none the less clear that at that time popular-style art-music, as well as some Hungarian folk-music, undoubtedly took over some stylistic idioms from the West; though not in the same way at every period, nor in the same way from every source. Even today, certain levels of Hungarian folk-music still seem to show more affinity with 17th-century German-Italian styles than with later European trends.

Finally we come to 'gipsy music', that is, to gipsy performance and ornamentation, which so strongly influenced the Romantics' attitude to Hungarian music in the 19th century. Here some sharp differentiation is necessary, since gipsy music and its style of performance is largely determined by the audience confronting it. Although the ornaments of Hungarian village gipsies show strong structural affinities with peasant folk-practice, the town gipsy employs the familiar brand of ornamentation, which break up sections of melody into minute festoons, and is derived from Arab-Indian ornamentation. (Bartók considered this style to be the remains of an earlier aristocratic tradition—i.e. a manner of performance once practised by the old Hungarian ruling class.[20])

5. *Music of North European peoples.* Basically this too consists of recently recorded folk-music material. According to information so far received, the elements of ornamentation are insignificantly few, apart from some rudimentary melismatic link-forms.[21] It is being disregarded in this brief survey for the moment.

★

Casting a backward glance over what has been said so far: what conclusions emerge from this regional classification of the formative processes underlying European melody? First, that in each of these regions—which do not necessarily follow racial or national boundaries—different musical impulses appear. The first region shows a drive towards spontaneously developing melody, the second, an exceptional dynamic impulse, the third, pronounced form-building tendencies, and the fourth, a unified conception of ornamental figuration. European musical culture has seemingly been compounded of these different layers. From them two main principles emerge, both of which require more detailed explanation:

1. *Ornamentation and Movement.* European music is divisible according to how much its cultures are affected by 'matter'—by the degree, that is, to which they adapt to their musical material, or more specifically, how they react to the rhythmical movement or decoration inherent in the musical idea. In more 'material' cultures, ornamentation either unfolds the melody spontaneously, or urges it along with the help of decoration, while in less 'material' ones it becomes largely responsible for the melody-structure. Latin-Romance music is the best example of the first type, and German music of the second. Oriental music, on the other hand, regards the 'substance' or 'matter' of music as changeable, and the moulding of it as accidental, valid for only one occasion (improvisation).

2. *Ornamentation and Polyphony.* The harmonically influenced cultures of the West developed the ornament in a decorative sense, yet on the other hand gave it structural importance through the polyphony of Central Europe; whilst Eastern homophony used it to spin out its motives into a unified texture. Ornamentation came in this way to assume basic structural importance in cultures which shape their musical forms out of the melody itself, that is, where the weight of the musical thought does not lie in multi-dimensional extension, in harmonic expansion, but concentrates instead on linear development and the one-dimensional pull of the melody (or melodies).

Hence East and West Europe differ as fundamentally in their musical thought as do North and South. In Southern Europe, melody is turned into yet another melody; melodies in this region do not merge, but develop out of one another. In the North (in Central Europe) one idea will develop another, but remain inside it. In the South, melodies flower continuously, in the North they constantly intertwine. The South encourages plastic and rounded shapes, whilst Northern forms develop organically, the result of elaboration. (The Italians invent forms, the Germans complete them.) In much the same way, Western musical thinking is opposed to Oriental thinking. Western homophony and polyphony use the ornament partly for movement and decoration, and partly for construction. But the aim is always a firmer idea of form. The Oriental ornament, on the other hand, not only acts as a stimulant and a unifier, but weaves the very fabric of which the music is made. Western ornamentation is like a fermenting agent: it summons up energies which are complex and much-ramifying, and compels them into a closed unity. The Oriental ornament is itself a supreme creator of form, realising inner unity by juxtaposition. In the West it appears inserted into structures which are monodic or contrapuntal,

261

but always polyphonic. Hence the ornament never takes up the whole space, but needs to be linked in and constructed. In the Orient it develops without extraneous additions, it is self-sufficient and self-explanatory. In the West the emphasis is on great polyphonic works, and forms built up of many sections; in the Orient it is a question of homophonic series of verses or variations (in other words, Europe prefers fixed forms and pre-established performance, whilst Asia prefers improvisation).

This brings yet another difficulty. If there is such great divergence in the way that musical ideas unfold—if they are governed by such different inner principles—does it not follow that musical structure itself has a different meaning in different cultures? And is it still possible to speak of a homogeneous history of European music, or of specialised subjects within it, of an international evolution of form? Can the sonata, for instance, be said to have a unified evolution, if Italian and German sonatas show basic differences, since German and Italian musical thought appear to be organised in a totally different way? In principle, every problem of priority (e.g. German symphonic forms, classical-romantic sonata literature in Italy, etc.) ought only to be determined within these limits.

But at present the range of the problem can hardly extend so far. In its primary state all music should supposedly be regarded as ornamentation, as an ever-flowing and freely improvised melodic texture, unfettered and unfixed. The different ways of applying it in the various regions seem to indicate that each community adopts a particular direction under pressure from the inner formative forces of its own particular culture. The younger the culture, and the more averse to all fixed forms, the greater seems to be the role of ornamentation, as a source, that is, of unfettered melody; cramped, rigid and atrophied ornaments denote a culture which is itself growing rigid and old. This provides a uniform way of assessing how the various cultures are related to ornamentation. Yet all European musical cultures obviously have the same common basis (polyphony, structural make-up, tonal system, and scales), otherwise they could not have collaborated on collective achievements, problems of form, etc. over a long stretch of time. They experienced individual artistic trends in a collective way and at about the same period, in spite of relative differences of time. Without shared basic principles, a reciprocal exchange of ideas would be quite unthinkable at any period—although a whole series of such connections clearly existed, particularly in the case of melody. (Obvious examples are the Italo-English link at the end of the 16th century, Flemish-German links in the 16th century, the Italo-English-Burgundian connection in the Middle Ages, the international sources from which motets were drawn, etc.[22]) The vagrant formulae[23] should also be mentioned here, models of diminution for the whole of Europe. There is also the often surprising influence exerted by various techniques (e.g. the Central European technique of florid elaboration, found in A. Gabrieli, Frescobaldi and the divisions of English music; the Neapolitan *fioriture* of Purcell, Handel[24] and J.C. Bach; the collective influence of Gregorian chant—not to mention the acceptance of 'Western' devices by Central Europe). A whole series of historical analogies offer themselves—the Baroque, for instance, which appeared in every European country, everywhere lent wings to different national drives and racial tendencies, forcing cultures of similar age to take a 'period direction' under the stimulus of a shared inspiration, to unite in a 'spirit of the period'.

Yet European cultures undoubtedly interpret and assess every current for themselves; they experience each trend in a radically different way, and in this new, 'individual' sense either develop it or turn away from it. In our opinion, the role played by single nations within the regions is still obscure and vague, yet we know that 'European unity' appears at all periods as the collective, harmonious result of a process of emanation from *divergent* giant organisms. What are, or were, these organisms? The attempt to penetrate more deeply into the 'personality' that lies behind their individual existence may also have the effect of clarifying the ultimate unity which emerges from their joint functioning.

NOTES

1. In *Studien zur Tanzmusik der Renaissance* (unpublished, but an extract appeared in the *Musical Quarterly* entitled "About Dance and Dance Music in the Late Middle Ages." *Musical Quarterly* XXVII, New York, 1941, pp. 289—305), O. Gombosi maintains that the formulae contained in the manuals of ornamentation were intended for *dilettanti*, and not for professional musicians (their education was in any case not very different). If this is true, they would have been written-out in order to provide technical training and preparation for whatever was considered essential by the practice of the day, regardless of improvisational skill. The living practice of ornamentation cannot in any case have been very different from the 'models': Fr. Severi (*Salmi passeggiati*, 1615) and Giovanni L. Conforti (*Breve e facile maniera d'esercitarsi a far passaggi*, 1593) emphasise expressly that their examples are meant to be improvised ("These are normally improvised" ... "They appear as though improvised" ... "these can be improvised"). Likewise, Zacconi (in the *Prattica di Musica*): "These may be sung as though improvised" ... "The models of *fioriture* are the written record of what was carried out freely and fluently in performance," wrote R. Haas (*Aufführungspraxis der Musik*, 1931, p. 117). They are all the more important in that a whole array of theorists (Guilelmus Monachus, Ortiz, Zacconi, Agazzari, Praetorius, Rousseau, Fuhrmann, Tosi, Marcello, Villeneuve, Agricola, Quantz, C.P.E. Bach, L. Mozart, Heinichen, Mancini, Hiller, Türk, Mosel) draw attention to the fact that the performer reshapes the ornamented part into an almost independent composition: "diminish the tenor part at will" *(facias tenorem diminutum sicut volueris)*, "write it afresh" *(escriviendo*

de nuevo), "form a melody of his own liking" *(formarsi un canto a suo modo)*, "invent new parts" *(compor nuove parti)*, "multiplicatio," "elaborate the material through a series of diminutions" *(travailler sur un sujet allant de diminutions en diminutions)*, "repeat in a different fashion" *(replicarle diversamente)*, "change all the arias" *(cangiar tutte le arie)*, "diminutions invented at will" *(diminuzioni a capriccio)*, "compose almost entirely new parts" *(fast ganz neue Stimmen komponieren)*, "apply individual invention to the written notes" *(eigene Erfindung über den vorgeschriebenen Noten anzubringen)*, "vary at will" *(willkürlich verändern)*, "vary the melody" *(formare un canto variato)*, "the invented parts" *(parti della mente creatrice)*, "change its form" *(changer la forme)*, "embellished with optional variations" *(durch willkürliche Veränderungen ausgezieret)*, "to improve on the upper part" *(der obern Stimme eine bessere Tour zu geben)*, "to surprise the hearer with new devices" *(die Zuhörer immer durch neue Erfindungen überraschen)*, "to improve on the melody" *(die Melodie verbessern)*, "as if to improvise a composition" *(gleichsam eine Komposition aus dem Stegreif)*, "to elaborate the notes and make a few dozen notes out of a single one" *(die Noten verkräuseln und aus einer Note ein paar Dutzend machen)*. At a later period (18th and early 19th centuries), the declarations of Quantz, C.P.E. Bach, G.D. Türk and I.F. Mosel have particular importance; e.g. Quantz, 1752: "If a player wishes to alter a passage, he should so execute it that the added part will be more agreeably melodic and its passage-work more brilliant than it is as it stands"; C.P.E. Bach, 1760: "A player must know how to vary almost any motive at the reprise"; G.D. Türk: *Klavierschule*. 1789, p. 325: "The variations must be . . . at least as good as the original melody"; F. Mosel, 1813: "The prevailing fashion . . . which in the arias . . . frequently leaves not a single bar from which the original melody may be deduced . . ." *Cp.* also H.-P. Schmitz: *Die Kunst der Verzierung im 18. Jahrhundert*. Kassel and Basel, 1955; also E.T. Ferand: "Embellished 'Parody Cantatas' in the early 18th century," *Musical Quarterly*. XLIV, 1958, pp. 40—64; in German in *Bericht über den Internat. Musikwissenschaftl. Kongress*. Wien, Mozartjahr 1956, published by E. Schenk, Graz—Köln, 1958, pp. 203—215. *Cp.* also: H. Chr. Wolff: "Orientalische Einflüsse in den Improvisationen des 16. und 17. Jh." *Kölner Kongressbericht*. 1958/1959, p. 303; I. Horsley: "The Diminutions in Composition and Theory of Composition." *Acta Mus*. 1963, p. 124.

2. R. Lach: *Studien z. Entwicklungsgesch. der ornamentalen Melopöie*. 1913, p. 637.

3. It is characteristic that where vocal and instrumental embellishments are concerned, De Bacilly, Agricola and Hiller only recognise a difference of expression and nuance, i.e. a difference of quantity and not of quality.

4. Lach, *op. cit.*, p. 266.

5. It is interesting that Mersenne, Couperin, Telemann, C.P.E. Bach and above all Quantz still acknowledge there to be a fundamental difference between French and Italian ornamentation. Colluccio Salutati was aware of the distinctively national flavour of the Italian way of singing as early as 1363, as was Joh. Burchardus in 1499. In the words of a 9th-century writer from St. Gallen, it is a case of *nimia dissimilitudo*.

6. In essentials, this technique is the same as that described by J. Handschin. He traces its beginnings in tropes of the Romance countries in the Middle Ages, finds it holding its own during the late Middle Ages in English music and peripheral areas of France—regardless of the dynamic function of ornamentation obtaining in Gothic music. Then it reappears in the music of the West European Renaissance (*ZMW* XI, 1928).

7. See also examples in Kuhn (*Die Verzierungskunst in der Gesangsmusik des 16—17. Jh.-s*. 1902, pp. 89 ff., 92 ff., 115 ff.) and in Haas (*Aufführungspraxis der Musik*. 1931, pp. 185 ff., 225 ff.), as well as the famous ornamented version of Corelli's Sonatas, op. 5.

8. See Lachmann's observations, according to which *maqam* and *raga* are "always implied,"

"exist solely in the sense of the Platonic 'Idea'," but with "the model appearing in a different way each time" (*Musik des Orients*. 1929, pp. 59—60); "It is thus an Oriental practice never to perform a melody twice in the same way" (Wellesz: *Byzant. Musik.* 1927, p. 66; Eng. ed.: *A History of Byzantine Music and Hymnography.* 2nd ed. revised and enlarged O.U.P., 1961).

9. *Cp.* Lach's notable observations, *op. cit.*, pp. 148—149, 286—288, 360—361; further Pedrell: *Folklore musical Castillan du XVIe siècle.* SIMG I, and *Cancionero mus. popular español.* 1921—1922, also Idelsohn: *Hebr.-orient. Melod.* IV, pp. 21—28, and Farmer: *Historical Facts for the Arabian Musical Influence,* 1930.

10. *Cp.* also the energetic stand taken by Jean Rousseau against "the embellishments which alter the pulse and the rhythm" *(Agréments qui altèrent la Mesure et le Mouvement)*; even in 1780, Hiller gives examples of ornamentation which can be adapted to any tempo "by extending the size of the bar"!

11. *Cp.* J. Beck: *Les Chansonniers des Troubadours et des Trouvères., Corpus Cant. Medii Aevi* II, 1927 (Transcription des chansons du Chansonnier Cangé), pp. 28—30. The typical clausula of the 'Lochamer Songbook' should also be included here.

12. *Cp.* Besseler's remarks quoted above.

13. K. Jeppesen: *Palestrinastil med saerligt henblik paa dissonansbehandlingen.* Köbenhavn, 1923, pp. 108—120.

14. *Cp.* also Paumann's dactylic 'paraphrases', etc.

15. *Cp.* Schering: *Zur instrumentalen Verzierungskunst im 18. Jahrhundert.* SIMG VI, further by the same writer: *Aufführungspraxis alter Musik.* 1931, p. 142. For Bach's sequences see E. Kurth: *Grundlagen des linearen Kontrapunkts.* 1917, pp. 230—233. The embellished versions of Telemann's and Benda's Violin Sonatas also show the same (German) characteristics.

16. Mozart elaborates his ornaments on strikingly few occasions, seemingly only in a few later works (e.g. *F minor Fantasy for Mechanical Organ,* K.V. 608) in order to obtain material for a *motif* (in the old German sense); it is interesting that in Mozart as in Beethoven this tendency coincides with their 'return to polyphony'. A similar process can be observed in the later works of Haydn, though much less clearly.

17. *Archiv für Musikwissenschaft* I, 1919, p. 497.

18. On the basis of recent researches I would divide native Hungarian ornamentation into two layers, one consisting of ornaments which act as structural links, and the other of figurated groups. The first comes from the East, the second from Baroque music.

19. Since this is relatively unexplored territory in Eastern European folk-music, more specific data would seem to be necessary here. Examples of Hungarian material, Bartók: *Hungarian Folk-Music.* (English ed. O.U.P, 1931) Nos. 21, 22, 40, 43, 55, 62, 158, 162, 202, 211, 226, 293, 294. Kodály: *Hungarian Folk-Music for voice and piano.* I, No. 3, II, No. 6, VII, No. 38, VIII, No. 43, X, No. 56. Bartók — Kodály: *Transylvanian Folk-Songs.* 1923, Nos. 26. 28, 50, 52, 64, 69, 76, 77, 87, 89, 95, 131, 144, etc. (comprising ornaments of 2—5 notes). The strange views held by some foreign researchers in this respect is illustrated by the so-called Hungarian 'folk-examples' which appear in R. Lach's book on ornamentation. He claims to hear 'primitive echoes' in them, yet without exception they are all semi-amateurish town songs and dances of the 1850's to the 1880's! For Kasan-Tartar analogies, see G. Schünemann's comments, *Archiv für Musikwiss.* I, 1919, pp. 510—511. See Hornbostel's article *Ch'ao't'ien tze* in the same review for some remarkable examples of Chinese ornamentation; still more interesting is the carefully compiled list by Liu T'ien-Hua in *Selections from the Repertoire of Operatic Songs and Terpsichorean Melodies of Mei Lan-Fang, Recorded in Both Chinese and European Notation* (Peiping, 1929, Preface) which resembles

Marchesi's tabulated lists of ornaments (R. Haas: *Aufführungspraxis der Musik*. 1931, pp. 225-230). For a Japanese equivalent of the 'homogeneous' East European style of ornamentation, see Tsuneyoshi Tsudzumi's work: *Die Kunst Japans*. 1929, pp. 320—321. A North Japanese and Javanese example in Lachmann's *Musik des Orients*. 1929, pp. 115—117, and p. 111. For Kirghiz material, see A. Zatajevitch: *1000 Pyesen Kirgisskovo Naroda*. Orenburg, 1925, Nos. 81, 195, 487, 851, 912, 921, 922, 927. Plenty of examples and analogous versions are to be found in Rimsky-Korsakov's Russian folk-song collection, Kolessa's Ukrainian collection, Lach's Turkish-Tartar collection, Bartók's Rumanian and Arabic collection and Idelsohn's Jewish collection. The descriptions and tabulated summaries at present available are not detailed enough to allow an assessment of the extent to which these characteristics are typical of certain areas. Folk-music research has only recently concerned itself with folk ornamentation.

20. See Bartók: "Neue Ergebnisse der Volksliedforschung in Ungarn." *Anbruch*, 1932, p. 41. Foreign 17th-century documents which probably reflect the performance traditions of the Hungarian upper class include Giovanni Picchi's *Ballo Ongaro* and *Padoana Ongara* (1620) and Poglietti's famous *"Hungarian Fiddle"* variation of 1677. They reveal the ornamental festoons reminiscent of present-day gipsy practice, rather than the closely moulded, homogeneous ornamentation typical of Hungarian folk-music.

21. See for example Launis: "Lappische Juoigos-Melodien." 1908, No. 615. "Suomen Kansan Sävelmiä." *Runosävelmiä* I, 1910, No. 580, 677/78, 690, 748/49, 782; *Laulusävelmiä* IV, 1933, No. 4730, etc.

22. *Cp.* among others Gennrich's study: "Internationale mittelalterliche Melodien." *ZMW* XII (1929), and Ludwig's article in Adler's *Handbuch der Musikgeschichte* (2nd edition, 1930).

23. See amongst others Schering's *Aufführungspraxis alter Musik*. 1931, pp. 129—130.

24. Whereas the ornamentation in Handel's keyboard suites—edited for publication by the composer—is markedly "German" in character.

MUSIC AND GEOGRAPHY

THE RISE AND FALL OF MUSIC CULTURES AND STYLES, SEEN IN TERMS OF GEOGRAPHY

Natural borders and music styles—art-music and coastal culture, folk-music and inland culture; the opposing laws governing their origin, spread and decay—the possibility of their merging—music and landscape—the life of border regions— the musical life-history of the continents—the law of diffusion—remains of early folk-music as evidence of human pre-history

I

Geography and musical history: are these two concepts related? Can some sort of connection be established between them? Faced with this question, a musicologist of the old school would probably reply with a sceptical shake of the head, and talk of Herder's or Humboldt's romanticism; but anyone familiar with more recent problems of musical history will not be surprised to find a connection between fields of research which, though remote from one another, are nevertheless complementary. Comparative musicology, the history of musical instruments and international research into melody draw not only upon ethnology, anthropology and history but make progressively greater use of geographical concepts and classifications. It is certainly no accident that in the last two or three decades there has been a steady increase in the number of musicological works, which in subject-matter and approach are strongly influenced by contemporary geographical research.[1] This infiltration of geography into musicology, however, amounts for the time being to little more than an occasional comment, a fleeting idea, a useful yet superficial analogy; anything more systematic will take time and will require much detailed research. The rough outline which follows is therefore merely designed to bring out a few of the main threads in world musical history as it has been enriched by geographical achievement.

2

It is well-known that even in the last century geography had ceased to content itself with merely 'describing the earth'; with the development of 'human' geography (anthropological geography) and in particular the geography of human civilisations, a direct link was established with ethnology, cultural history and other strictly intellectual fields of scientific research. This cultural geography investigates the influence of natural phenomena and particularly landscape on human behaviour, and is also interested in man himself as a geographical entity. Hence it has developed certain basic principles which are valid for music historians too.

The point of departure may perhaps be stated in these simple terms: *the manner as well as the direction in which cultural processes develop are largely determined by natural factors.*

What are these natural factors? In quantity as in variety they are legion, for they range from interrelated continents to mountain-chains, from the course of a river to the location of a marsh; connecting links and impediments, bridges and dams, are equally relevant. For each of these factors may determine or divert the course along which some product of the human mind—whether seen or unseen, material or spiritual—is transmitted from one community to another, from one populated area to another, or indeed from one way of life to another. That music (although with certain limitations, as will be seen) is also one of these products—these inter-changing, fluctuating products, which can be communicated or deflected—was only discovered by folk-music research in recent years, in the form of comparative musicology. Today we know that the basic ideas underlying human melody, the most ancient forms of melody, relatively few of which are still extant, may survive thousands of years, whereas the more temporary, transitory forms, the variants, are legion, but comparatively short-lived and limited in range. In the main, the same holds good for the basic principles of instrumental music, and the various forms they may assume in different regions. This explains how melody and tonal system, the principle of intonation and instrumental form, and even the absolute pitch of certain instruments as standards of acoustics (gender, marimba, xylophone and pan-pipes) can cover immense distances, reaching from one end of the earth to another, and can strike deep roots in the soil of one race or culture, yet shallow roots in another. We can get a faint idea of the extent of this "traffic" if we imagine how many hundred thousands of human beings have been travelling about on earth since the beginning of time, and how many melodies those hundreds and thousands of people have carried and carry with them from one place to another; not that the migration of a group of human beings necessarily implies a migration of style, but it does mean that the style has undergone a change in its environment. This does not, however, present anything like a true picture of the way that music spreads, for in such a migration melody is the smallest organism, the simplest form of life, but not an indivisible basic unity. It is a cell, not an electron. Tonal system, melody, construction and rhythm, on the other hand, are basic principles, which within one and the same melody can be the products of various cultures. Although in themselves they are mere abstractions, they are, nevertheless, extremely hardy and adaptable: they circulate round the world, easily combining, but always ready to separate and re-group themselves. Better than any other field of research, the history of melody thus exemplifies the natural law of *pseudo-morphosis* by which old forms become wedded with new substance (e.g. the fusion of new scales with old melody-shapes and rhythms). (In Hungary and Turkey-in-Asia, for example, pentatonic scales and transposed melody-lines are found in close alliance as well as independently; in a large part of Western and Eastern Europe these two principles are almost mutually exclusive; the structural principles of Gregorian chant were taken over by numerous major melodies of the Western Middle Ages, etc.) But what is it that determines how these elements spread and ramify in the course of their migration? Obviously neither the ethnologist nor the music historian can hope to find the answer without the help of cultural geography.

The prime need is to concentrate on the *system of natural highways and barriers,* in which may lurk the unknown new basic principles governing the life-span of music. All cultural geographers are more or less agreed about the nature of this system, and of how it controls the life of earth and of human beings: the principal laws governing human culture can be acquired from an orographical and hydrographical map of the earth's surface. So the first thing is to consider the significance of the world's mountain- and water-systems in relation to the development of cultural products.

Generally speaking, it is water which spreads and diffuses a culture, mountains which check and preserve it. Water in its two forms—as a river it creates a link between remote land-areas, as a sea or a lake it sometimes divides and sometimes joins. (As Ratzel points out: at the outset it separates, but later it creates closer and closer links.) Mountains also have a twofold significance: as walls of rock that halt progress, and as plateaux that give protection. A mountain range plays a double role: for those who wish to cross it, it is an obstacle, but for those who want to travel along the foot of it, it is a guide. Islands and peninsulas separate and breed a sense of isolation. Plains, steppes and deserts not only give free play to the forces they engender but they can also isolate, stifle and eventually destroy these same forces. Highlands, valleys and basins also separate, yet at the same time conserve racial characteristics. The chief breeding-grounds, the real cradles of culture are the oases, river-valleys, estuaries, mountain-slopes, the high plateaux of the temperate zones, well-watered hilly landscapes, the natural junctions of natural highways. Woods and savannahs, deserts and mountain-valleys are the places where 'half-cultures', the nomadic way of life, are born and are arrested in their development. And lastly the most natural and most self-contained units are islands and continents enclosed by sea, but only so long as they are difficult or even impossible of access. As soon as man has learned the secret of sea-faring, the island unit may become an archipelago, and the concept of a closed continent may give way to that of a block comprising several continents. From then on the sea speeds up rather than retards the process of communication; two coastlines separated by an ocean are often closer to each other than the two extremities of a steppe, or the two slopes of an alpine range.

So in the last resort, the importance of every natural phenomenon to human culture depends on the extent to which it facilitates or inhibits, speeds up or slows down man's instinctive urge to move about the world. When to this urge to move is added the fact that the habitable regions encompass the earth's surface with a network of long interconnected strips and "contain the areas of obstruction,"[2] then human civilisation appears as a planned geographical organism with a natural tendency to expansion. And where nature stifles man's urge to move, as on the ice-fields of the Arctic or in tropical jungles, civilisation is also unable to survive for long.

3

But we have already progressed from Nature to Man, and even as far as Man's intellectual activity; and that is no small distance. In moving from the world of nature to the world of the mind, we pass through the various forms of human society, through a gradually changing environment; behind the changes in mental processes we can glimpse changes in the forms of life. As Hornbostel and Lachmann put it, "Styles can only migrate with their bearers,"—and even if this is not completely acceptable in a wider sense, it does reveal *one* important law, which is that the reality of human life and human groups must be sought in the changing phenomena of culture. Universal human life is also to be found behind music; we only lack ways and means of measuring the one by the other.

So far it has been necessary to record a series of facts, which are well known to geographical specialists, in order to devise new laws for musical history on the basis of this system of natural and cultural laws.

Let us turn now to the history of music and try to present under this heading the whole history of music, a 'biography' of music which embraces the whole of humanity, the whole earth, the whole history of the world—not just a single chapter, an isolated detail, a colourful episode, which, because of the inescapable limitations of our European situation and professional outlook, we have come to regard as the *whole*, as a universe in itself.

Let us now observe how the first great music cultures emerged down the valleys of the Hoang-Ho, the Euphrates and the Indus, and up the valley of the Nile, that is to say, in the territories of ancient river-cultures, and, later on, along the coasts of the Greek peninsula. And how later on the thousand-year-old music centres of present-day Europe came to be developed: round the Lake of Constance, on the banks of the Seine and the Loire, in the valley of the Arno, between the Maas and the Schelde, then on the Italian coast and in the triangle formed by the Rhine, Elbe and Danube. All these are 'water-centres', river networks, coastlines, well-watered hilly landscapes or coastal regions.

It almost seems as though the life of music were in some way bound up with water. Yet this is only true of developed music-cultures, and as a result of urban civilisation. The earth also abounds in other forms of music, the 'barbaric', semi-cultured forms of primitive folk-music, of nomadic and peasant music. And the life of this music is subject to quite other laws than those which govern the great music-cultures.

They generally emanate from wooded mountainous regions, enclosed valleys, high plateaux which are difficult of access, the farms of steppe-lands, remote villages, moorland cottages and alpine shepherd huts. Mongolian, Scottish, Indian, Hungarian, Spanish and Turcoman folk-music, Rumanian, Russian and Negro peasant music—all the world's folk-music that is extant and still developing—seems essentially an inland product, the product of *closed territories*, by contrast with the winged, soaring music of the open water-regions and coastal strips. From the point of view of cultural geography, woods, plateaux and marshes seem to be equally *closed* territories, although in another sense they represent nomadic freedom (and it should be remembered that almost one third of the mainland is still covered by forests). It is surely no accident that coastal civilisations have been responsible for the most ruthless forest-clearance, for they not only need the timber but are intent also upon uprooting the 'primeval bush', the natural element and the home of barbarism, the jungle of nomadic chaos. Strangely enough, the nomadic way of life is more apt to preserve linguistic and other traditions than urban life[3]; here ideas of freedom and isolation directly confront each other: the immobile way of life faces the mobile, the traditional the progressive, the instinctive the conscious.

Folk-music differs from art-music in the way it is disseminated and in the courses it follows; folk-music comes down from the mountains or approaches the coasts from the moorlands. Art-music sets out from the coasts to conquer the interior. And the most striking thing is that, although these two musical forms move in opposite directions, the element of location is common to both.

271

All styles expand and disperse along mountain-ranges, rivers and sea-boards. All styles settle and survive in plateaux, basins, peninsulas and islands. The border areas generally have a double function: in some cases styles are rigidly conserved, in others they intermingle and lose their initial identity.

So, where a style spreads, it tends to follow the same course as popular migrations, along the rivers, inland seas and mountain-ranges. The main obstacles in the way of such stylistic migrations are those which also hold up popular migrations, namely oceans, deserts and such mountain-ranges as lie across their path. The highest degree of stylistic unity is achieved by sea-girt continents, islands and peninsulas, valleys and high plateaux: all regions enclosed by natural as well as racial boundaries.

In actual fact styles are already governed at birth by characteristic and decisive geographical laws. At what point, at what stage of growth, at what level of geographical expansion does the isolated impulse develop into a style? A style begins to emerge when some community accepts it as their natural language and at an advanced level; when it encounters another style, when it proves itself in conflict, when it influences and is itself influenced. And as it can only exert an influence and be influenced itself if it has a complete, organic unity of its own, which is *in touch with* the surrounding world and yet *distinct* from it, this means that it is subject to the time-honoured laws governing the progress of human culture. So in historical terms an impulse develops into a style, when the impulse, as a self-contained unit, oversteps its narrow geographical bounds, when it ceases to be an oral-type variant or an individual speciality: when the verses of a poet become the voice of his town, when Landino becomes Florence, Jannequin Paris, when a German cantata-form emerges from the works of German composers or a typical regional folk-song from an isolated new idiom.

Style, by definition, has a geographical identity, in which the common traditions of the community find expression, but it derives its identity primarily from its contact with other such entities. In the last analysis, its vitality can only be gauged by the energy it then displays in its urge to develop and to combat other styles. It is at this point that we begin to speak of a Florentine or a Neapolitan opera-style, of a Transdanubian type of recruiting music, of a German or Romance style, a 'Northern' or Southern dialect of Gregorian chant (already recognised in the Middle Ages) or of a Berlin type of Rococo song. And the vitality of a style can also be gauged by the degree of rivalry, friction and fusion between various geographical areas; how, for instance, Vienna (about 1770) learned from Mannheim, and how between 1640 and 1740 the influence of Rome, Florence, Venice and Naples spread to Paris, how the Italian madrigal (about 1590) was transplanted to London; and how one nation's folk-music will influence another's ... So far as inner construction is concerned, these two types of music come into being in very different ways. It is an essential condition of *folk-music* creation that it cannot take an individual or specific form, but draws on a communal source of supply and adapts itself to ready-made traditional forms, which it can only change over a period of centuries, and even then as part of a collective effort and only to a limited extent; only in this way can it become the natural, homogeneous expression of a living community. The stylistic origin and growth of *art-music* produce more visible upheavals, are more personal, more closely associated with individuals and with 'history'. It follows from this that folk-music creation favours the formation of *types*, which survive as such in the communal consciousness, either in a variety of forms, which have no particular regional association, or else in forms occurring in many regions. Art-music creation is more or less an *individuum*, the product of a uniform perception, and is more closely linked with place and performer. Yet the gulf dividing these two ways of life is even deeper and wider: the same sharp distinction applies equally to the laws which govern their diffusion. To give only one example: the *few melodies that extensive areas have in common inthe field of folk-music and folk-cults* always reflect ancient traditions and preserv e primitive traits (Hungarian dirges, the Arab-Romanic *Hora Lunga*, the Slovak *Detwanska*, the Chinese Hymns of Confucius). In art music, on the other hand, richly woven, grandiose stylistic forms are invoked from the outset. Here the appeal is not to the instinct for conservation but to the urge to build and mould, not to conformity but to deviation, not to the 'roots' but to the foliage (Gregorian chant, *folia, romanesca, bergamasca*). Moreover this is an example which serves to emphasise *common* characteristics: art-music is not subject to continuous change, whereas folk-music, like every traditional cultural product in daily use by many people over long periods of time, is subject to constant change. Only the ritual folk-melodies already mentioned are an exception, in that they occupy a fixed, insular position in this ever-changing flow.

Thus it seems hard to find principles and perspectives which are common to the historical development of both folk-music and art-music. All the same, at a certain stage in their development, both begin to radiate energy and acquire dynamic properties, at which point they enter the sphere of cultural geography on an equal footing—although in many respects their inherent energies work against each other. This forward development, by pursuing a specific course, also acquires its own law, shape, and individual character; only now are its place and its sphere of influence established on the inhabited globe, as a result of earlier encounters and conflicts; for everything that occupies space, and everything that blazes a trail for itself, leaves its mark on the earth's surface.

These phenomena of space-filling and of interaction give rise to certain other complex questions, which now need to be discussed.

18

4

What is the importance of the dual role of border-zones and the conflicting trends of art- and folk-music in the development of music as a whole? And what conclusions can we hope to draw from them in relation to the growth, consummation and decline of musical cultures? Let us consider these problems in order.

The idea of *peripheral survival* is not new: it has already been put forward by Herder, Ritter, Darwin, Richthofen and others, and Sachs has recently created a whole system on this theory. Its basic idea is that the marginal areas of a style or culture always conserve the earlier stages of the particular style or culture, since these phases have already been preserved and crystallised at a time when they have been completely forgotten by the centre from which they first emanated (where fashions change more quickly, or where change as such is more constant and more rapid). "The farther removed a cultural phenomenon is from the centre of its cultural source, the farther back lies the past from which it stems," writes Curt Sachs. The weak point of this theory lies in the blatant paradox that in fact not only the older, stagnant phases of a style are to be found on the margin of a style's living space, but also—and to the same degree—the later, declining phases. Celtic pentatonicism was forced to retreat to the wooded mountainous regions of Wales, Scotland and Brittany, the old Hungarian pentatonic style and musical ornamentation into Transdanubia, as well as to Transylvania and Moldavia—just as the oldest Hungarian language is spoken in Slavonic and Moldavian villages, and, for example, the most ancient Turkish language has survived on the borders of the old Turkish-speaking area, amongst the Chuvash and Yakut peoples; traces of the old Greek melody-style may be found today in Rumelia, Southern Morea and the Aegean islands; the oldest elements of Italian musical folklore—musical instruments and tunes—appear to have survived in Sardinia and Sicily[4]; primitive elements of Rumanian folk-music have been discovered in Bihar, Máramaros and Bessarabia.

It is also possible to add some data about art-music: the French-Burgundian music style of the Middle Ages was preserved into the 16th century in music centres beyond the Elbe and in the southern part of Germany—long after it had gone out of use in its own homeland; even today a researcher may encounter early medieval *organum*, not on French or English soil, where it flourished a thousand years ago, but in Iceland; the melodies of French *trouvères* can be heard today in Catalonia; Goudimel's choral method still survives after 250 years ... in Sárospatak (N.E. Hungary); and the hurdy-gurdy, so beloved in Central Europe eight hundred years ago, roves around Spanish, Swedish, Russian and Hungarian villages today as a beggar's instrument. All of this is striking evidence of the 'conservative soul' of peripheral areas; relics of ancient times are everywhere preserved not in the centres, but in the border-lands and places of refuge. The borderlands offer the best facilities for actual separation from the centre and for isolation. (The same is true of political history: when the original inhabitants of conquered territories are driven from their settlements, they take refuge in inaccessible borderlands. Was not the ancient way of life in the Carpathian Basin long preserved by the border-dwellers?) But there is also a reverse side to the medal. The disruption and confusion which beset pentatonicism in Central Asia can best be observed in Hungary at one extreme and Indonesia at the other. Rumanian folk-music has to thank its borderlands not only for the conservation of its primitive elements, but also for its extremely diverse foreign admixtures—Ukrainian, Transylvanian (Székler), Russian and Southern Slav. There are Spanish elements in the melodies of the South of France; and the austere styles of the Renaissance, as well as Flemish and Roman polyphony, disintegrate not in their places of origin, but in the provinces, in the countryside and abroad, where they reappear in new forms. It is a known fact that the primitive styles usually stagnate in islands and peninsulas, but they also disappear or become deformed more easily on islands (as for instance in the 'peripheral islands' of Australasia). So here the border territories provide the closing stages, and bring decay and death-agony! There are numerous examples to show that the peripheral zones are places of refuge not only for primitive forms but also for relics and fragments. What is more, because of the great distances of space and time involved, the peripheral zones are always primarily the scene of decisive *changes*. An example of this is the change in function of wandering musical instruments. The rudimentary Negro harp has not the same importance as its more developed Egyptian ancestor; and the organ, stemming from the South-East, was very probably transformed in the course of the Middle Ages from an open-air instrument into an instrument for chamber and church music—because of the climate of Central Europe. Hence the peripheral zones are both faithful and unfaithful to traditions: why this ambiguity, this paradox? And if it is true that living and dominant styles spread fairly evenly throughout a continent, and in fact circulate most easily on coastal areas, how is it that a moribund style needs to be studied in the 'coastal areas' and not in the place where it originated, flourished and came to fruition?

The answer is contained in the question: if we have missed high noon, we can only look towards the dusk. And yet if dusk always represents the day's history, it also marks its death. The dual role of peripheral zones can perhaps best be illustrated and explained by the position of a world-conquering style such as Arabic music. On the fringes of this music, e.g. in N.W. Africa (the Maghreb area) or in the oases of Algeria, Tunisia and Egypt,[5] the ancient Arabic, pre-Arabic and related traditions appear side by side, in the same place.

The border country is, as elsewhere, a dumping-ground for *everything*, a region in which, as it were, the blood-stream slows down and turns back, and where it can in consequence be most clearly observed; where "the arteries are in process of hardening." Perhaps it cannot be asserted of any single living style that it is in a state of quiescence, that it has completely settled and crystallised; no, because inner movement, continuous precipitation, fragmentation and fluctuation are the inevitable conditions of organic life. The organism is alive, and so it burns and burns up other things, so it consumes and is itself consumed; at every moment its balance is upset, and in every moment it strives to regain it; it ebbs and flows, grows tense and relaxes, rears up and sinks down; it is always 'under way', its whole essence lies in movement. Thus every living style eliminates, and every living style wears itself down, crumbles and breaks apart; the waves are *constantly* pulling towards the perimeter, the old material is *constantly* driven towards the borderlands. (In principle this slow drifting process probably takes place in all living communities in the same way—but in practice the process is strongly influenced by geographical and other factors; for not every region is equally receptive, adaptable and resistant.) In general, *everything* is swept to the outside edge, both the old material and the new, the 'pure' archaic as well as the more modern mixture[6]; the significance of the border-zones lies precisely in the fact that (in principle) everything may be found there, and that this *everything* also includes the ancient tradition which in the meantime has been lost at the centre. They break up and preserve at the same time: Janus-like, they guard both life and death.

5

Closer study of the second problem, the idea that folk-music and art-music *move in opposite directions*, will also lead away from the sphere of geographical enquiry. It has been seen that art-music develops and thrives on interconnected coastal strips; it is dependent for its growth on the waters of the earth's temperate zones and on open regions. 'More primitive' folk-music, on the other hand, flourishes in the earth's dry basins, and its development is generally similar to that of the valley-cultures. The former symbolises the seething, stirring motions of life on the earth, the latter its pent-up, massed energy. Seen from this standpoint, art-music and folk-music would not be stages of development, not younger and older sisters in the world of human culture, but rather opposing principles—comparable, in general terms, to urban civilisations and the nomadic way of life, to individual consciousness and mass instinct—manifestations of radically different modes of living. What for one spells birth, for the other spells death; what for one means decay brings the other prosperity.

So when mature civilisations at their zenith recall their nomadic antecedents, and when mature art-music seeks renewal in ancient folk-music, this could be no more than nostalgia, regression, a dream—destiny would not be affected by it. Is this what happens? Quite clearly it is not.

Here perhaps the first ray of light is thrown on the origin and decline of musical cultures and styles. A new art-music culture, that is, a conscious cultivation of music, normally originates along the same route that is followed by an expanding 'coastal culture'; for coastal regions adopt an individual, organic cultural life more readily than inland regions. These 'slumber' longer, that is, they preserve the 'barbarian' forms of life for a longer period. Consider, for instance, the history of European music; when Atlantic culture took over from Mediterranean culture, Western European music wrested the leadership from the ancient world of Southern Europe; in the Middle Ages German music was the last to emerge (after that of Italy, France, England, Spain and the Netherlands) and even then only in South Germany, along the Lake of Constance, the Rhine and the Danube; after that it was the turn of the further Danube basin and still later the disparate countries of East Europe. In 800 A.D. the arbiter of European musical life was Rome, about 1200 it was Paris, around 1800 Vienna; a regular musical life only really began in Hungarian, Polish and Russian towns in the 19th century. So far as European semi-popular types of music are concerned (or more precisely, types closely approximating to the accepted social standard), the art of minstrelsy which flourished from the 12th to the 17th century—troubadour poetry, *Minnesang, Meistergesang*, epic narrative, *Dumka-bylina*—shows the same chain formation, stretching from Scotland eastwards to the Crimea.

Possibly the sharp differences[7] between the melodic dialects of the European continent are somehow connected with the different points of time at which art-music came to life. The development of an art culture only becomes possible when a society has reached a certain level of maturity, but this level can vary in different spheres, so that art-music establishes quite a different melody-style in the national tradition of every people. The growth of art-music and folk-music is closely connected; they gravitate towards each other, in some ways they complement each other. Neither of them stands still; each strives to expand towards the breeding-ground of the other. 'Art-music culture', which sets out from the coasts and river-valleys, gradually penetrates the forests and climbs the mountain-slopes; finally it reaches the high plateaux, the broad inland plains, the great river-basins and the remote valleys. 'Folk-music' comes down from above and finally reaches the busy civilised coasts. Here the two great streams can be seen approaching from opposite directions and intermingling. Somewhere they meet—the art-music stream from the 'open' regions and the primitive culture from the 'closed' zones. And, if this meeting-point is acces-

277

sible, it can enter into the blood stream of the world's music: a folk-music culture may change into an art-music culture, if the life of the steppes or the high plateaux can be transformed into an urban or coastal life. (At another level this would confirm the law by which old high-cultures originate from a mixture of different peoples: barbarians from the mountains—mounted herdsmen and soldiers—mixing with civilised plain-dwellers—farmers and peasants.[8])

A complex state of balance has to be achieved: for the centres, the regions of art-music, endeavour to absorb and dominate, while the peripheral zones, the folk-music regions, try to preserve or level up, to fragment or disperse. A harmonious and productive relationship is seldom possible and then only for a relatively short time; but where such a relationship does emerge, the focal point of a *great* art-music culture has been created. (So it was in India about the time of Christ's birth, in Greece three hundred years earlier, in France about 1200, in Italy about 1500, in Germany about 1700.) As has been pointed out, art music occupies the central position in such a symbiosis whilst folk-music takes to the peripheral zones. Wherever such an association occurs, it binds the dialects together and gives them unity. For it frequently happens in folk-music, too, that at certain points in time the homogeneous, new style which owes its existence to just such an organic fusion, superimposes itself upon a variety of old dialects. (A case in point is Hungarian folk-music, in which the four dialect-regions of oral peculiarities, identified by Bartók, clearly only refer to an early stage of development.[9]) In the field of art-music, however, the meaning of such generalisation immediately becomes clear when, for example, we ask how many representatives of the 'Roman School' were born in Rome, how many Viennese classical masters in Vienna. Hence the linking process unifies and organises, particularly where a focal point of art-music attracts a region of folk-music, or vice versa, where peripheral areas of folk-music form a common art-music centre at their point of contact. The active elements then accumulate in the peripheral zones, they are blended and moulded in the centres (in the towns), they *spread* along the 'coasts' and either disintegrate or stagnate again in the peripheral zones. This dual movement, which is sometimes centripetal and sometimes centrifugal, appears to be the heart-beat of every living musical organism. If the movement ceases or becomes one-sided, if the material is only distributed outwards and not inwards any more, then the music culture has grown old, and its life-balance is at an end. And its death is simply final disappearance of this life-balance, a reversion to anarchy by the constituent parts; the substance at the centre disperses, the vital arteries dry up and the 'barbaric' border-zones are all that is left. So for a time 'inorganic matter' becomes 'organic', only to relapse again into the inorganic, as in all other spheres of life, in the endless cycle of life and death.

The laws which govern the decline of a musical style are still unknown, but it seems as though this ageing process were particularly closely connected with the absorption or decay of peripheral zones, and an excessive increase in central functions. Thus in the 19th century, German-French major music assumed a metropolitan character, just as Arabian *maqam* music had done in the 10th—12th centuries. The reverse process, where rural and barbaric elements take the upper hand, would only be apparent in the context of nomadic invasions, of folk-migrations, in other words when new styles come into existence; but an upsurge of 'folkish' music is sometimes brought about by the emergence of a new social layer. For a newly emergent layer of this kind is just a 'peripheral' element, pouring its own contribution into the central maelstrom.

Perhaps the most unusual development occurs when these opposing principles are transformed one into the other. The music of the Balkans and of Western Asia are good examples. The early art-music cultures in the Balkans were flooded by several nomadic streams, and in this nomadic metamorphosis the music spread outwards from the ancient centres. (Byzantine music reached the Russian plains in this way.) The musical history of Western Asia, on the other hand, shows how 'semi-cultured' music developed into 'maritime' art-music, into world-music, when it reached the coast—the regular route by which *hinterland cultures* in the Mediterranean world reached the great centres. (Judaean music of the 2nd and 3rd centuries, Arabic music of the 7th and 8th centuries are examples of this.) Under the same heading come changes in historical significance, where a musical product loses its original folk-character and, caught in the cultural framework of a world-religion, reaches peoples who take it over as a sort of art-music (Gregorian, Moslem and Buddhist liturgies), or, as in the case of Indian music, where the product of an old indigenous culture shrinks to a dialect under Western influence, that is, under the impact of a new and alien culture. Contrast and concord meet in all forms and at all stages throughout world history.

*

The cradle of the *great* early music cultures was, therefore, not high mountains or steppes but water-networks, well-watered hilly country, lakesides or sea-coasts, or more precisely, the human settlements there. The most 'individual' cultures developed in the 'most adaptable' regions; they did not choose the Himalayas or the ocean, but the Chinese coastline or the Nile Valley, Attica (S.E. Greece) or Burgundy, the mountain-slopes of Italy or South Germany. All these regions adapted themselves to the character of their inhabitants, and since they bore the "visible signs of tomorrow's cares" (Brunhes), the plans of human communities and of human periods of time, they became linked with these communities and periods. It is no accident that every period discovers certain types of landscape; they represent its conquests and achievements, and reflect to some extent its essential nature, of which they are an organic part. Moreover, music is able to convey the atmosphere of landscapes, cultures, or epochs—"for the Western musician the world is full of Wagnerian forests and Mozartian gardens, of Vivaldi's lagoons, Schubert's highroads and Debussy's seas." Art-music conjures up this atmosphere with conscious deliberation and with more obvious individual effort than folk-music, which moves at a slower tempo and lives according to a much broader concept of time.[10]

6

In conclusion, let us take a look at the continents and consider music as a spiritual bridge linking the four corners of the globe.

Asia's musical history resembles the *radii* of a circle. One must assume that round the central point lies a primitive, semi-nomadic inner circle: East and West Asia were equally enriched by it. Yet it was the South-West (Mesopotamia) which first achieved a higher degree of music culture, followed by the eastern coastline (China) and afterwards by the South (India). The coastal areas of the South-East and South-West continued throughout to act as vital links: the first with Australia, Oceania and America, the second with Europe and Africa. This process of radiation from an Asian centre occupied some 3,000—3,500 years.

The development of music in Europe is more aptly described as a *parabola*. The line of high-culture begins in the South-East, in Asia Minor, passes through the Southern (European) peninsulas, then appears on the West European coasts and the inland river-regions; finally it reaches East Europe and here, at the highest point of Central Europe, the curve of history turns back again towards Asia.[11] It is as if this curve follows roughly the same course as the central mountain-range of the European continent, the Alps—"Europe's backbone," as Reclus calls it—in a broad, semicircular sweep. This semicircle represents 2,000 to 2,500 years of development.

The musical graph of Africa is best compared to a *hyperbola*. It begins somewhere in the Eastern hemisphere, the first impulses coming from Southern Asia, and possibly at the same time in the West as a result of Atlantic influence (at the "points of Euro-African colonial contact": Frobenius). The flame of high culture blazes up in the North-East, and considerably later in the North-West, following a foreign (Arab) invasion; the central block preserves intact the relics of the oldest Eastern cultures and those of the Nile Valley. The time-span of this hyperbola cannot be measured, but our estimate is about 3,000 years.

America shows a more longitudinal formation, the same *zig-zag* line in a north-to-south direction, which is followed on the map by its vast mountain-range, the Cordilleras. The indigenous chain of music culture (which makes repeated contact with the semi-nomadic impulses infiltrating from the West) is more or less identical with the western coastline; its earliest centres are the great high plateaux (Mexico, Peru) and it impinges on barbaric regions on either side. The immigrant (European, African) music cultures in North and South America come in by way of the eastern plain or the hilly country, and between the two by way of the Central American archipelago. Whereas the divergences in Eurasia were between North and South, here they are between East and West. The latitudinal balance has become a longitudinal one. The time-span of this culture-curve is about 2,000 years.

So the growth of music cultures in both the Old and the New World reflects the same universal laws of cultural geography — the decisive importance of mountains and river networks, of inland and coastland formations. And wherever there is a stratum of conscious art-music culture, it coincides with the slender stratum of conscious human culture, which is barely more than a few thousand years old.

The most important style-regions (the world language of music) can be classified geographically as follows:

a. *Primitive styles* ('Pendulum melody', 2- and 3-note formulae, basic rhythms): in the Polar zones and the tropics, as well as in the temperate zones of the Southern hemisphere. (Pygmies, hoarding peoples, fishing and hunting peoples; only a small proportion of nomadic peoples, who have probably degenerated from a higher cultural level.)[12]

b. *Pentatonic system:* in the Celtic zone of Western Europe, on the line extending from the Danube to the Yellow Sea (Eurasian steppe regions), in Melanesia and Polynesia, in the entire Red Indian zone of America, in Central Africa. These areas are also, very largely, the areas in which the oldest types of plants were first cultivated (plant cultures).

c. *Maqam and Raga styles* (chromaticism, melody-models): in the subtropical zone of the Ancient World (North Africa, Western and Southern Asia) from the Atlas Mountains (North Africa) to the Malayan peninsula (20—50° Northern latitude). Generally speaking, this comprises the continent of the ancient Orient, the south-eastern *Oikumene* (later Islam), where oases and settlements first checked the surge of nomadic folk-migrations. Regions influenced include Southern and Eastern Europe.

d. *Major-minor style of melody:* in the temperate zone of Europe, from the Thames to the Volga, from the Pyrenees and Sicily to the Danube (40—60°

Northern latitude). Essentially the zone of 'ancient Indo-Germanic' culture, of European agrarian civilisation; the closest link appears to be between major music and the early Germanic settlements. Regions directly affected: Anglo-Saxon areas and Latin America.

It is clear from this that the older a musical style, the more widely it is dispersed, and (as today located) the more independent of race and climate; the younger it is, and the more pronounced as a cultural phenomenon, the more compact and the more closely linked to climatic (as well as to racial and social) boundaries. The living space of the *maqam* style coincided on the whole with that of Islam, that of major music with that of Christianity or of the white race; but there is reason to associate pentatonic styles more closely with the earliest high-cultures of the Ancient and the New World, whilst primitive music covers a very much wider field. This much is clear: the old music-cultures spread, while the new remained compact. So the process of development is that *the original compactness of the style becomes loosened with time : the musical language breaks up and disperses*. Styles, these organically developing 'linguistic' entities of music history, are carried off and destroyed by migrating groups; this is a truly natural process, like diffusion and erosion. So geography teaches us that musical life is just as expansive as cultural life in general: in its historical development it knows no frontiers.

*

But the most important laws of geography and even of geology are encountered when the intercontinental links between the earliest music-cultures are studied in terms of historical continuity and tribal survival; in general, when a search is made for the element in music which is *not* expansive and diffuse, but compact and constant. Music has much to show here that has been lost in other fields, precisely because only a relatively narrow sector of it, that of highly developed music-cultures, enters the sphere of 'historical consciousness'. Although the 'barbaric' world of folk-music is not without its historical side, and is enriched by the admixture of elements from above, which have sunk down into it, its deepest layer is nevertheless largely primitive and prehistoric. It is still not possible to determine what is changed in the course of its existence, and what remains the same. Sometimes the structure is preserved, sometimes the scale, and sometimes the ornamental turns in the melody. Art-music too is full of these 'survival-revival' elements, but folk-music must be regarded as more conservative, because in it, as has been seen, there is a more binding and general tradition of basic principles. This keeps alive a greater variety of elements and brings out the dominant part, the basic pattern, the main stem.

It is not yet known how far this basic pattern, this *reservatio organica* which tended always towards preservation and the fulfilment of a definite function coincides with basic traditions in human societies, how far it assumes a folk-character, or how interchangeable it is. But this much is certain, that in folk-music there is more and more evidence of primitive historical links and kindred relationships. It is perhaps even possible to venture the hypothesis that here and there in music the oldest memories of man linger on. When recent research reports the existence of the same primitive elements (pendulum melody) in the melodic world of the dwarf-peoples, the Pygmies, from Central Africa to Australia, one is immediately reminded that in geological antiquity this region of the Southern hemisphere—which today is largely under the sea—was still a single continent. If the music of North Africa is so closely and organically linked with the music of Western Asia in its older as well as in its more recent forms, it must be remembered that, geologically speaking, this region does not belong to Africa but to Asia. The melodic and instrumental world of Melanesia and Australia is directly related to South-East Asia, since this whole continent, together with the Indonesian islands, was once connected with the Asian mainland. The musical links between Siberia and North America should not come as a surprise: the original inhabitants of this continent migrated from Northern Asia, probably across the mainland; their western links are still evident to this day, particularly where the history of instruments is concerned. But this is all the more reason for thinking that there may be a certain relationship between the primitive instruments (the oldest forms of clapper, xylophone and bowed instruments) of the ancient peoples of East Africa and India; that there is growing musical evidence, far beyond the Malayan folk-migrations, of a connection between Indonesia and Central Africa. And now and then there are signs of a relationship between the primitive styles in the whole area south of the Tropic of Capricorn—for these continents and archipelagos were once closer together, and it is possible that they were the scene of the oldest human migrations. It is possible that primitive humanity spread over the earth's surface at a time when the continents were still one, or that they penetrated to distant parts of the earth over the sea, which now separates the continents, at a time which far precedes historical culture. Any such meeting of musical dialects thus means nothing less than that *folk-music in many parts of the world is an 'inheritance of Atlantis': a legacy of prehistoric times*, one of the earliest manifestations of human life, heralding our most ancient connections with Earth. Hence every researcher, who is concerned with Man's past and interested in his historical endeavours, potentialities and prospects, should apply himself with ever greater zeal to music, in the hope of obtaining answers to many questions which other manifestations of human culture leave unsolved, because their memory is more superficial and does not go so far back.

7

To summarise the main points of this 'musical geography':

a. The life of music is bound up with the natural formation of the earth's surface.

b. Regions which are enclosed from the point of view of cultural geography favour the preservation of musical styles in isolation, while the open regions encourage a more rapid circulation, a more conscious centralisation and transformation of musical styles. So the art-music cultures become part of the life of open regions, while primitive forms of folk-music cling to that of closed inland regions.

c. The growth and character of both these basic forms often take opposite directions: they take each other's place, draw on each other's resources and are able to reach a state of equilibrium, a fruitful co-existence.

d. In this state of equilibrium, the material collected in the peripheral areas is shaped into integrated musical language by the (art-music) centre, distributed and dispersed through the network of highways, and either conserved or destroyed by the half-civilised peripheral zones.

e. Diffusion is the most important process in musical history; over thousands of years all styles are scattered across the globe, and the longer they survive, the more diffuse they become.

f. Archaic folk-music is, however, a vehicle for the oldest human links, for the earliest conditions of human life.

A later 'musical geography', illustrating all these facts in greater detail, would doubtless reveal the existence of new laws determining the life-history of music; they will show clearly that music is much more deeply and firmly rooted in the life of human culture and its problems than our cultural sciences have so far suspected.

NOTES

1. Three articles by E. von Hornbostel began the series ("Die Probleme der vergleichenden Musikwissenschaft." *Zeitschr. d. Internat. Musikgesellschaft*, 1906; "Über ein akustisches Kriterium für Kulturzusammenhänge." *Zeitschr. f. Ethnologie*, 1911; and "Die Massnorm als kulturgeschichtliches Forschungsmittel." *W. Schmidt-Festschrift*, 1928); see also R. Lach: *Die vergleichende Musikwissenschaft, ihre Methoden und Probleme.* 1924; C. Sachs: *Geist und Werden der Musikinstrumente.* 1929; idem, *Vergleichende Musikwissenschaft in ihren Grundzügen*, 1930; idem, "Prolégomènes à une préhistoire musicale de l'Europe." *Revue de Musicologie*, 1936; Béla Bartók: *The Folk-Music of the Magyars and Neighbouring Peoples.* 1935; in French, *La Musique populaire des Hongrois et des peuples voisins.* 1937;

B. Szabolcsi: "Five-Tone Scales and Civilisation." *Acta Musicologica*, 1944 (Chap. XIII of present volume is an enlarged version of this article). See also G. de Gironcourt: *La géographie musicale*. Nancy, 1934, and Jaap Kunst: *Ethno-Musicology*. Den Haag, 1955. (Relevant remarks already appear in 16th and 17th century literature, in the works of Zarlino and Kircher.) A similar direction is shown in architectural studies, particularly since Strzygowski. All the same, it is worth noticing that the initial impulse came from musicians (Grétry: *Essais sur la Musique* II, 1797; Wagner: *Kunst und Klima*. 1850), naturally under the influence of 18th-century philosophers.

2. Pál Teleki: *A gazdasági élet földrajzi alapjai* [The geographical basis of economic life]. I, 1936, pp. 175—176 (in Hungarian), and Ratzel: *Völkerkunde*. I, 1885, p. 19.

3. See *Ethnogr.*, 1937, pp. 4—5 (L. Tamás); A. Kirchhoff: *Mensch und Erde*, Leipzig, 1901, pp. 45—46. *Cp.* W. Barthold: *12 Vorlesungen über die Geschichte der Türken Mittelasiens*. Berlin, 1935, 40, pp. 214—215, for the theory which seeks to connect racial interbreeding with settlement, the abandoning of the nomadic way of life.

4. See for example G. Fara: *Canti di Sardegna*. Milano, 1923, and A. Favara: *Canti della terra e del mare di Sicilia. Ibid.*, 1921.

5. See B. Bartók: "Die Volksmusik der Araber von Biskra und Umgebung." *Zeitschr. f. Musikwiss.*, 1920; R. Lachmann: "Die Musik in den tunesischen Städten." *Archiv. f. Musikwiss.*, 1923; B. Schiffer: *Die Oase Siwa und ihre Musik*. Bottrop, 1936.

6. Here are some Hungarian examples. Even today, Hungarian art-songs and operetta-melodies undergo characteristic transformation in the villages of Bukovina (now Rumania). (See the communication of P. Balla, *Ethn.*, 1935, pp. 139—141; Huszka's operetta-waltz mentioned there reached also further to the North as a Polish-Jewish 'folk-song'; see Idelsohn: *Hebräisch-orientalischer Melodienschatz* IX, 1932, No. 234.) Last-century *ländlers, chansons*, and operetta-melodies today form the basis for Transylvanian folk-dances in the county of Csík (now Rumania). (S. Vámszer-Bándy: *Székely táncok* [Transylvanian Dances]. Kolozsvár-Cluj, 1937.) In Bukovina in 1914, on the other hand, Kodály came across the *Árgirus* melody, probably stemming from the 16th century! Architecturally speaking, K. Gerstenberg provides interesting examples of the *new* style arising out of border-zones in his *Ideen zu einer Kunstgeographie Europas*, Leipzig, 1922, p. 14. In the field of philology, see 'laws' deduced by M. Bartoli "Le norme neolinguistiche e la loro utilità per la storia dei linguaggi e dei costumi." *Atti della Soc. Italiana per il progresso delle scienze*. Roma, 1933, p. 157, resp. J. Jordan (*An Introduction to Romance Linguistics*. London, 1937, p. 276). They maintain that isolated areas (islands, mountains) preserve older forms of language; borderlands (such as the Iberian peninsula, Dacia) preserve more ancient forms than the central areas (Gaul, Italy); linguistic forms scattered over a wide area are older than those contained in a smaller one, etc. For counter-arguments deduced from territories of Romance philology (borderlands as innovators) see Jordan, *op. cit.*, p. 277.

7. See previous chapter of present work. For the geographical nature of stylistic trends in art-music, see comments by J. J. Moser (*Musiklexikon*. 1935, p. 546): "About 1500, Germany and England were still largely under the influence of Dufay, while Italy, Flanders and France were already fully committed to Josquin; the Viennese classical style had already spread all over Germany about 1800 ... while Italy was still experiencing Baroque and Rococo, and France was already feeling its way towards early Romanticism ..."

8. F. Ratzel: *Völkerkunde* I, (1885) p. 19, and III, (1888) pp. 6—7, 35, 52; A. Hettner: *Der Gang der Kultur über die Erde*. 2nd ed. Leipzig—Berlin, 1929, pp. 76—77, 88; M. Granet: *Danses et légendes de la Chine ancienne*. Paris, 1926, pp. 3—23.

9. Bartók: *Hungarian Folk-Music*. Eng. ed. O.U.P., 1931, VIII. A map showing how the stylistic features of Hungarian folk-song have spread and intermingled is—for the time

being—only possible on the lines which Bartók here envisages. G. Lükő's plea that it be modified in the light of the special relations linking the dialect regions of Moldova and Szamos-Upper Tisza needs supporting by more detailed evidence (see *A magyar parasztzene történetéhez* [A history of Hungarian peasant music]. Debrecen, 1937). With time a more detailed system of musical dialects will presumably be elaborated on the lines set out by Gyula Prinz (*Magyar Földrajz* [Hungarian Geography] I, 1936, p. 295). The history of settlements and the geography of music are undoubtedly complementary in this respect.

10. Naturally enough, it was music of romantic and late-romantic complexion which first conjured up European landscapes with a conscious feeling for colour and atmosphere. (The musical landscapes of Schubert, Schumann, Mendelssohn, Wagner, Liszt, Berlioz, Verdi, Mussorgsky, Borodin, Smetana, Grieg, Debussy, Delius, De Falla, Vaughan Williams; in Hungary Erkel, later Kodály and Bartók.) The connection between music and landscape was first made in Oriental philosophies, that is, in books about Taoism (Chuang-tze, about 300 B.C.: music of the earth and the sky, flute songs of the forest, melodies of plants, seasons and celestial bodies). Scattered elements of this cosmology still survive in the mystical ideas of music held by Neo-Platonists. That it sometimes turns up in more recent histories of music (Bücken and others) is on the other hand a reversion to the 18th and 19th century 'Theory of Environment' (of which Taine's *Italian Journey* is a particularly good example), rather than to this school of the history of ideas. An interesting Oriental-romantic version, found in a Chassidic source-work, is quoted by Idelsohn in *Hebr.-orient. Melodienschatz* X, 1932, X: "Every melody, every forest, every cliff, every tree, and every plant, from a rose to a blade of grass, emanates its own special melody . . . The shepherd learns his songs from the fields where his flock find pasture, from the mood of meadow or mountain-side, and when he changes pasture, the character of his song changes too." So far as the author is aware, in the field of romantic fiction, Tieck and Jean Paul are the pioneers of such *paysages musicales*. *Cp.* also R. Wustmann: *Musikalische Bilder*. 1907; B. Szabolcsi: "Zene, táj és korszak" [Music, Landscape and Epoch]. *Magyar Írók Könyve*, 1937.

11. Here is a short 'biographical' sketch of Europe in the light of recent musicological research: Europe, 'the musical continent *par excellence*', 'the homeland of conscious musical culture'. Ethnically speaking, European music is rooted in three culture-regions, of which the precise boundaries are still uncertain. There was a Scandinavian region in the North, a Celtic one in the West, and a Mediterranean one in the South. The first region is characterised by major music and polyphonic propensities, the second by a heritage of pentatonic melody, and the third by strong diatonic sense with a highly developed instrumental and theoretical culture. For a long time Eastern Europe remained a direct part of Asia. The Mediterranean region, more highly organised, was the first to develop a high-culture. This was followed about 1200 by France in the Atlantic region, and by the Netherlands in the late Middle Ages. Italy took the lead during the 16th and 17th centuries, as did Germany during the 18th and 19th. The countries of Eastern Europe developed their art-music very considerably between 1820 and 1900. In spite of shared basic principles (tonal system), these cultures were sharply differentiated by their musical thought, which produced completely different artistic results. Ancient Mediterranean culture evolved a homophonic melody-style and a theoretical system, Rome in the early Middle Ages organised Gregorian chant; French and English medieval music achieved the first large-scale polyphonic structures, and even arrived at secular art-song; the Netherlands perfected polyphonic technique. Italy shaped present-day musical forms, and her work was then taken up by the entire Western world. Germany set the crown on this achievement, and between 1700 and 1890 gave it free rein in two great Classical movements and in Romanticism. During the course of the 19th century, Italy came to the fore again in opera, while France experienced a stylistic

revolution which was new and instrumental in character. The Slav countries, Hungary and Scandinavia contributed to folk-Romanticism during the 19th century, and during the 20th to musical reforms inspired by folk-music.

12. In "The Music of the Fuegians", *Ethnos*, Stockholm, 1948, p. 95, Hornbostel maintains that peoples whose primitive music styles are related may once have been neighbours in Central and Northern Asia. This would have been before more recent folk-migrations (of present-day Australian peoples, or of tribes of Indian stock passing through the Bering Straits) had pushed them progressively further south to southern tips of continents: to Tasmania, South-Eastern Australia, the Andaman Islands and Ceylon, or to the Tierra del Fuego and California.

INDEX

To keep this index within bounds, some compression has been necessary. Single references to tribal and anthropological classifications have been omitted, especially in Chapter I and the Appendix. Further, footnotes have been indexed only where new points from the main text are discussed, or important single new points developed.

ouvert-clos formula 117

toccata 80, 94
Todesca 101
Tolstoi S. L. 216
tonality 37 et seq, 51, 171, 190
tonal systems (primitive) 14 et seq, 28 et seq
tonality (major) 51 et seq
Tosi, P. F. 122, 123, 245
tonus lascivus 47
Traetta 175
tragédie lyrique 120
Traybenreiff-Tritonius, Peter 70
Tromboncino 65
tropos spondeiazon 29
troubadour melodies 41, 42, 55f, 88, 251
troubadour poetry 277
trouvère music 46, 49, 55f, 274
tuning systems (primitive) 14
Türk, Daniel 123, 124, 245
twelve-note music 188, 189, 190
Tye, Christopher 103

Umlauff 134
ungaresca 101
Urbs beate Jerusalem 42

Vanhal 127, 150, 163
Vaqueiras, Rambaut de 51
Várad songbook 71
Vargyas, Lajos 207
variations 254
Vatican 41, 42
vaudeville 118
Vaughan Williams, Ralph 186
Vavilov, N. I. 232
Vedic hymns 20, 21, 33
Vega, C. 221
Velazquez, Diego 77
verbunkos 252, 259
Verdi, Giuseppe 86, 101, 165, 168, 175, 176, 177, 183, 185, 195, 210
  Aida 177, 179, 180
  Ballo in Maschera 179, 180
  Don Carlos 168, 179, 180
  Falstaff 178, 179, 180
  Forza del Destino 161
  Lombardi 179
  Macbeth 161
  Otello 101, 179
  Requiem 161, 179

Rigoletto 168, 179, 180
Simone Boccanegra 168
La Traviata 178
Il Trovatore 179
Veris ad imperia 50
Viadana 79
Vicentino 80
victimae paschali laudes 59, 60, 61
Viennese school 47, 98, 133 et seq, 147, 156, 278
Viéville, Lecerf de la 131
Villani, F. 59
villanella 83, 101
Villeneuve, Josse de 122
villota 61, 63, 65
virelay melodies 51
Virgil 70
Vitali 87
Vivaldi, Antonio 90, 95, 96, 98, 100, 104, 119, 152, 160, 256, 280
Vogelweide, Walther von der 60
Volkston 135
Voltaire
  Dictionnaire philosophique 201
Vondel 102

Wagenseil, Georg 126, 127, 133
Wagner, E. D. 244
Wagner, Peter 38, 46, 247, 257
Wagner, Richard Wilhelm 59, 77, 86, 165, 167, 170 et seq, 179 et seq, 185, 190, 192, 202, 203, 211, 256, 279
  Lohengrin 177
  Meistersinger 168, 170, 180, 254
  Tetralogy (Ring) 165, 170
  Tristan 59, 168, 172, 188
  Walküre 161
  essay: Oper und Drama 202
Wagner, Siegfried 181
Walker 202
waltz 133, 209
Walsingham variations 103
wandering minstrels 59
wazne 19
Wapare 'sing song' intonation 12
Watteau 110, 111, 127, 213
Weber, Carl Maria von 161, 164, 171, 185, 256
  Euryanthe 164

MUSIC EXAMPLES

The numbers in italics refer to music examples in the Notes

309

LIST OF PLATES